The New Busy Man's Bible

a New Age Approach to
Christian Fundamentals

A Special
Study and Enlightenment Toolset
for the "Last Generation"

compiled by

M. Lee Morris

with inspiration and excerpts of

George Washington Cable

Body Mind Book Publishers

Body Mind Book Publishers
111 Conroe Dr.
Conroe, TX 77301

Printed in U.S.A.

In Appreciation and Memory of George Washington Cable,

Who wrote the following brilliant lines over 100 years ago!

Rules are risky things, soon worn out,
easily spoiled, and, however good,
bad as soon as they obscure our view of principles.

To call a thing right without feeling it right, is wrong.
To try to feel it right merely because it has been called right,
is to yield that homage to authority which God has nowhere given us any right
to yield to anything but that which we see to be true and right.

Never conclusively call an interpretation of God's Word your own
because your church or mine declares or denies it,
but only when you could not help but call it your own
if all the churches on earth forbade it.

It is a sad perversion of the true art of teaching,
and saddest when the things taught are those of the Bible,
for a teacher, either directly or by implication,
to ask his pupils to pay assents and consents
in advance of convictions imparted.

the noblest and most indispensable part
of real study is not hard study,
but hard thinking,

Truth itself, God's pure eternal truth,
simply discovered, observed, and emotionally reverenced,
is but treasure still buried.
"The kingdom of God cometh not by [mere admiring] observation " of it.

No follower of Christ may hope to profit any soul to whom he teaches the Bible
except when he so teaches it as to widen and intensify the Christ-life in the
affections and daily actions of his learners.
This is the whole final purpose of the Bible.

it is a hundred times easier to get the essentials of Christianity
into "the pupil's" head by way of his heart
than into his heart by way of his head.

Too many "of us unconsciously satisfy ourselves
with trying to teach the Bible, instead of
simply using the Bible to teach Christianity."

CONTENTS

Prologue – The Busy Man's Bible's Cable Connection i
Prologue portion to be read after completing study iv
Introduction xiv
How to Use the B.M.B. ("Use Cases") xvii
How to Use Internal Reference Notations xviii

BMB CORE - SECTION ONE: Chronological Overview Of Events And Characters

Creation - The Beginning 1
The Fall of Mankind 2
The First Judgment and Salvation of the Human Race 2
God's Covenant With Abraham 3
Jacob Usurps Esau 3
Joseph and Israel Sold Into Egypt 4
Moses the Deliverer 4
God Make Himself a Name Through Moses 5, 6
What is in a Name? 7
God's Presence - Physical & His Name's 8
God's Revelation of Himself to Us
The Divine Nature of God 9, 10
The Physical Nature of God 11, 12
Man as God's Offspring – "Triune" Nature 13
The Spirit of Truth 14
Historical Recap Through Moses' Time 15
The Ten Commandments 16
Transition from Moses to Joshua 16, 17
Joshua Taking the Promised Land 18
Judges Period (& Ruth) 19
Samuel and King Saul 20
King David and King Solomon 21, 22
The Kingdom Divided 23
Elijah and Elisha 23, 24
Samaria Lost and resettled; Prophesy of those taken to Babylon 25
King Hezekiah and Prophesy of Imminent Judgment 25
Judah in Babylon (Shadrach, Meshach, and Abed-Nego) 26A
Daniel and the Spirit Realm, Lions Den and Prophecy 26B, 27
Proven Prophesy and Prophetic Style (Daniel) 28-29
Return From Captivity 30
The Name of The LORD (recap of history) 31, 32
Prophecies of Messiah 33-37
(+ Clues to When Christ was Born) 35B, 37
Messiah Arrives (Clues to When) 37
John the Baptizer 38
Jesus' Ministry of Signs of His Deity 38, 39
Christ's Crucifixion and Resurrection 40
Apostolic Signs Start: The Day of Pentecost 41
Early Church Growth by Strength of Signs 42

Peter Uses "Keys" for Samaria and Gentiles 43
Paul and Barnabas Go to the Gentiles 43
More Boldness of the Church Through Signs 44
Recap of Significance of Signs in God's Plan 45
Notes on the "Name" of Christ 45
Baptism 45, 46
Character Study of Paul 47
Paul – Strong + Weak + Timothy; Was he the Last Apostle? 48
Paul's Instructions about Signs and Gifts 49, 50
"Tongues" 50
Warnings About False Doctrines, and Imitations of Signs 51
Examples of Demonic Activities and Imitations 52
Character Study of Satan / Lucifer 53, 54
Prophesies of Last Days
- Looking Ahead - the End Without Warning 55
- "Rapture" ("Yanking out") of the Church 56
- Daniel's 70 Weeks Outline 57
- Time of Jacob's Troubles 58-62
- God's Two Witnesses 60
- End of Tribulation; "Second Coming" 62, 63
- End of 1,000 Year Reign 64, 65
- Final Judgment 65
- Eternity and New Jerusalem 66-68

BMB CORE - SECTION TWO:
Sequential Topical Studies

Sin 71
Sin and Condemnation Under Law 72
Consequences of Sin: Death 73
- Atonement by Christ 73
Salvation Through Christ 74
Predestination/Election 75, 76
Faith and Salvation 77
Assurance of Salvation 77, 78
Hope of Salvation 79
Grace and Liberty 80
Faith Manifested by Works 81
Human Religion 82
The Conscience/Heart 83
Law of Liberty and Conscience 84
Snares of the Devil 85, 86
Watch for Christ's Return 86
The Battle of Spirit vs. Flesh 87
Sanctification – Spirit and Truth 88
- From The World and Its Riches 88
Separation (Sanctification) of Christians 89
Christian "Walk" Warnings and Lifestyle guidance 90
Love 90

Warnings of Defilement.. 91
Positive Commands.. 92
Punishment/Chastisement of Believers.. 92
Trials and Temptations of Believers.. 93
Spiritual Growth.. 94
The Word (Food) of God 95-98
Prayer: Fellowship With Our God
  Examples of the Basics.. 99, 100
  Instructions on Prayer.. 101
  Principles – Fasting and Public.. 102
  Requirements for Prayer.. 103
  Principles of Prayer.. 103-106
Life in the Church Family.. 107, 108
Support of the Church.. 109
Male/Female Principles of Church.. 109, 110
Family Principles.. 111, 112
Marriage.. 113
Principle of Submission.. 113
Principles of Governments in the World.. 114
Missionary/Evangelism.. 114

BMB CORE - Special Topic Highlights

Pride vs. Humility.. 115
"Beatitudes" - "Kingdom of God".. 115
Christology.. 116
Angels, Heaven.. 117-118
Genealogy of Christ.. 118
Dinosaurs in the Old Testament Days.. 119, 120
Creation Misc. and Geological Effects of the Great Flood.. 120
Miscellaneous.. 121, 122
The Real "Generation" Gap.. 123
Principles of Child Raising.. 123
BLANK PAGES FOR NOTES.. 124,125

About the Author and BMB Challenges

Excerpts from the Original *Busy Man's Bible*.. 126
About the Original Author - George Washington Cable.. 136
Busy Man's Bible Challenges - Leisure Learning Time Entertaining 140
Thought Exercises (aka "Stretching The Truth Accurately")..
  Dimensions of Truth 145
  Challenging Others to Think – Against PC Propaganda 147
  What's Wrong With the Church? 151
  Fractally Thinking – An Extra-Biblical Challenge.. 153

TOPICAL INDEX.. 159
INDEX OF BIBLE PASSAGES.. 163
RearFace – Preface for reading book from rear.. R-1
Re-Dedication – (To Those Learning This Backwards and Forwards)....... R-0

Prologue

(The Busy Man's Bible's Cable Connection)

In 1891, George Washington Cable published his book, ***The Busy Man's Bible*** *AND How to Study and Teach It*, in which he proposed an approach to the Bible more radical than any I had ever imagined to have been spoken so long ago; yet so intuitively and irrefutably obvious were his arguments as to convict me of my shyness in espousing that same approach over a hundred years later. Although I knew in my heart and mind that I was "supposed to" publish my "Busy Man's Bible" study book years ago, I still questioned myself and God as to why, until I read his book.

So you may ask, "Why is *The New* ***Busy Man's Bible*** needed?" I think it's because we need to get to where the learning and sharing of the truth is as attractive and effective, if not as fun, as the entertainment industries' viral spreading of confusion and deceptions in our world today. It seems that those who want to profit by enslaving or immobilizing us with lies have too well learned and implemented the teaching methods that Cable espoused – that the way to get a truth, or, in this case, untruth into a pupil's, or victim's, head, is by getting it into their heart first. (George Cable said that an intimate student teacher relationship was critical for teaching, so I will try to be as personal in "talking" to **you** as I can, and hope we can "chat" at BusyMansBible.com.)

We tend to hold on to something, right or wrong, true or false, good for us or bad or even deadly, after we become emotionally invested in it; and on the other hand, if we are not emotionally invested in it, others can use our emotions, fears and desires and easily lead us away from what might even hold the truest and richest rewards for our lives. Consider that the logical contra-positive of "the truth shall set you free" is "If your spirit is not free, you have believed lies". Lies are chains that you attach where wings belong!

So what can we do about it? George Cable stressed that "hard thinking" combined with a heart-felt connection with a teacher was the best, and maybe the only successful way for a student to gain a truly life changing knowledge. I like to call it "heart thinging" when something new is taken to heart, and becomes (a heart thing) alive there.

One particular statement of his caught my attention right off. He said

"To call a thing right without feeling it right, is wrong."

This has an amazing similarity to the words of the Koan Zen masters recorded centuries prior to Cable. Their most common retort to their students that gave good answers was,

"That may be true, if you do not know it yourself, it does you no good."

Upon meditating on this for a while, I decided that perhaps there is more similarity between that Zen practice and the kind of Christianity George Cable was promoting, than there is in many denominations today. HERESY! NO, really, wait a minute. The obvious similarity is that both religions had a problem getting disciples to learn truth so as to get it deep into their heart and make a difference in their lives. The problem in both camps is that students learn how to earn their teachers' approval with good answers. Zen meditation was similar to the type of prayer and protracted meditation on the Law that Jews were supposed to do, at least in that the goal was to bring the student to God consciousness and a changed life. The difference with Zen goals was and is that they are seeking a god of dissipation instead of the God of substance and Truth. I think this idea deserves more discussion.

I suspect that a little knowledge of Koan Zen practice, for comparison, may actually give us more understanding and practical application on the subject of George Cable's sub-title, "How to Study and Teach <the Bible>". First we need to know a little about Zen, and the Koan practice, in particular.

Within the Zen Buddhist religion, Koan practice was like a new age form of Zen, that brought in the idea that some stories were worthy of being codified as actual doctrine. Prior to that Zen only suggested that one empty one's head of all opinions and meditate on any, almost random idea or question, often chosen by their teacher, repeating it over and over until you transcended normal thinking and contacted some higher essence of the concept, and of your own self seeking perspective.

Note that all quotes from Wikipedia are not restricted by copyright, and according to their own rules, may be copied freely per their website link: "http://en.wikipedia.org/wiki/Wikipedia:Copyrights".

To find some basics about "Zen" you can go online to Wikipedia ("http://en.wikipedia.org/wiki/Zen"), which says

"<Zen> de-emphasizes both theoretical knowledge and the study of religious texts in favor of direct, experiential realization through meditation and dharma practice."

About Koan practice ("http://en.wikipedia.org/wiki/Koan") it says

"A kōan (literally 'public case') is a story or dialogue, generally related to Zen or other Buddhist history; the most typical form is an anecdote involving early Chinese Zen masters. These anecdotes involving famous Zen teachers are a practical demonstration of their wisdom, and can be used to test a student's progress in Zen practice. kōans often appear to be paradoxical or linguistically meaningless dialogues or questions. But to Zen Buddhists the kōan is 'the place and the time and the event where truth reveals itself unobstructed by the oppositions and differentiations of language.'" ...

Example

"Two hands clap and there is a sound; what is the sound of one hand?"

English-speaking non-Zen practitioners sometimes use kōan to refer to an unanswerable question or a meaningless statement. However, in Zen practice, a kōan is not meaningless, and teachers often do expect students to present an appropriate response when asked about a kōan. Even so, a kōan is not a riddle or a puzzle. Appropriate responses to a kōan may vary according to circumstances; different teachers may demand different responses to a given kōan, and a fixed answer cannot be correct in every circumstance. One of the most common recorded comments by a teacher on a disciple's answer is: "Even though that is true, if you do not know it yourself it does you no good." The master is looking not for an answer in a specific form, but for evidence that the disciple has actually grasped the state of mind expressed by the kōan itself.

Thus, though there may be so-called "traditional answers" (kenjo) to many kōans, these are only preserved as exemplary answers given in the past by various masters during their own training. In reality, any answer could be correct, provided that it conveys proof of personal realization.

One of the more amazing parallels is that which I see when considering the Christian goal to have "Christ live in me." First, from the Koan wiki page:

"If you are thinking about Buddha, this is thinking and delusion, not awakening. One must destroy preconceptions of the Buddha. Zen master Shunryu Suzuki wrote in *Zen Mind, Beginner's Mind* during an introduction to Zazen, 'Kill the Buddha if the Buddha exists somewhere else. Kill the Buddha, because you should resume your own Buddha nature.'"

That sounds much like Oswald Chambers in *My Utmost For His Highest*. (He stressed being non-self-conscious. I highly recommend you read it.) It appears that some Zen principles echo an essence of Christianity that has mostly vanished from modern Christian practice and commercial products. Consider the following passages from the Bible:

I Corinthians 6:

17 But he who is joined to the Lord is one spirit with Him.

Galatians 5:

24 And those who are Christ's have crucified the flesh with its passions and desires.

Galatians 2:

20 "I have been crucified with Christ; it is no longer I who live, but Christ lives in me;

If you read the "Excerpts from the Original *Busy Man's Bible*" I have provided for you in the back of this book, I think you will see that George Cable was something like a "Zen master of Christianity" way ahead of his time. (But that is a subject for a follow-up book *New Age Christian Fundamentalism* still being written.) The most interesting parallel to me was that the true goals of both Cable and the Zen masters, were for students to receive spiritually discerned information – truth from God versus well, I'm not going into that discussion pit now.

Now wait a minute!

To be true to the spirit of this book, I must stop here and officially ask that you skip over the rest of this Prologue, and begin your Bible study. Just use all of your own thinking and analytical abilities, trying to leave behind all the presuppositions and predispositions you might have accepted from anyone, no matter how trustworthy they are, because, well – just go back and reread the quotes from George Cable on the Dedication page in the front of this book – just figure out why for yourself! You can read this Prologue later.

Proceed to page xiv "Introduction" – Return here later.

Now, if you are not yet decided and committed to critically reading the Bible passages present in this book, or are not yet convinced that you might need or have time to read this book, let me offer a little more background.

I was once tempted to write an allegorical novel, to illustrate the sad state of Bible study and attitude towards truth today. I couldn't get in to it, though, because it was just too painfully close to what has really happened.

Just briefly, …

> Imagine the life of the "holy keepers of the secret knowledge of eternal life" living in a time, where those who were taught the secret, were seen to grow and develop an unshakeable joy and strength from their hope, individually and in community; so much so that almost everyone wanted to have what they had.
>
> There were many others, those who were already quite happy with themselves and their lot in this life, who were bothered when they saw those keeper-teachers of what appeared to be a new "religion" reaping great power and wealth from the gratitude and zeal for sharing that sprang up in those who were receiving the eternal truth. Many of them, perhaps even a power hungry primitive consortium of political and entertainment industries that were losing influence to the spreading new religion, then infiltrated and learned to become truth merchants, repackaging and reselling a heavily gold plated happy pill kind of religion, that taught people to act out and enjoy all the feelings they would have if they actually owned the secret of eternal life. The key to their success was in planting in their hearts the belief in the happy effects of knowing the secret, and yet preventing the actual truth of the secret from becoming alive in their heart. They were thus able to build huge, endless profiteering empires from the business secret of integrating the old-fashioned religion products of guilt and shame into a cyclical relationship with one's personal journey of rediscovery of the joy and happy feelings of religious success and pride.

OK, maybe I'm being a little bit cynical, but I don't really think so. Cynical is believing that the proper use of knowledge is to control and profit from others, and that the proper power of faith is in believing that if you say a lie often enough and convincingly enough, it will become accepted as truth, and that the proper perspective on religion is that worship is the ultimate entertainment power principle behind those ideas of knowledge and faith. Cynical, is my friend Pete, professor of Marketing at UNO in the Eighties, teaching "THE LAW OF SUPPLY AND IDIOTS" which says that "There are more idiots than you can ever supply, so invest only in marketing to them!"

Uh-Oh, I better lighten up here or I'll stop being entertaining and lose you! Or worse yet, have you take me too seriously.

Back to the main discussion at hand. One side of the problem today is that there is too much of people taking the wrong ideas to heart, without any hard thinking, and with too much pressure, affirmation and other emotional manipulation, by peers, authorities, and greedy, merciless pleasure providers. The result is that ideas are implanted in the heart and mind, and are only as permanent as the depth of the emotional hooks used to snag the lazy minds.

The other side of the problem is that even the real "keepers of truth" long ago found that the dissemination of truth is a source of prestige, profit and power, and thus have worked to keep control of the flow, and to taint that flow just enough with their brand of authority to prevent it from ever feeling owned by the consumer. Those that actually "hunger and thirst for righteousness" are fed in a manner so as to keep them dependent and unfulfilled as well as make them self-replicating like an evangelical virus, wherein there are many new mutations into new competing strains, but hardly a chance at someone evolving into a truly new level of life.

The pursuit of Bible knowledge has become known as either a tedious, divisive self-mortifying pursuit for individuals or a prestigious competition for pious professionals, and very few of today's young minds and hearts are being drawn toward either. Instead, they, along with a lot of older, cynical minds, are being drawn mostly to a "New Age Lite" religion, of spiritual ideas that free their heart from their mind, and join them to "liteminded", affirming, self-help seekers.

I personally feel more comfortable in a "new age" style "community" than in the old fashioned religious social clubs I grew up in. However, there is just not enough real Truth in their wildly popular New Age philosophies, much less new truth. They are all merely new fads based on old religions to compete in the religion business market for the massive profits, power and prestige. The old time religion has become more like new age entertainment, which in turn, has become more like the old school religious establishment!

I think it not so terribly presumptuous to believe that George Cable, if here, would agree with my proposition, that what is really needed now is a "**New Age Christian Fundamentalism**" (I have been working on a book by that name for some years now) which takes the original Christian truths of Love, Peace, Hope and Faith, etc., that can be understood logically as being the truths the Bible was meant to impart, and fit those into the popular "New Age" religious seekings, replacing the structural emptiness there of Nihilism and hedonistic mini-self worship, and creating a "new thing" in the empty hearts of those who have what I call the "spiritual handicap" - a capable, logical mind tied to a healthy heart. Notice that I am not saying that this will be easy for those people whose heart is not healthy, and whose mind thus cannot accurately grasp or adequately hold on to the truth. That brings me back to George Cable's and my premise on how real learning happens.

Here is a story to help explain the ideas of hard thinking and heart thinging:

When I was a young boy, one of the most challenging experiences of the Boy Scouts was that of building a transistor radio from a kit. That exercise taught some motor skills like soldering, twisting and crimping, clearly not as physical as hiking, chopping trees, or building campfires, yet still quite exiting in the almost miraculous result of producing music from a bunch of seemingly random wires and little gadgets. In the Fifties, a transistor radio was something most kids could only wish for, so the prospect of ending up with such a technological marvel induced a seriousness of focus in trying to understand and follow the directions carefully in hopes of reaping the fruit of success. I feel certain that the lessons learned by children doing such an exercise, of dissecting information, following instructions and planning work with foresight and understanding - what George Cable called "hard thinking" and I call "heart thinging" - were foundational in many successful careers, whether in teaching, engineering, construction, entertainment or any endeavor requiring one's mind to be busy and logical.

In my teen years a more amazing metaphor occurred, when my best friend Greg and his big brother built the most amazing FM Stereo receiver from a kit – the Heathkit. The Heathkit Corporation sold a kit that, when built, was the finest FM receiver stereo system available at the time. If you were a true audiophile you had no choice but to build your own, or pay someone lots of cash to build it for you, from the Heathkit kit. Despite being a task very uncommon apart from electrical engineering school, I'm sure many people were motivated to build a Heathkit receiver only by a desire for listening and bragging enjoyment. However, they learned on order of magnitude much more than the Boy Scout radio exercise of skills and thinking, and I suspect their lives were greatly affected by the experience.

There were two radically different responses and directions taken away from the same experience. Greg's big brother became an E.E. and was very successful in the business world. Greg, however, applied those same skills in hobbies such as restoring old sports cars, and became a professional musician and then a very successful music teacher in a junior high school!

WHAT HAPPENED THERE ? ! ? ! ?

I propose, and I believe George Cable would agree, that Greg's big brother was typical of those who, when they discovered studying the Bible, were fascinated with and proud of the abilities to analyze and correctly interpret the meaning and intent of the Holy Scriptures, and choose to master and use those skills, either professionally or as lay leaders in the church.

They went to "Bible College" and learned to do what the authoritative teachers taught, and to think what they thought; however, the truths that they gathered became tools they adopted, rather than passions they lived. Their passion was in finding, possessing, and showing the truths to others, not in having the truths possess and control them.

Greg, on the other hand, after completing the stereo, listened more to the spirit of the work and music, than to the quality of the music and work; and was changed, not only by the power of the music, but by an experience that had convinced his heart to correctly value truth and the benefits to one's life from a developed ability to seek, find and hold on to truth. This truth, that had become alive in his heart, had to be shared in teaching – the kind of teaching that hopes to impart an understanding of the reality and power of truth, and the proper manifestation of it in the life's work for which you were designed.

George Cable encouraged all of us, busy men and women (note, he made it clear he was NOT speaking only to men!) to recognize and fulfill our calling to use our abilities to study the Bible in such a way that its truths take hold strongly in our heart and transform our life, and affect those around us. His understanding of the human brain and soul are remarkable, considering he was an accountant and an author, not a psychiatrist or theologian. He instructed us to not be distracted into learning facts that are not so important or cannot be so firmly believed as to change our soul to be more like Jesus. I propose that there are levels of truth (see Pg. 145), which I found to be best illustrated with concentric circles, or spheres, with core truth principles at the center, spiritually discerned, and with observable or deducible facts on the outside surface, and then in between those are layers for realms of truth that are more spiritual and foundational, and dependent on inner foundations and observation and specific application out towards the surface.

In this NBMB I propose that you super busy men and women of today need first to get a taste for the product I propose you to build, much like Greg and his brother, who had listened to a Heathkit stereo and developed a lust to own one before attempting to build one. The bulk of this NBMB is meant to "prime the pump" in helping you, busy man or woman, to hopefully experience hearing the transformational truths that comes from "rightly dividing the word of God" and then be driven to do what you were meant and designed to do - "Be diligent" at studying and even teaching the Bible.

In the rear of this book you find a few extra sections for reference:

"Excerpts from the Original *Busy Man's Bible*"

"About the Original Author - George Washington Cable"

"*Busy Man's Bible* Challenges - Leisure Learning Time Entertaining Thought Exercises" (aka "Stretching the Truth Accurately")

Although, it is not at all necessary, and even seemingly self contradictory, I suggest that you consider reading the excerpts provided (on pages 126-135) from George Cable's BMB, prior to reading through the scripture sections of this book. I believe the need for hearing his approach is as strong now as when George Cable's original book was first written, in order to repurpose busy people like you into becoming the right kind of Bible students. Since it is so important to know your teacher, I hope you will enjoy reading more about him in the rear of this book, and then even some of his fiction works.

Most of the passages in this BMB are arranged so that they flow nicely as you read each column on a page. The intent and hope is that the optimal use of the BMB is simply reading it, one page or column at a time, out loud, and listening for what God is saying in the Word, expecting to hear and gain wisdom and knowledge from the "word of God" which "is alive and powerful" (Heb.4:12) and "able to make you wise for salvation" (II Tim.3:15); because, prior to each reading, you go first to God in a simple prayer for wisdom, per James 1:5, reflecting on your need for that wisdom and God's faithfulness for providing it. As you read do not read the passage labels or notes, or anything except the "word of God" until you have read all the passages on the page. Then, after a pause for listening for any questions or answers or urgings that spring from the reading, look back over the page to notice the labels of the passages and any notes, and see if that stirs you to want to follow the off-page references, and/or reread passages on the page.

Of course you should pause any time as you read and you hear a question or other inspired thought, at least to note it so you can come back to it later. If you are reading aloud then speak your question out, or exclaim your praise or thanks or joy at what you hear. I suspect you have already discovered that when you read something with your eyes while you hear it with your ears, it at least doubles your understanding and retention. Let your study time turn into a conversation with the "word of God" and your heart and mind. As George Cable said to us,

"Don't be afraid of your own originality;
there's no strong chance that you have enough of it to be afraid of."

(Have confidence in your intelligence and skills of thoughtful inquiry, having developed and proven them in your successful, busy business of life.)

At this point I hope you have now decided to read the Bible study portion of this book, as I tried to suggest about 5 pages back. I really want you to read the "BMB core" passages as presented, front to back, with nothing more in your mind about me than that I am some data analyst who wants you try what I think is an "optimized" presentation of the basic and vital information in the Bible. Oh, and that I would like it if you might then go to the "BusyMansBible.com" website to share your feedback with me and, hopefully, others as I hope to make this into a Wikipedia like project and a "New Age Christian Fundamentalist community" ☺.

Now, again I say: Please skip to page xiv "Introduction".

If you are someone who just wants to know more "about the author" then I ask you one more time, to try reading the BMB core first then come back here. If you must know something about me, please go and try reading the "Re-Dedication" page at the rear of the book, where I expressed my true heart and quirkiness, and, I think, expose more about me than what follows here. (So much so that my wife made me move that dedication to the back, and come up with another one ☺.) Or, here is a little more "about the author" :

It has been 30 years since I first decided that this type of Bible study resource was needed, and that I felt obligated, if not "called" by God, to attempt it. I had experienced a phenomenal career rise in only a few years, due to my God-given talents and skills for doing large scale data analysis and data modeling, and I felt that it was my duty to attempt to use those "gifts" for God's Kingdom. In 1979 I was at the forefront of the engineering business world's field of Data Modeling and Database design. I had fallen into one opportunity after another to prove that I had a unique ability to analyze and organize huge masses of data into efficient, useful, enterprise data repositories, and I was well noticed, appreciated and rewarded.

I greatly enjoyed my work of analyzing large complex business processes and the related profusion of data, then discovering the inherent structures that best presented logical and useful views for understanding and improving the business. It is always fun to do something for which you are particularly suited. It was even more fun since my abilities enabled me to really impress my bosses, and the many others involved in the standardization and automation efforts that I was leading for a huge, global corporation. However, having been a very serious student of the Bible since early childhood, I could not help seeing the huge opportunity, not to mention the fun, of organizing the key content of the Bible into an optimal database layout, by applying the data analysis and modeling techniques that made me successful at work. No worldly job could be any way close to the fun of getting to use my skills and natural abilities to do to the Bible as I did for the mountains of engineering project and reference data. When I started in on that project, it was the most fun I have had yet in life. I did not even seem to need sleep, and in a just a few years, just in my spare time, I was done.

Yes, I have been quite perplexed by my failure to actually publish this in the 25 years since I first completed it in 1984. Perhaps even more surprising to me than that is how the business of Christian publishing has become so huge during that time, and yet, has not produced any product that fills what I still believe to be an important need – a comprehensive and optimized primer of the Bible that facilitates and encourages the person who feels too busy for spiritual studies, to attack it themselves, in their spare time.

Well, this is not my biography, so I'll skip to now. I was in church last Sunday (Feb.1, 2009), and the message that morning was about how Abraham and Sarah had to wait 25 years from the time they were promised a son by God, until that promise actually was fulfilled. The preacher talked about how God had meant it as a time for building their character and perspective, and much more. However, Abraham and Sarah decided to try to bring about the fulfillment of God's promise by the only means that they could see to do, and thus spawned a race that was a metaphor for the wrong results that come of being impatient for the visible, public success one knows has been promised by God, and trying to make it happen by our own power.

While sitting in church that Sunday, considering the message, I thought I "heard" God clearly "tell" me that it has now been 25 years since I finished the initial version of my "Optimized Bible Study Source", and that this year would be the time for Him to complete the work He had started, and to actually publish and produce "fruit" from this book. Twenty-five years ago I firmly believed that God had promised me that He was going to use the book that I very certainly felt He had mightily helped me to put together. I can't say I literally heard the word "promise" from God's voice, but I believed it was His firm plan, because I had experienced what I believe was God's powerful help in choosing and arranging the Bible verses. It was an amazing, exhilarating, "mountaintop" experience. I'll share that experience here briefly, despite the risk of being seen as a real weirdo by some, just to help you understand why I felt so certain.

After feeling "called" as mentioned above, I had spent a year reading through other translations of the Bible. I found out about the New King James Version, published by Thomas Nelson Inc., and really liked it. My uncle, Henry M. Morris Jr., told me that it was the very best translation available, having been very involved in the project and well acquainted with the people on the team, and their abilities and work ethic. I particularly liked that even the basic first printing contained footnotes describing any variations in alternate source texts, while staying true to the style and texts used by the old King James Version, unless there were clear reasons to use a better source.

After making a first pass through the NKJV, cover to cover, marking selections to be used, I then bought a second copy, and started from the beginning again, and physically cut out each passage. The second copy was needed, because often passages chosen were on opposite sides of the same page. Then with each passage freshly cut, in my hand I would ask, "OK, where does this one go?" and place it either in an envelope already labeled, or make a new envelope for it.

That was fun, but nothing compared to the six week exercise of building the final structures and page layouts. After a most painful experience and operation I "got" to stay home and rest for 6 weeks. During that time I was able to use a huge dining room floor and table to layout the 123 pages and go through all the clippings of passages, one by one, asking, "OK, where does this one go?"

I was absolutely amazed at how easily I was "drawn" (it almost felt like having my gaze, and then my head pulled) towards the page, on the floor or on the table, where the passage belonged.

Well, that was probably way too much detail about my actual method and experience in putting together the first version of this book. But I would really like to encourage everyone, not just those who are analytical, to go through the same or a similar exercise for the sheer joy of the close walk with the Holy Spirit of Jesus Christ that happened as I sought to "rightly divide the Word of God" for long hours at a time. I know people who run marathons, and they insist that the pleasure I get from an hour or two, at most, of walking and/or running, cannot begin to compare to the euphoria that kicks in during the latter miles of a marathon.

I think it is probable that my experience in building my Optimized Bible Database (the very first title of the first compilation) might be enjoyed by any who give their heart, soul and body to the task, and not just a personal, one time prophetic like anointing as indeed it felt to me.

So, why did I have to wait 25 years before I could publish more than the ten or so copies I made and gave away back then?

Oh, there are so many things on which I could put the blame:
my fear of failure, my fear of success, my relationship failures,
my business successes, or, how about my
I'm-simply-satisfied-with-deep-dark-humor-and-enabling-relationships-martyring self, my laziness, my procrastination ("never put off today what you can put off putting off until tomorrow!"), my – oh, never mind! Uh, slipping back into my old ways am I?

Looking back over the past 25 years, I can see that God had to change me in two major dimensions to bring me to where I might make the final cut of this book and publish it. No, one of those dimensions was not Bible knowledge or theological discernment and analysis. I had the "benefit" (?) of an intensive theological education as a teen, actively attending Berachah Church in Houston, where Bob Theme taught the most rigorous imaginable systematic theology. If you know anything about him at that time, you will understand that, as well as what I would be lacking from that experience.

Perhaps it is a good thing that life worked out so that I "escaped" "organized" religion (business) into a successful, "secular" business career, and did not gather for myself all of the letters like PhD after my name, like my uncle and cousins did. I strongly believe that the biggest problem in Biblical studies is and has been that the common student has been trained to learn what the "theologians" tell them about the Bible, and end up believing what they have "learned" because of their letters and reputation. After I left Berachah Church, I found out that Bob Theme even went so far as to say individuals could not and should not try to understand the Bible any way other than from his teachings. Whoa! I'm glad I escaped that!

So, reigning in my rambling again, let me just say that I would prefer to go and present my New Busy Man's Bible where the witness of the Holy Spirit and the attraction of the Word Of God draws me, rather than where I may gain admittance based on any worldly credentials or personnel references by man. With this book, I am not asking you to trust and follow my spiritual and theological insights in reading and studying the Bible, but only to learn, or at least get a taste from me, of the skills of data analysis and organization to help you in digesting the Bible, as was meant by Paul when he wrote to tell Timothy to study, "be diligent … rightly dividing the Word of God".

Now, about the book as it is today - I am truly amazed at the timing of how God's plans play out. I settled on "The Busy Man's Bible" (BMB) as the new title for this book almost a year ago, and although I could think of no better new title, I felt it was not exactly right. I felt I could not start the publishing ball rolling until I had a firm commitment to a title. It amazes me that I did not do a Google search for that title until after the Sunday message about the 25 year wait, and, until my wife tells me she thinks I need to find a new title because she found a book already published by that name. I then went to my laptop and found the book, and saw that it is not in copyright because it was published in 1891 by George Washington Cable. It was subtitled "How to Study and Teach It" and even before I read it, I knew in my heart that I had discovered the "missing link" of and foundation for my own "New Busy Man's Bible". After reading his BMB, I knew if I had read it 30 years ago, my BMB would have logically come about in response to his call.

I have some more to say about George Cable in the "Introduction" that follows. I put it there because, as I said ten pages ago, I wanted you to skip these ten pages and start with the "Introduction." I did not want you to miss out on the background information on George Cable, or the basic explanation of this new BMB. I do thank you for reading all my personal viewpoint, even though I hope it does not taint your appreciation of the BMB core Bible passage sections, but helps you to feel more comfy exchanging ideas with me.

The last bit I want to include here in this "optional" background, is about my design goals for the BMB core.

The core content of the BMB was selected with the hope to bring together at least a minimum set of essential Bible passages everyone should at least read, in order to have a basic understanding of God and reality as presented in the Bible. The BMB aspires to have the structure that maximizes the comprehension and utilization of the Bible doctrines that all people should know. I have attempted to place all the Bible passages within a structure that is built upon a complete and accurate understanding of the essential data and how it will be used and applied, just as in business information systems. As with such databases in business, the proper use of the BMB should bring about a new and deeper understanding of the subject material, which is God, and our relationship with God as revealed in the Bible.

Most importantly, PLEASE NOTE: The BMB is **absolutely not** intended to be treated as a finished book. This book is meant for you to use as a starting point for your own database of Bible verses and notes. Notes and references, and other verses should be added as needed for your own specialized study areas. For me, this should become 122 "wiki" pages on BusyMansBible.com.

INTRODUCTION

The New *Busy Man's Bible* (BMB) promotes and supports an alternative approach to studying, teaching, and referencing the Bible. This book echoes the calling of the 1891 book, *The Busy Man's Bible*, by George W. Cable, in proposing the approach of using, in Bible study, the same methods used by busy business men and women for accurately discovering and making use of the meaning and purpose of communications and reference information in their busy daily endeavors, whether as employer, employee, or in running a household. This new book also agrees with George W. Cable's core point – that the heart of the Bible is about changing the human heart, to produce the "Christ life" in you, and thus the methods of gaining Bible knowledge must be very personal and yield an emotional bond to your heart. I think that George Cable's arguments and the Bible passages presented in this new BMB respectfully defeat all of the objections of the religious establishment about common man not being able to discern the spiritual truths of the Bible apart from a teacher. If you really "need" to know it (i.e. for a truth to have spiritual life value in you), you must figure it out on your own, from the spirit of truth!

George W. Cable wrote his *The* ***Busy Man's Bible*** *- and How to Study and Teach It* to encourage busy men and women to study the Bible in the only way one can truly digest and assimilate God's Word so as to make it alive and powerful in one's own life – by methodically reading and thinking as they would if trying to successfully process business information and instructions from an employer or customer. He so eloquently encouraged us to do our own analysis and thinking in learning God's Word and God's will for our life, rather than simply submitting to dogma and the interpretations of others, and merely saying (to ourselves) that we believe them because of their authority, when in truth, our actions will only be driven by that which we believe to be true no matter who else might say otherwise.

In the "Prologue (The Busy Man's Bible's Cable Connection)" I have tried to give some long overdue credit and thanks to George Washington Cable for his progressive, almost revolutionary and "New Age" thinking and wonderful eloquence. I think that when you taste the sample of his work in the back of this book, you will want, as I did, to seek out and read the entire original book, as well as want to find and read his other wonderful historical fiction books. (Please read Prologue pages iv - xiii after the next 130 pages.)

I was surprised to find out what an important literary figure he was. After the "Excerpts from the Original *Busy Man's Bible*" in the back of this book, you will also find a section "About the Original Author", where I provide some biographical excerpts about George Washington Cable. I was rather surprised to find out what a complicated man he was.

For instance, the LSU Press book page about George W. Cable – *A Biography* by Arlin Turner, says,

"George Washington Cable, compared in his lifetime to Dickens and Daudet and praised in Moscow as a disciple of Turgenev, was more than a local colorist of Creole days in New Orleans. He was a crusader as well—and a crusader for a dangerously unpopular cause."

Even more amazing, to me, is that I cannot find any mention of his Busy Man's Bible in any biographical article on the internet. For instance, the NNDB.com website lists the following :

Is the subject of books:

George W. Cable, 1962, BY: Philip Butcher
George W. Cable: A Biography, 1966, BY: Arlin Turner
Critical Essays on George W. Cable, 1980, BY: Arlin Turner (ed.)
A Genius in His Way: The Art of Cable's Old Creole Days, 1988, BY: N. J. Rutherford

Author of books:

Old Creole Days (1879, short stories)
The Grandissimes (1880, novel)
Madame Delphine (1881, novel)
Dr. Sevier (1884, novel)
The Creoles of Louisiana (1884, nonfiction)
The Silent South (1885, essays)
Bonaventure (1888)
The Negro Question (1888, essays)
The Cavailier (1901, novel)
Loves of Louisiana (1918, novel)

George Cable was unquestionably of extreme intelligence, and quite popular with post modern liberal "thinkers" of his time. However, he was out in his own boat when it came to his deep and strong Christian beliefs in the reality of Jesus as the living savior who lives inside His "believers" who will live eternally as God's children, far from his liberal friends and organized religions. He was radically non-traditional in his approach to the Bible in that he believed the Bible to be literally logical and laden with spiritual truth that should be directly transforming intelligent people within a community, rather than to be mysteriously used by a priestly class to control and have power over a community. And he wasn't afraid to say so openly, even in a book!

I'm guessing that in his early years of writing fiction, his strong passions against slavery and those who enabled it, caused him to pollute his stories in an unconscious, perfectionistic attempt to force feed his convictions upon a populace, instead of giving them the credit, as he later did in his BMB, for being able to figure out and respond rightly on their own, when the important truths were passionately fed to their minds through their hearts, as his beautiful, descriptive fiction no doubt could have done. (Take a breath. ☺)

I wish a political/social historian, or literature/journalism historian, or whoever, would take an interest in this rare man's story and help us all learn something about the dynamics and dangers of Political Correctness and propaganda, and the idealistically good intentions of intelligent, loving literary leaders. I'm not sure who the right person would be; I just don't think it is I. At the very least, there must be a lesson to be learned about how things worked to prevent the powerful transformative truths in his BMB from being accepted by the two philosophical camps that existed then and continue to hold power and battle each other today. But now, back to this new BMB.

The motivation behind building the New BMB was not an inspired, noble New Age crusade like Cable's, but rather a simple technical answer to the challenge of proving that the Bible's information is indeed logical and can be "rightly divided" by an non-seminary trained data analyst. The goal was to build an optimized database of the Bible that one should have available in order to make good use of (i.e. properly interpret) any portion of the Bible.

In constructing analogous databases for large business or engineering enterprises, I used the advanced art form of data analysis in discerning the data architecture, where the analyst actually tries to learn from the data, by attempting to "let the data tell you" its inner and often hidden truths, structures and uses. My hope for this book is to teach you this approach by presenting you with the results of my many years of analysis of the actual data of the Bible, as well as many of the "existing users" and old study "systems."

Just as for business systems, the goal of this database is to arrange, store and index a large amount of data in a manner to provide the most efficient "user friendly" access to it by the anticipated users. The modern term for how a database system will be used is "Use Cases", and I have listed some of these on the next page. The users (techie term "actors") include the following:

- Anyone truly wanting to know the basic message of the Bible
- New Christians just getting started in the "Christ life"
- Christians at home confronted by cult evangelists who misuse scripture
- Bible student preparing for the ministry
- Teachers and Ministers preparing lessons and messages
- Front line evangelists witnessing to the world

Putting aside all that technical stuff, the New BMB, unlike other Bible study courses or commentaries, makes little use of explanatory comments, but allows the Bible to reveal its own truths. Unlike a concordance or other topical Bible reference books, the BMB is specially designed to be read from front to back. It is short enough to make this an easy task. Doing so provides a unique benefit, much like training wheels for learning to navigate and explore the Word, and thus the "Mind of God," uncluttered by the comments of humans, and illuminated only by the "Spirit of Truth" as you read.

How To Use The B.M.B. ("Use Cases")

The following are the "design Use Cases" of the BMB. (Remember, I'm an Information Technology Geek. (See "www.en.wikipedia.org/wiki/Use_case")

1. An initial straight through reading of at least the top third of each column is probably the optimum use of time for the beginning student of the Bible. This is the quickest way to build an organized knowledge of the basics of the Bible and gain a basic understanding of God's perspective on history and life, before attempting your own study of the entire Bible.

2. A straight through study of the BMB will provide the serious student with a unified perspective of doctrinal subject materials that are often dealt with as disjointed doctrinal topics. This is accomplished by coherently focusing on doctrinal topics within a thorough presentation of the central unifying theme of the Bible: God Establishing His Name and plan for our salvation. Reread short passages together with the one before and after it in the same column, until you understand why they are together. Expect, and of course allow "the spirit of truth in your heart: to help you understand.

3. A study focusing on one or more of the topics found in the Table of Contents offers the student an optimum set of verses arranged in an optimum order, to allow rereading and comparisons of passages without the distractions of turning a lot of pages. The serious student is encouraged to then dig deeper using the Strong's and Young's concordances and other Bible versions, in finding related passages to add to those in the BMB for each subject.

4. As a reference source on subjects listed in the Index of Topics (in the back of the book), the BMB presents verses in the context described in #2 above. The BMB is intended to be a "sparse matrix" frame of reference into which other verses can be fit in order to aid in their proper interpretation. In depth study as in #3 above should build out this framework, as the student of the Bible grows in wisdom and knowledge.

5. The BMB is hoped to be a great source for choosing verses for a lesson, sermon, or for memorization. (This is a big reason for using the NKJV.)

6. The BMB should also be a must read for non-believers who seriously want to investigate what the Bible really says on any of the listed topics, for whatever reason. However, be aware that the Bible should be considered in order to make any fair report or assessment of the Bible's content.

The BMB, just like the Bible, will provide spiritual growth only to those who honestly and earnestly seek the truth with their heart, using their whole mind. Start each study time sincerely asking the Spirit of Truth for wisdom and understanding to grow you and produce spiritual fruit.

Though this database would make a great computer resource for Bible projects, it was specifically designed and laid out in this physical book form to make it most useful to all who can read and make notes. Analogous to computerized data, the physical positions of each passage on a page, and page within the book, constitute an optimum arrangement of the data. Each page was planned and "human engineered" to provide the most efficient access to useful scriptures, whether reading straight through, studying topically, or casually looking for a key memory verse. For example, a quick reading of just the first (or even 1 inch of) passage on top of each column is meant to give the reader the maximum impact when one is in a hurry. The top verses on the page or column for each subject will generally make the best memory verses.

Even though the BMB was optimized to be read from front to back, in doing so you will encounter several cross-references to passages elsewhere in the BMB. This is somewhat like a data-warehouse "Fact table" having a relationship to another "fact" that is important enough to be represented by a pointer to the key organizing attribute of the related fact. Following these links is very important when focusing on one particular subject, but they should also be followed when encountered in a second sequential reading.

Syntax of the Internal References

A cross-reference note may have four parts to it:

1. Page number
2. Column designator ("A" or "B")
3. Passage number(s)
4. A sub-passage indicator

A period will be found to end each of the above parts. The term "passage" refers to one or more verses on a page not separated by a chapter number designation followed by a colon. A "sub-passage" indicator will either be an actual verse number (e.g. "v4") or a letter (e.g. "a" or "b") that serves as a count of sub-passages. In the latter case a sub-passage will consist of one or more verses separated from other verses in the same chapter by a blank line and no chapter designation. When counting passages, note that there is always whitespace and a chapter number designation separating passages. Usually the book name will precede the chapter number. Examples of cross-references follow:

[see also Pg. 94]
[see also Pg. 90 A.]
[see also Pg. 96.A.1.]
[see also Pg. 95.B.1,2.] (list of passages)
[see also Pg.103.A.1-3v4\ (1 "through" verse 4 of "3")
[see also Pg 11.B.2. & 12.A.1.] (2 Ref. pages)

The Index of Topics also uses the above syntax.

Section One

Chronological Overview of Events and Characters

Creation - The Beginning

Hebrews 11
3 By faith we understand that the worlds were
framed by the word of God, so that the things
which are seen were not made of things which are
visible.

Genesis 1:
In the beginning God
created the heavens and the earth.
2 The earth was without form, and void; and
darkness was on the face of the deep. And the
Spirit of God was hovering over the face of the
waters.
3 Then God said, "Let there be light"; and there
was light.
4 And God saw the light, that it was good; and
God divided the light from the darkness.
5 God called the light Day, and the darkness He
called Night. So the evening and the morning
were the first day.
6 Then God said, "Let there be a firmament in
the midst of the waters, and let it divide the
waters from the waters."
7 Thus God made the firmament, and divided the
waters which were under the firmament from the
waters which were above the firmament; and it
was so.
8 And God called the firmament Heaven. So the
evening and the morning was the second day.
9 Then God said, "Let the waters under the
heavens be gathered together into one place, and
let the dry land appear"; and it was so.
10 And God called the dry land Earth, and the
gathering together of the waters He called Seas.
And God saw that it was good.
11 Then God said, "Let the earth bring forth
grass, the herb that yields seed, and the fruit tree
that yields fruit according to its kind, whose seed
is in itself, on the earth"; and it was so.
12 And the earth brought forth grass, the herb
that yields seed according to its kind, and the tree
that yields fruit, whose seed is in itself according
to its kind. And God saw that it was good.
13 So the evening and the morning were the third
day.
14 Then God said, "Let there be lights in the
firmament of the heavens to divide the day from
the night; and let them be for signs and seasons,
and for days and years;
15 "and let them be for lights in the
firmament of the heavens to give light on
the earth"; and it was so.
16 Then God made two great lights; the greater
light to rule the day, and the lesser light to rule
the night. He made the stars also.
17 God set them in the firmament of the heavens
to give light on the earth.
18 and to rule over the day and over the night, and
to divide the light from the darkness. And God
saw that it was good.
19 So the evening and the morning were the fourth
day.
20 Then God said, "Let the waters abound with an
abundance of living creatures, and let birds fly
above the earth across the face of the firmament
of the heavens."
21 So God created great sea creatures and every
living thing that moves, with which the waters
abounded, according to their kind, and every
winged bird according to its kind. And God saw
that it was good.
22 And God blessed them, saying, "Be fruitful and
multiply, and fill the waters in the seas, and let
birds multiply on the earth."
23 So the evening and the morning were the fifth
day.
24 Then God said, "Let the earth bring forth the
living creature according to its kind: cattle and
creeping thing and beast of the earth, each
according to its kind"; and it was so.
25 And God made the beast of the earth according
to its kind, and everything that creeps on the
earth according to its kind. And God saw that it
was good.
26 Then God said, "Let Us make man in Our
image, according to Our likeness; let them have
dominion over the fish of the sea, over the birds
of the air, and over the cattle, over all the earth
and over every creeping thing that creeps on the
earth."
27 So God created man in His own image; in the
image of God He created him; male and female
He created them.

Genesis 2:
7 And the LORD God formed man of the dust of
the ground, and breathed into his nostrils the
breath of life; and man became a living being.
<see Pg. 110.B2!>

Genesis 3:
1 Now the serpent was more cunning than any
beast of the field which the LORD God had
made. And he said to the woman, "Has God
indeed said, 'You shall not eat of every tree of the
garden'?"
4 Then the serpent said to the woman,
"You will not surely die.

A. 1. Adam's Sin
A. 2. Sinful World

Genesis 3: (Man cursed)

5 For God knows that in the day you eat of it your eyes will be opened, and you will be like God, knowing good and evil."

6 So when the woman saw that the tree was good for food, that it was pleasant to the eyes, and a tree desirable to make one wise, she took of its fruit and ate. She also gave to her husband with her, and he ate.

12 Then the man said, "The woman whom You gave to be with me, she gave me of the tree, and I ate."

17 Then to Adam He said, "Because you have heeded the voice of your wife, and have eaten from the tree of which I commanded you saying, 'You shall not eat of it' :

" Cursed is the ground for your sake;
In toil you shall eat *of* it
All the days of your life.
18 Both thorns and thistles
it shall bring forth for you.
And you shall eat the herb of the field.
19 In the sweat of your face you shall eat bread
Till you return to the ground,
For out of it you were taken;
For dust you *are*,
And to dust you shall return."

20 And Adam called his wife's name Eve, because she was the mother of all living .

21 Also for Adam and his wife the LORD God made tunics of skin, and clothed them.

22 Then the LORD God said, "Behold, the man has become like one of Us, to know good and evil. And now. Lest he put out his hand and take also of the tree of life, and , eat, and live forever"

<see Pg.110.B3 for Woman's Curse>

Genesis 6:

1 Now it came to pass, when men began to multiply on the face of the earth, and daughters were born to them,,

2 that the sons of God saw the daughters of men, that they *were* beautiful; and they took wives for themselves of all whom they chose.

3 And the LORD said, "My Spirit shall not strive with man forever, for he *is* indeed flesh; yet his days shall be one hundred and twenty years."

4 There were giants on the earth in those days, and also afterward, when the sons of God came in to the daughters of men and they bore *children* to them. Those *were* the mighty men who *were* of old, men of renown.

5 Then the LORD saw that the wickedness of man *was* great in the earth, and *that* every intent of the thoughts of his heart *was* only evil continually.

B. <u>THE FLOOD</u>

<see also Pg 120.B.>

6 And the LORD was sorry that He had made man on the earth, and He was grieved in His heart.

7 So the LORD said, "I will destroy man whom I have created from the face of the earth, both man and beast, creeping thing and birds of the air, for I am sorry that I have made them."

8 But Noah found grace in the eyes of the LORD. *

Genesis 7:

1 Then the LORD said to Noah, "Come into the ark, you and all your household, because I have seen that you are righteous before Me in this generation.

8 Of clean beasts, of beasts that are unclean, of birds, and of everything that creeps on the earth.

9 two by two they went into the ark to Noah, male and female, as God had commanded Noah.

10 And it came to pass after seven days that the waters of the flood were on the earth.

11 In the six hundredth year of Noah's life, in the second month, the seventeenth day of the month, on that day all the fountains of the great deep were broken up, and the windows of heaven were opened.

12 and the rain was on the earth forty days and forty nights.

23 So He destroyed all living things which were on the face of the ground: both man and cattle, creeping thing and bird of the air. They were destroyed from the earth. Only Noah and those who were with him in the ark remained alive.

24 And the waters prevailed on the earth one hundred and fifty days.

Genesis 9:

9 "And as for Me, behold, I establish My covenant with you and with your descendants after you,

10 "and with every living creature that is with you: the birds, the cattle, and every beast of the earth with you, of all that go out of the ark, every beast of the earth.

11 "Thus I establish My covenant with you: Never again shall all flesh be cut off by the waters of the flood; never again shall there be a flood to destroy the earth."

12 And God said: "This is the sign of the covenant which I make between Me and you, and every living creature that is with you, for perpetual generations:

13 "I set My rainbow in the cloud, and it shall be for the sign of the covenant between Me and the earth.

*****<*see Pg. 25B4 God's opinion of Noah.*>

Abrahamic Covenant

Genesis 15:

18 On the same day the LORD made a covenant with Abram, saying,
"To your descendents I have given this land, from the river of Egypt to the great river, the River Euphrates –

Genesis 17:

3 Then Abram fell on his face, and God talked with him, saying:
4 "As for Me, behold, My covenant is with you, and you shall be a father of many nations.
5 "No longer shall you name be called Abram, but you name shall be Abraham; for I have made you a father of many nations.
6 "I will make you exceedingly fruitful; and I will make nations of you, and kings shall come from you.
7 "And I will establish My covenant between Me and you and your descendants after you in their generations, for an everlasting covenant, to be God to you and your descendants after you.
8 "Also I give to you and your descendants after you the land in which you are a stranger, all the land of Canaan, as an everlasting possession; and I will be their God."

10 "This is My covenant which you shall keep, between Me and you and your descendants after you: Every male child among you shall be circumcised;

Genesis 22:

15 Then the Angel of the LORD called to Abraham a second time out of heaven,
16 and said: "By Myself I have sworn, says the LORD, because you have done this thing, and have not withheld your son, your only son,
17 "in blessing I will bless you, and in multiplying I will multiply your descendants as the stars of the heaven and as the sand which is on the seashore; and your descendants shall possess the gate of their enemies.
18 "In your seed all the nations of the earth shall be blessed, because you have obeyed My voice."

(Prophecy of Messiah)

Jacob & Esau

Genesis 25

32 And Esau said, "Look, I am about to die; so what profit shall this birthright be to me?"
33 Then Jacob said, "Swear to me as of this day." So he swore to him, and sold his birthright to Jacob.

Genesis 27

6 So Rebekah spoke to Jacob her son, saying, "Indeed I heard your father speak to Esau your brother, saying,
7 'Bring me game and make savory food for me, that I may eat it and bless you in the presence of the LORD before my death.'
8 "Now, therefore, my son, obey my voice according to what I command you.
9 "Go now to the flock and bring me from there two choice kids of the goats, and I will make savory food from them for your father, such as he loves.
10 "Then you shall take it to your father, that he may eat it, and that he may bless you before his death."

36 And Esau said, "Is he not rightly named Jacob? For he has supplanted me these two times. He took away my birthright, and now look he has taken away my blessing!" And he said, "Have you not reserved a blessing for me?"
37 Then Isaac answered and said to Esau, "Indeed I have made him your master, and all his brethren I have given to him as servants; with grain and wine I have sustained him. What shall I do now for you, my son?"

Genesis 35:

10 And God said to him, "Your name is Jacob; your name shall not be called Jacob anymore, but Israel shall be your name." So He called his name Israel.
11 Also God said to him: "I am God Almighty. Be fruitful and multiply; a nation and a company of nations shall proceed from you, and kings shall come from your body.
12 "The land which I gave Abraham and Isaac I give to you; and to your descendants after you I give this land."

Israel & Joseph

Genesis 32:

24 Then Jacob was left alone; and a Man wrestled with him until the breaking of day.
25 Now when He saw that He did not prevail against him, He touched the socket of his hip; and the socket of Jacob's hip was out of joint as He wrestled with him.
26 And He said, "Let Me go, for the day breaks." But he said, "I will not let You go unless You bless me!"
27 So He said to him, "What is your name?" And he said, "Jacob."
28 And He said, "Your name shall no longer be called Jacob, but Israel; for you have struggled with God and with men, and have prevailed."
29 Then Jacob asked Him, saying, "Tell me Your name, I pray." And He said, "Why is it that you ask about My name?" And He blessed him there.

Genesis 37:

28 Then Midianite traders passed by; so the brothers pulled Joseph up and lifted him out of the pit, and sold him to the Ishmaelites for twenty shekels of silver. And they took Joseph to Egypt.

Genesis 45:

26 And they told him, saying, "Joseph is still alive, and he is governor over all the land of Egypt." And Jacob's heart stood still, because he did not believe them.

Genesis 46:

3 And He said, "I am God, the God of your father; do not fear to go down to Egypt, for I will make of you a great nation there.
4 "I will go down with you to Egypt, and I will also surely bring you up again; and Joseph will put his hand on your eyes."

Genesis 50:

17 'Thus you shall say to Joseph: "I beg you, please forgive the trespass of your brothers and their sin; for they did evil to you." '. Now, please, forgive the trespass of the servants of the God of your father." And Joseph wept when they spoke to him.

20 "But as for you, you meant evil against me; but God meant it for good, in order to bring it about as it is this day, to save many people alive.

B1, 2 430 years
B3 – 6 Moses

Galatians 3:

117 And this I say, that the law, which was four hundred and thirty years later, cannot annul the covenant that was confirmed before by God in Christ, that it should make the promise of no effect.

Exodus 12:

40 Now the sojourn of the children of Israel who lived in Egypt was four hundred and thirty years.

<see also Pg. 121. B.1.2. >

Exodus 6:

5 "And I have also heard the groaning of the children of Israel whom the Egyptians keep in bondage, and I have remembered My covenant.
6 "Therefore say to the children of Israel: 'I am the LORD; I will bring you out from under the burdens of the Egyptians, I will rescue you from their bondage, and I will redeem you with an outstretched arm and with great judgments.

Exodus 4:

10 Then Moses said to the LORD, "O my Lord, I am not eloquent, neither before nor since You have spoken to Your servant; but I am slow of speech and slow of tongue."

Numbers 12

3 (Now the man Moses was very humble, more than all men who were on the face of the earth.)
6 Then He said, "Hear now My words:
If there is a prophet among you,
I, the LORD make Myself known to him in a vision
And I speak to him in a dream.
7 Not so with My servant Moses;
He is faithful in all My house.
8 I speak with him face to face,
Even plainly, and not in dark sayings;
And he sees the form of the LORD.
Why then were you not afraid
To speak against My servant Moses?"

Establishing the Name of the LORD (Moses & Egypt)

Psalm 9:

10 And those who know Your name will put their trust in You;

Psalm 135:`

13 Your name, O LORD, endures forever,
Your fame, O LORD, throughout all generations.

Exodus 3:

14 And God said to Moses, "I AM WHO I AM." And He said, "Thus you shall say to the children of Israel, 'I AM has sent me to you.' "

15 Moreover God said to Moses, "Thus you shall say to the children of Israel: 'The LORD God of your fathers, the God of Abraham, the God of Isaac, and the God of Jacob, has sent me to you. This is My name forever, and this is My memorial to all generations.'

Exodus 6:

2 And God spoke to Moses and said to him:
"I am the LORD.

3 I appeared to Abraham, to Isaac, and to Jacob, as God Almighty, but by My name, LORD (YHWH), I was not known to them.

Exodus 9: TO EGYPT

14 "for at this time I will send all My plagues to your very heart, and on your servants and on your people, that you may know that there is none like Me in all the earth.

15 "Now if I stretched out My hand and struck you and your people with pestilence, then you would have been cut off from the earth.

16 "But indeed for this purpose I have raised you up, that I may show My power in you, and that My name may be declared in all the earth.

Exodus 3:

6 Moreover He said, "I am the God of your father – the God of Abraham, the God of Isaac, and the God of Jacob." And Moses hid his face for he was afraid to look upon God.

Deuteronomy 28:

58 "If you do not carefully observe all the words of this law that are written in this book, that you may fear this glorious and awesome name, THE LORD YOUR GOD,

Hebrews 12:

29 For our God is a consuming fire

Note that the Bible teaches us that the term Name applies to all that is known about someone. The Name of the Lord is a primary theme of the Old Testament. All works done by God's power (all good) are added to His Name (thus in it). See also these refs :>

Name	*Blaspheme*	*Prayer*	*Word*
Pg 45 A.3-6	*Pg. 122 B 2,3*	*Pg. 104 A. 4-5*	*Pg. 95 B.3*

Exodus 10:

1 Now the LORD said to Moses, "Go in to Pharaoh; for I have hardened his heart and the hearts of his servants, that I may show these signs of Mine before him,

2 "and that you may tell in the hearing of your son and your son's son the mighty things I have done in Egypt, and My signs which I have done among them, that you may know that I am the LORD."

Exodus 6:

7 'I will take you as My people, and I will be your God. Then you shall know that I am the LORD your God who brings you out from under the burdens of the Egyptians.

Exodus 14:

18 "Then the Egyptians shall know that I am the LORD, when I have gained honor for Myself over Pharaoh, his chariots, and his horsemen."

31 Thus Israel saw the great work which the LORD had done in Egypt; so the people feared the LORD, and believed the LORD and his servant Moses.

Isaiah 63:

12 Who led them by the right hand of Moses,
With his glorious arm,
Dividing the water before them
To make for himself an everlasting name,

Exodus 14:

21 Then Moses stretched out his hand over the sea; and the LORD caused the sea to go back by a strong east wind all that night, and made the sea into dry land, and the waters were divided.

Exodus 3:

6 ...'I Am the LORD; I will bring you out from under the burdens of the Egyptians, I will rescue you from their bondage, and I will redeem you with an outstretched arm and with great judgments.'

<see also Pg 122. A.4>

Proclaiming the Name of the LORD

Psalm 68:

1 Let God arise, Let His enemies be scattered;

4 Sing to God, Sing praises to His name;
Extol Him who rides on the clouds,
By His name YAH, …

Psalm 105:

7 He is the LORD our God;
His judgments are in all the earth.
8 He has remembered His covenant forever,
The word which He commanded, for a
thousand generations,
9 The covenant which He made with Abraham,
And His oath to Isaac,
10 And confirmed it to Jacob for a statute,
To Israel for an everlasting covenant,
11 Saying, "To you I will give the land of Canaan
As the allotment of your inheritance,"
12 When they were but few in number,
Indeed very few, and stranger in it.
13 When they went from one nation to another,
From one kingdom to another people,
14 He permitted no one to do them wrong;
Yes, he reproved kings for their sakes,
15 Saying, "Do not touch My anointed ones,
And do My prophets no harm."
16 Moreover He called for a famine in the land;
He destroyed all the provision of bread.
17 He sent a man before them –
Joseph – who was sold as a slave.
18 They hurt his feet with fetters,
He was laid in irons.
19 Until the time that his word came to pass,
The word of the LORD tested him.
20 The king sent and released him,
The ruler of the people let him go free.
21 He made him lord of his house,
And ruler of all his possessions,
22 To bind his princes at his pleasure,
And teach his elders wisdom.
23 Israel also came into Egypt,
And Jacob sojourned in the land of Ham.
24 And he increased His people greatly,
And made them stronger than their enemies.
25 He turned their **heart** to hate His people,
To deal craftily with His servants.
26 He sent Moses His servant,
And Aaron whom He had chosen.
27 They performed His **signs** among them,
And wonders in the land of Ham.

28 He sent darkness, and made it dark;
And they did not rebel against His word.
29 He turned their waters into blood,
And killed their fish.
30 Their land abounded with frogs,
Even in the chambers of their kings.
31 He spoke, and there came swarms of flies,
And lice in all their territory.
32 He gave them hail for rain,
And flaming fire in their land.
33 He struck their vines also, and their fig trees,
And splintered the trees of their territory.
34 He spoke, and locusts came,
Young locusts, without number,
35 And ate up all the vegetation in their land.
And devoured the fruit of their ground.
36 He also destroyed all the **firstborn** in their
land,
The first of all their strength.
37 He also brought them out with silver and gold,
And there was none feeble among his tribes.
38 Egypt was glad when they departed,
For the fear of them had fallen upon them.
39 He spread a cloud for covering,
And fire to give light in the night.
40 The people asked, and He brought quail,
And satisfied them with the bread of heaven.
41 He opened the rock, and water gushed out;
It ran in the dry places like a river.
42 For He remembered His holy promise,
And Abraham His servant.
43 He brought out His people with joy,
His chosen ones with gladness.
44 He gave them the lands of the Gentiles,
And they inherited the labor of the nations.

Psalm 106:

8 Nevertheless He saved them for His **name**'s
sake,
That He might make His mighty power known.
9 He rebuked the Red Sea also, and it dried up;
So He led them through the depths,
As through the wilderness.
10 He saved them from the hand of him who
hated them,
And redeemed them from the hand of the
enemy.
11 The waters covered their enemies;
There was not one of them left.

<see also Pg 52.B.1-26. >

What's In a Name?

*Before proceeding chronologically we will dig more into who God is. The Bible is His revelation of himself to us. These passages show that in Bible times there was a lot more to a name than just a few special words. The power in His name caused Israel (and us) to "seek God's face" – His fellowship, etc. The Bible let's us build appreciation, fear, awe, trust and hope responses to any short name, logo, or icon that points to the person of the Lord who told Moses His name is **YWWH – "I AM"**.*

Psalm 99:

8 You answered them, O LORD our God;
You were to them God-Who-Forgives,

Psalm 105:

1 Oh, give thanks to the LORD!
Call upon his name;
Make know his deeds among the peoples.
2 Sing to Him, sing psalms to Him;
Talk of all His wondrous works.
3 Glory in His holy name;
Let the hearts of those rejoice who seek the LORD.
4 Seek the LORD and His strength;
Seek His face evermore.
6 Remember His marvelous works which He has done,
His wonders, and the judgments of His mouth.

Exodus 34:

5 Then the LORD descended in the cloud and stood with him there, and proclaimed the name of the LORD.
6 And the LORD passed before him and proclaimed, "The LORD, the LORD God, merciful and gracious, long-suffering, and abounding in goodness and truth.
7 "keeping mercy for thousands, forgiving iniquity and transgression and sin, by no means clearing the guilty, visiting the iniquity of the fathers upon children and the children's children to the third and fourth generation."

Deuteronomy 32:

3 For I proclaim the name of the LORD:
Ascribe greatness to our God.
4 He is the Rock, His work is perfect;
For all His ways are justice,
A God of truth and without injustice;
Righteous and upright is He.

Joshua 24:

19 But Joshua said to the people, "You cannot serve the LORD, for He is a holy God. He is a jealous God; He will not forgive your transgressions nor your sins.

Exodus 34:

14 "(for you shall worship no other god, for the LORD, whose name is Jealous, is a jealous God),

II Samuel 7:

23 "And who is like Your people, like Israel, the one nation on the earth whom God went to redeem for Himself as a people, to make for Himself a name – and to do for You great and awesome deeds for Your land – before Your people whom You redeemed for Yourself from Egypt, from the nations and their gods?

Ezekiel 36:

22 "Therefore say to the house of Israel, 'Thus says the LORD God: "I do not do this for your sake, O house of Israel, but for My holy name's sake, which you have profaned among the nations wherever you went.
23 "And I will sanctify My great name.

Daniel 2:

20 Daniel answered and said:
"Blessed be the name of God forever and ever,
For wisdom and might are His.
21 And He changes the times and the seasons;
He removes kings and raises up kings;
He gives wisdom to the wise
And knowledge to those who have understanding.
22 He reveals deep and secret things;
He knows what is in the darkness,
And light dwells with Him.

Jeremiah 23:

6 In His days Judah will be saved,
And Israel will dwell safely;
Now this is His name by which He will be called:
THE LORD OUR RIGHTEOUSNESS
7 "Therefore, behold, the days are coming," says the LORD, "that they shall no longer say, 'As the LORD lives who brought up the children of Israel from the land of Egypt,'
8 but, 'As the LORD lives who brought up and led the descendants of the house of Israel from the north country and from all the countries where I had driven them.' And they shall dwell in their own land."

A. God's physical presence

Exodus 24:

1 and they saw the God of Israel. And there was
under His feet as it were a paved work of sapphire
stone, and it was like the very heavens in its
clarity.
11 But on the nobles of the children of Israel He
did not lay His hand. So they saw God, and they
ate and drank.
17 The sight of the glory of the LORD was like a
consuming fire on the top of the mountain in the
eyes of the children of Israel.

Exodus 33:

18 And he said, "Please, show me Your glory."
19 Then He said, "I will make all My goodness
pass before you, and I will proclaim the name
of the LORD before you. I will be gracious to
whom I will be gracious, and I will have
compassion on whom I will have compassion."
20 But He said, "You cannot see My face; for no
man shall see Me, and live."
21 And the LORD said, "Here is a place by Me,
and you shall stand on the rock.
22 "So it shall be, while My glory passes by, that I
will put you in the cleft of the rock, and will
cover you with My hand while I pass by.
23 "Then I will take away My hand, and you shall
see My back; but My face shall not be seen."

Daniel 7:

9 "I watched till thrones were put in place,
And the Ancient of Days was seated;
His garment was white as snow,
And the hair of His head was like pure wool.
His throne was a fiery flame,
Its wheels a burning fire;
10 A fiery stream issued
And came forth from before Him.
A thousand thousands ministered to Him;
Ten thousand times ten thousand stood
before Him.
The court was seated,
And the books were opened.

<see also Pg. 27.B.2>

Hebrews 12:

18 ...that mountain that may not be touched
and that burned with fire, and to blackness
and darkness and tempest,
19 And the sound of a trumpet and the voice
of words, so that those who heard it begged
that the word should not be spoken to them
anymore.
21 And so terrifying was the sight that Moses
said "I am exceedingly afraid and trembling."

B. God's Name's presence

Zechariah 10:

12 "So I will strengthen them in the LORD,
And they shall walk up and down in His name,"
Says the LORD.

II Chronicles 7:

16 "For now I have chosen and sanctified this house,
that My name may be there forever; and My eyes
and My heart will be there perpetually.

Deuteronomy 12:

2 "You shall utterly destroy all the places where the
nations which you shall dispossess served their gods,
on the high mountains and on the hills and under
every green tree.
3 "And you shall destroy their alters, break their
sacred pillars, and burn their wooden images with
fire; you shall cut down the carved images of their
gods and destroy their names from that place.
4 "You shall not worship the LORD your God with
such things.
5 "But you shall seek the place where the LORD your
God chooses, out of all your tribes, to put His
name for His habitation; and there you shall go.

II Chronicles 6:

18 "But will God indeed dwell with men on the
earth? Behold, heaven and the heaven of heavens
cannot contain You; how much less this temple
which I have built!

Deuteronomy 4:

32 "...now concerning the days that are past, which
were before you, since the day that God created
man on the earth, and ask from one end of heaven
to the other, whether any great thing like this has
happened, or anything like it has been heard.
33 "Did any people ever hear the voice of God
speaking out of the midst of the fire, as you have
heard, and live?
34 "Or did God ever try to go and take for Himself
a nation from the midst of another nation, by trials,
by signs, by wonders, by war, by a mighty hand
and an outstretched arm★, and be great terrors,
according to all that the LORD your God did for
you in Egypt before your eyes?
35 "To you it was shown, that you might know that
the LORD Himself is God; there is none other
besides him.
36 "Out of heaven He let you hear His voice,
that He might instruct you; on earth He showed
you His great fire, and you heard his words out
of the midst of the fire.

★*<see also Pg.5 B.6. & Pg. 22.A.2-36>*

God Is Revealed To Us

Having learned of God's Name
We now look deeply to know Him more fully in the next six pages.

His Divine Nature

Isaiah 45:

5 I am the LORD, and there is no other;
There is no God besides Me.

I Timothy 6:

16 who alone has immortality, dwelling in unapproachable light, whom no man has seen or can see, to whom be honor and everlasting power. Amen.

Isaiah 55:

8 "For my thoughts are not your thoughts,
Nor are your ways My ways," says the LORD.
9 "For as the heavens are higher than the earth,
So are my ways higher than your ways,
And My thoughts than your thoughts.

Romans 11:

33 Oh, the depth of the riches both of the wisdom and knowledge of God! How unsearchable are His judgments and His ways past finding out!

34 *"For who has known the mind of the Lord?*
Or who has become His counselor?"
35 *"Or who has first given to Him*
And it shall be repaid to him?"

36 For of Him and through Him and to Him are all things, to whom be glory forever. Amen.

II Peter 3:

8 But, beloved, do not forget this one thing, that with the LORD one day is as a thousand years, and a thousand years as one day.
9 The LORD is not slack concerning His promise, as some count slackness, but is longsuffering toward us, <u>not willing that any should perish but that all should come to repentance.</u>

Hebrews 4:

13 And there is no creature hidden from His sight, but all things are naked and open to the eyes of Him to whom we must give account.

James 1:

17 <u>Every good gift and every perfect gift is from above</u>, and comes down from the Father of lights, with whom there is no variation or shadow of turning.

Isaiah 57:

15 For thus says the High and Lofty One
Who inhabits eternity, whose name is Holy;

Psalm 19:

1 The heavens declare the glory of God;
And the firmament shows His handiwork.

Acts 15:

18 "<u>Known to God from eternity are all His works.</u>

Psalm 90:

4 For a thousand years in Your sight
Are like yesterday when it is past,
And like a watch in the night.

Psalm 68:

33 To Him who rides on the heaven of heavens, which were of old!

Psalm 147:

4 He counts the number of the stars;
He calls them all by name.
5 Great is our LORD, and mighty in power;
His understanding is infinite.

Jeremiah 51:

15 He has made the earth by His power;
He has established the world by His wisdom,
And <u>stretched out the heaven</u> by His understanding.
16 When He utters His voice –
There is a multitude of waters in the heavens:
"He causes the vapors to ascend from the ends of the earth;
He makes lightnings for the rain;
He brings the wind out of His treasuries."

Isaiah 45:

6 That they may know from the rising of the sun to its setting
That there is none besides Me.
I am the LORD, and there is no other;
7 I form the light and create darkness,
I make peace <u>and create calamity</u>;
I, the LORD, do all these things.'
8 "Rain down, you heavens, from above,
And let the skies pour down righteousness;
Let the earth open, let them bring forth salvation,
And let righteousness spring up together.
I, the LORD, have created it.

More About the Author of the Bible

I Timothy 2:

3 For this is good and acceptable in the sight of God our Savior,
4 who desires all men to be saved and to come to the knowledge of the truth.

Romans 1:

19 because what may be known of God is manifest in them, for God has shown it to them.
20 For since the creation of the world His invisible attributes are clearly seen, being understood by the things that are made, even His eternal power and Godhead, so that they are without excuse,

Jeremiah 23:

24 Can anyone hide himself in secret places, So I shall not see him?" says the LORD; " Do I not fill heaven and earth?" says the LORD.

I Chronicles 28:

9 "As for you, my son Solomon, know the God of your father, and serve Him with a loyal heart and with a willing mind; for the LORD searches all hearts and understands all the intent of the thoughts. If you seek Him, He will be found by you; but if you forsake Him, He will cast you off forever.

Exodus 33:

11 "Say to them: 'As I live,' says the LORD God, 'I have no pleasure in the death of the wicked, but that the wicked turn from his way and live. Turn, turn from your evil ways! For why should you die, O house of Israel?'

Isaiah 57:

15 "I dwell in the high and holy place,
With him who has a contrite and humble spirit,
To revive the spirit of the humble,
And to revive the heart of the contrite ones.
16 For I will not contend forever,
Nor will I always be angry;
For the spirit would fail before Me,
And the souls which I have made.
17 For the iniquity of his covetousness
I was angry and struck him;
I hid and was angry,
And he went on backsliding in the way of his heart.
18 I have seen his ways, and will heal him;
I will also lead him,
And restore comforts to him < humans>
And to his mourners. < angels? >

Isaiah 40:

12 Who has measured the waters in the hollow of his hand,
Measured heaven with a span
And calculated the dust of the earth in a measure?
Weighed the mountains in scales
And the hills in a balance?
13 Who has directed the Spirit of the LORD,
Or as His counselor has taught Him?
14 With whom did He take counsel, and who instructed Him,
And taught Him knowledge,
And showed Him the way of understanding?
25 "To whom then will you liken Me,
Or to whom shall I be equal?" says the Holy One.
26 Lift up your eyes on high,
And see who has created these things,
Who brings out their host by number;
He calls them all by name,
By the greatness of His might
And the strength of His power;
No one is missing.
27 Why do you say, O Jacob,
And speak, O Israel:
"My way is hidden from the LORD,
And my just claim is passed over by my God?"
28 Have you not known?
Have you not heard?
The everlasting God, the LORD,
The Creator of the ends of the earth,
Neither faints nor is weary.
There is no searching of His understanding.

I Kings 19:

8 So he arose, and ate and drank; and he went in the strength of that food forty days and forty nights as far as Horeb, the mountain of God.
11 Then He said, "Go out, and stand on the mountain before the LORD." And behold, the LORD passed by, and a great and strong wind tore into the mountains and broke the rocks in pieces before the LORD, but the LORD was not in the wind; and after the wind an earthquake, but the LORD was not in the earthquake;
12 and after the earthquake a fire, but the LORD was not in the fire; and after fire a still small voice.
13 So it was, when Elijah heard it, that he wrapped his face in his mantle and went out and stood in the entrance of the cave. And suddenly a voice came to him, and said, "What are you doing here, Elijah?"

The Physical (3-D) Side of God: Jesus

Colossians 2:

9 For in Him dwells all the fullness of the
Godhead bodily;

Acts 17:

24 "God, who made the world and everything in
it, since He is Lord of heaven and earth, does
not dwell in temples made with hands.
25 "Nor is He worshipped with men's hands, as
though He needed anything, since He gives to
all life, breath, and all things.
26 "And He has made from one blood every
nation of men to dwell on all the face of the
earth, and has determined their preappointed
times and the boundaries of their habitation,
27 "so that they should seek the LORD, in the
hope that they might grope for Him and find
Him, though He is not far from each one of us;
28 "for in Him we live and move and
have our being, as also some of your
own poets have said, 'For we are also
His offspring.'
29 "Therefore, since we are the offspring of
God, w ought not to think that the Divine
Nature is like gold or silver or stone, something
shaped by art and man's devising.
30 "Truly, these times of ignorance God
overlooked, but now commands all men
everywhere to repent,
31 "because He has appointed a day on
which He will judge the world in
righteousness by the Man whom He has
ordained. He has given assurance of this
to all, by raising Him from the dead."

Hebrews 1:

1 God, who at various times and in different
ways spoke in time past to the fathers by
the prophets,
2 has in these last days spoken to us by His Son,
whom He has appointed heir of all things,
through whom also He made the worlds;
3 who being the brightness of His glory and the
express image of His person, and upholding
all things by the word of His power, when He
had by Himself purged our sins, sat down at
the right hand of the Majesty on high,

Deuteronomy 11:26b

LORD your God, His greatness and His
mighty hand and outstretched arm –

Mark 13:

31 "Heaven and earth will pass away, but
My words will by no means pass away."

< *see Pg.5B5 & Pg.33A1, 37B3, 75B6* >

Colossians 1:

15 He is the image of the invisible God, the
firstborn over all creation.
16 For by Him all things were created that are
in heaven and that are on earth, visible and
invisible, whether thrones or dominions or
principalities or powers. All things were
created through Him and for Him.
17 And He is before all things, and in Him
all things consist.

John 1:

1 In the beginning was the Word, and the Word
was with God, and the Word was God.
2 He was in the beginning with God.
3 All things were made through Him, and
without Him nothing was made that was made.
4 In Him was life, and the life was the light of men.
10 He was in the world, and the world was made
through Him, and the world did not know Him.
11 He came to His own, and His own did not
receive Him.
12 But as many as received Him, to them He
gave the right to become children of God,
even to those who believe in His name:
13 who were born, not of blood, nor of the will of
the flesh, nor of the will of man, but of God.
14 And the Word became flesh and dwelt among
us, and we beheld His glory, the glory as of the
only begotten of the Father, full of grace and
truth.

Isaiah 40:

10 Behold, the LORD God shall come with a
strong hand,
And His arm shall rule for Him;
Behold, His reward is with Him,
And His work before Him.
11 He will feed His flock like a shepherd;
He will gather the lambs with His arms,

<*see alsoPg.8B5 & Pg.4B3 & Pg.40A1*>

Isaiah 52

10 The LORD has made bare His holy arm
In the eyes of all the nations;
And all the ends of the earth shall see
The salvation of our God.

Deuteronomy 7: <*see Exodus 15:6, 12*>

19 "the great trials which your eyes saw, the signs
and the wonders, the mighty hand and the
outstretched arm by which the LORD your
God brought you out.

The Son and the Father Are One!

(see Pg 78 A.3.30)

Revelation 3:
14 'These things says the Amen, the Faithful and True Witness, the Beginning of the creation of God:

John 14:
6 Jesus said to him, "I am the way, the truth, and the life. No one comes to the Father except through Me.
7 "If you had known Me, you would have known My Father also; and from now on you know Him and have seen Him."
8 Philip said to Him, "Lord, show us the Father, and it is sufficient for us."
9 Jesus said to him, "Have I been with you so long, and yet you have not known Me, Philip? He who has seen Me has seen the Father; so how can you say, 'Show us the Father'?
10 "Do you not believe that I am in the Father, and the Father in Me? The words I speak to you I do not speak on My own authority; but the Father who dwells in Me does the works.
11 "Believe Me that I am in the Father and the Father in Me, or else believe Me for the sake of the works themselves.

John 12:
44 Then Jesus cried out and said, "He who believes in Me, believes not in Me but in Him who sent Me.
45 "And he who sees Me sees Him who sent Me.
46 "I have come as a light into the world, that whoever believes in Me should not abide in darkness.
47 "And if anyone hears My words and does not believe, I do not judge him; for I did not come to judge the world but to save the world.
48 "He who rejects Me, and does not receive My words, has that which judges him – the word that I have spoken will judge him in the last day.

I Timothy 2:
5 For there is one God and one Mediator between God and men, the Man Christ Jesus,
6 who gave Himself a ransom for all, to be testified in due time,

I Timothy 4:
10 For to this end we both labor and suffer reproach, because we trust in the living God, who is Savior of all men, especially of those who believe.

John 5:
18 Therefore the Jews sought all the more to kill Him, because He not only broke the Sabbath, but also said that God was His Father, making Himself equal with God.*

John 8:
56 "Your father Abraham rejoiced to see My day, and he saw it and was glad."
57 Then the Jews said to Him, "You are not yet fifty years old, and have You seen Abraham?"
58 Jesus said to them, "Most assuredly, I say to you, before Abraham was, I AM."

John 17:
9 "I pray for them. I do not pray for the world but for those whom You have given Me, for they are Yours.
10 "And all Mine are Yours, and Yours are Mine, and I am glorified in them.
11 "Now I am no longer in the world, but these are in the world, and I come to You. Holy Father, keep through Your name those whom You have given Me, that they may be one as We are.
12 "While I was with them in the world, I kept them in Your name. Those whom You gave Me I have kept; and none of them is lost except the son of perdition, that the Scriptures might be fulfilled.
13 "But now I come to You, and these things I speak in the world, that they may have My joy fulfilled in themselves.
14 "I have given them Your word; and the world has hated them because they are not of the world, just as I am not of the world.

John 6:
33 "For the bread of God is He who comes down from heaven and gives life to the world."
34 Then they said to Him, "Lord, give us this bread always."
35 And Jesus said to them, "I am the bread of life. He who comes to Me shall never hunger, and he who believes in Me shall never thirst.

I John 4:
12 No one has seen God at any time. If we love one another, God abides in us, and His love has been perfected in us.
13 By this we know that we abide in Him, and He in us, because He has given us of His Spirit.

** To the Jews a son was equal to his father and could carry on the same name. This metaphor was well suited to deliver Christ's message: "I Am God!"*

We are God's Offspring.
Note our own Triune nature.

<see also Pg.14B2 & Pg.96.A.1>

Genesis 1:

26 Then God said, "Let Us make man in Our image, according to Our likeness; let them have dominion over the fish of the sea, over the birds of the air, and over the cattle, over all the earth and over every creeping thing that creeps on the earth."
27 So God created man in His own image; in the image of God He created him; male <u>and</u> female He created them.

James 1:

18 Of His own will He brought us forth by the word of truth, that we might be a kind of firstfruits of His creatures.

I John 3:

1 Behold what manner of love the Father has bestowed on us, that we should be called children of God! Therefore the world does not know us, because it did not know Him.
2 Beloved, now we are children of God and it has not yet been revealed what we shall be, but we know that when He is revealed, we shall be like Him, for we shall see Him as He is.

Romans 8:

18 For I consider that the sufferings of this present time are not worthy to be compared with the glory which shall be revealed in us.
19 For the earnest expectation of the creation eagerly waits for the revealing of the sons of God.
20 For the creation was subjected to futility, not willingly, but because of Him who subjected it in hope;
21 because the creation itself also will be delivered from the bondage of corruption into the glorious liberty of the children of God.

John 20: ** *<** See note Pg. 14.A.1>*

17 Jesus said to her, "Do not cling to Me, for I have not yet ascended to My Father; . . .' "

Ephesians 4:

23 And be renewed in the spirit of your mind.

Zechariah 12:

1 . . .Thus says the Lord, who stretches out the heavens, lays the foundation of the earth, and forms the spirit of man within him:

Proverbs 20:

27 The spirit of a man is the lamp of the Lord, Searching all the inner depths of his heart.

More about the three-faceted (Triune) nature of God and man.

John 1:

18 No one has seen God at any time. The only Begotten Son, who is in the bosom of he Father, He has declared Him.

Philippians 1:

19 For I know that this will turn out for my salvation through your prayer and the supply of the Spirit of Jesus Christ,

I John 5:

7 For there are three who bear witness in heaven: the Father, the Word, and the Holy Spirit; and these three are one.
8 And there are three that bear witness on earth: the Spirit, the water and the blood; and these three agree as one.

I Thessalonians 5:

23 Now may the God of peace Himself sanctify you completely; and may your whole spirit, soul, and body be preserved blameless at the coming of our Lord Jesus Christ.

I Corinthians 2:

10 But God has revealed them to us through His Spirit. For the Spirit searches all things, yes, the deep things of God.
11 For what man knows the things of a man except the spirit of the man which is in him? Even so no one knows the things of God except the Spirit of God.

John 17:

20 "I do not pray for these alone, but also for those who will believe in Me through their word;
21 "that they all may be one as You, Father, are in Me, and I in You; that they also may be one in Us, that the world may believe that You sent Me.

<Note Christ's desire for believers.>

22 "And the glory which You gave Me I have given them, that they may be one just as We are one: *< per Pg. 82.B.1>*

Jeremiah 17:

9 "The heart is deceitful above all *things*, and desperately wicked; who can know it?
10 I the lord, search the heart, I test the mind, Even to give every man according to his ways, According to the fruit of his doings. "

<see also Pg.51B1& 100B3>

God - The Spirit of Truth

The Holy Spirit is the Spirit of Christ. (pg.13B2), aka "Spirit of truth." Aka "spirit of wisdom" (pg.17B5). The spirit of Jesus, was on earth in Him, and now in His offspring.

I Peter 1:

10 Of this salvation the prophets have inquired and searched diligently, who prophesied of the grace that would come to you,
11 searching what, or what manner of time, the Spirit of Christ who was in them was indicating when He testified beforehand the sufferings of Christ and the glories that would follow.*
12 To them it was revealed that, not to themselves, but to us they were ministering the things which now have been reported to you through those who have preached the gospel to you by the Holy Spirit sent from heaven – things which angels desire to look into.

John 15:

26 "But when the Helper comes, whom I shall send to you from the Father, the Spirit of truth who proceeds from the Father, He will testify of Me.
27 "And you also will bear witness, because you have been with me from the beginning.

John 15:

14 "You are My friends if you do whatever I command you.
15 "No longer do I call you servants, for a servant does not know what his master is doing; but I have called you friends, for all things that I heard from My Father I have made known to you.

John 16:

7 "Nevertheless I tell you the truth. It is to your advantage that I go away; for if I do not go away, the Helper will not come to you; but if I depart, I will send Him to you. *
8 "And when He has come, He will convict the world of sin, and of righteousness, and of judgment:
9 "of sin, because they do not believe in Me;
10 "of righteousness, because I go to My Father and you see Me no more;
11 "of judgment, because the ruler of this world is judged.
12 "I still have many things to say to you, but you cannot bear them now.
13 "However, when He, the Spirit of truth, has come, He will guide you into all truth; for He will not speak on His own authority, but whatever He hears He will speak; and He will tell you things to come.

I John 5:

6 This is He who came by water and blood – Jesus Christ; not only by water, but by water and blood. And it is the Spirit who bears witness, because the Spirit is truth.

John 14:

16 "And I will pray the Father, and He will give you another Helper, that He may abide with you forever,
17 "even the Spirit of truth , whom the world cannot receive, because it neither sees Him nor knows Him; but you know Him, for He dwells with you and will be in you.
18 "I will not leave you orphans; I will come to you.
25 "These things I have spoken to you while being present with you.
26 "But the Helper, the Holy Spirit, whom the Father will send in My name, He will teach you all things, and bring to your remembrance all things that I said to you.
27 "Peace I leave you, My peace I give to you; not as the world gives do I give to you. Let not your heart be troubled, neither let it be afraid.
28 "You have heard Me say to you, 'I am going away and coming back to you.' If you loved Me, you would rejoice because I said, 'I am going to the Father,' for My Father is greater than I.

Ezekiel 11:

5 Then the Spirit of the LORD fell upon me, and said to me, "Speak! 'Thus says the LORD: "Thus you have said, O house of Israel; for I know the things that come into your mind.

I John 4:

6 We are of God. He who knows God hears us; he who is not of God does not hear us. By this we know the spirit of truth and the spirit of error.
7 Beloved, let us love one another, for love is of God; and everyone who loves is born of God and knows God.
8 He who does not love does not know God, for God is love.
9 In this the love of God was manifested toward us, that God has sent His only begotten Son into the world, that we might live through Him.
10 In this is love, not that we loved God, but that He loved us and sent His son to be the propitiation for our sins.
11 Beloved, if God so loved us, we also ought to love one another.

* < *See also Pg. 78.A.4.5/Pg. 91.A.2/Pg. 113.A.2/ Pg.88A.1-2!* >

Historical Recap (Name)

Acts 7:

2 And he said, "Men and brethren and fathers,
listen: The God of glory appeared to our father
Abraham when he was in Mesopotamia, before
he dwelt in Haran.
3 "and said to him, 'Get out of your country
and from your relatives, and come to a land
that I will show you.'
4 "Then he came out of the land of the
Chaldeans and dwelt in Haran. And from
there, when his father was dead, He moved him
to this land in which you now dwell.
5 "And God gave him no inheritance in it, not
even enough to set his foot on. But even when
Abraham had no child, He promised to give it
to him for a possession, and to his descendents
after him.
6 "But God spoke in this way: that his
descendants would sojourn in a foreign land,
and that they would bring them into bondage
and oppress them four hundred years.
8 "Then He gave him the covenant of
circumcision; and so Abraham begot Isaac and
circumcised him on the eighth day; and Isaac
begot Jacob, and Jacob begot the twelve
patriarchs.
9 "And the patriarchs, becoming envious, sold
Joseph into Egypt. But God was with him
10 "and delivered him out of all his troubles,
and gave him favor and wisdom in the presence
of Pharaoh, king of Egypt; and he made him
governor over Egypt and all his house.
11 Now a famine and great trouble came over all
the land of Egypt and Canaan, and our fathers
found no sustenance
12 "But when Jacob heard that there was grain in
Egypt, he sent out our fathers first.
13 "And the second time Joseph was made
known to his brothers, and Joseph's family
became known to the Pharaoh.
14 "Then Joseph sent and called his father Jacob
and all his relatives to him, seventy-five people.
15 "So Jacob went down to Egypt; and he died,
he and our fathers.
16 "And they carried back to Shechem and laid
in the tomb that Abraham bought for a sum of
money from the sons of Hamor, the father of
Shechem.
17 "But when the time of the promise drew near
which God had sworn to Abraham, the people
grew and multiplied in Egypt
18 "till another king arose who did not know
Joseph.
19 "This man dealt treacherously with our people,
and oppressed our forefathers, making them
expose their babies, so that they might not live.
20 "At this time Moses was born, and was well
pleasing to God; and he was brought up in his
father's house for three months.
21 "But when he was set out, Pharaoh's daughter
took him away and brought him up as her own
son.
22 "And Moses was learned in all the wisdom of
the Egyptians, and was mighty in words and deeds.
23 "But when he was forty years old, it came into
his **heart** to visit his brethren, the children of
Israel.
24 "And seeing one of them suffer wrong, he
defended and avenged him who was oppressed,
and struck down the Egyptian.
25 "For he supposed that his brethren would have
understood that God would deliver them by his
hand, but they did not understand.
29 "Then, at this saying, Moses, fled and became a
sojourner in the land of Midian, where he had two
sons.
30 "And when forty years had passed, an **Angel** of
the LORD appeared to him in a flame of fire in a
bush, in the wilderness of Mount Sinai.
31 "When Moses saw it, he marveled at the sight;
and as he drew near to observe, the voice of the
LORD came to him,
32 "saying, 'I am the God of your fathers – the God
of Abraham, the God of Isaac, and the God of
Jacob.' And Moses trembled and dared not look.
33 'Then the LORD said to him, "Take your sandals
off your feet, for the place where you stand is holy
ground.
34 "I have certainly seen the oppression of my
people who are in Egypt; I have heard their
groaning and have come down to deliver them.
And now come, I will send you to Egypt." '
35 "This Moses whom they rejected, saying, 'Who
made you a ruler and a judge?' is the one God sent
to be a ruler and a deliverer by the hand of the
Angel who appeared to him in the bush.
36 He brought them out, after he had shown
wonders and **signs** in the land of Egypt, and in
the Red Sea, and in the wilderness forty years.

Ten Commandments
Then to the "Promised Land"

Exodus 20:

1 And God spoke all these words, saying:
2 "I am the LORD your God, who brought you out of the land of Egypt, out of the house of bondage.
3 "You shall have no other gods before Me.
4 "You shall not make for yourself any carved image, or any likeness of anything that is in heaven above, or that is in the earth beneath, or that is in the water under the earth;
5 you shall not bow down to them nor serve them. For I, the LORD your God, am a jealous God, visiting the iniquity of the fathers on the children to the third and fourth generations of those who hate Me,
6 but showing mercy to thousands, to those who **love** Me and keep My commandments.
7 "You shall not take the **name** of the LORD your God **in vain**, for the LORD will not hold him guiltless who takes His name **in vain.***
8 "Remember the Sabbath day, to keep it holy.
9 Six days you shall labor and do all you work,
10 but the seventh day is the Sabbath of the LORD your God. In it you shall do no work; you, nor your son, nor your daughter, nor your manservant, nor your maidservant, nor your cattle, nor your stranger who is within your gates.
11 For in six days the LORD made the heavens and the earth, the sea, and all that is in them, and rested the seventh day. Therefore the LORD blessed the Sabbath day and hallowed it.
12 Honor your father and your mother, that your days may be long upon the land which the LORD your God is giving you.
13 "You shall not murder.
14 "You shall not commit adultery.
15 "You shall not steal.
16 "You shall not bear false witness against your neighbor.
17 "You shall not covet your neighbor's house; you shall not covet your neighbor's wife, nor his manservant, nor his maidservant, nor his ox, nor his donkey, nor anything that is your neighbor's.
18 "Now all the people witnessed the thunderings, the lightning flashes, the sound of the trumpet, and the mountain smoking; and when the people saw it, they trembled and stood afar off.

*** *Note how "in vain" means referring to the Lord without considering His whole name (and its power); and thus being careless or vain in doing so.***

Deuteronomy 4:

2 "You shall not add to the word which I command you, nor take from it,...

9 "Only take heed to yourself, and diligently keep yourself, lest you forget the things your eyes have seen, and lest they depart your **heart** all the days of your life. And teach them to your children and your grandchildren,
10 "*especially concerning* the day you stood before the LORD your God in Horeb, ...
12 "And the LORD spoke to you out of the midst of the fire. You heard the sound of the words, ...

<see Pg.72B and Deuteronomy 10: 12-13>

Joshua 5:

6 For the children of Israel walked forty years in the wilderness, till all the people who were men of war, who came out of Egypt were consumed, because they did not obey the voice of the LORD – to whom the LORD swore that He would not show them the land which the LORD had sworn to their fathers that he would give us, "a land flowing with milk and honey."

John 1:

17 For the **law** was given through Moses, *but* grace and **truth** came through Jesus Christ.

Taking the Promised Land

Deuteronomy 2:

34 "We took all his cities at that time, and we utterly destroyed the men, women, and little ones of every city; we left none remaining.

<(NOTE KILLING of "innocents"?)>

Deuteronomy 3:

4 "And we took all his cities at that time; there was not a city which we did not take from them: sixty cities, all the region of Argob, the kingdom of Og in Bashan.
5 "All these cities were fortified with high walls, gates, and bars, besides a great many rural towns.
6 "And we utterly destroyed them, as we did to Sihon king of Heshbon, utterly destroying the men, women, and children of every city.

8 At that time the LORD separated the tribe of Levi to bear the ark of the covenant of the LORD, to stand before the LORD to minister to Him and to bless in His name, to this day. "

Some Final Instructions of Moses

Deuteronomy 4:

15 "Take careful heed to yourselves, for you saw no form when the LORD spoke to you at Horeb out of the midst of the fire,
16 "lest you act corruptly and make for yourselves a carved image in the form of any figure: the likeness of male or female,
17 "the likeness of any beast that is on the earth or the likeness of any winged bird that flies in the air,
18 "the likeness of anything that creeps on the ground or the likeness of any fish that is in the water beneath the earth.

Deuteronomy 2:

9 . . . 'DO not harass Moab, . . . because I have given Ar to the descendants of Lot *as* a possession.'"
10 (The Emin had dwealt there in times past, a people as great and numerous and tall as the Anakim. 11 They were also regarded as giants,. . .

19 . . . 'the people of Ammon, do not harass them . . . because I have given it to the descendants of Lot *as* a possession.'"
20(. . .giants formerly dwealt there. But the Ammonites call them Zamzummim,
21 a people as great and numerous and tall as the Anakim. But the LORD destroyed them before them,. . .
22 just as He had done for the descendants of Esau, who dwealt in Seir, when He destroyed the Horites . . .

Deuteronomy 7:

16 "And you shall destroy all the peoples whom the LORD your God delivers over to you; your eye shall have no pity on them; nor shall you serve their gods, for that will be a snare to you.

Deuteronomy 31:

24 So it was, when Moses had completed writing the words of this law in a book . . . 25 that Moses commanded the Levites, who bore the ark of the covenant of the LORD, saying : 26 "Take this Book of Law, and put it inside the ark. . . as a witness against you; . . . 29 For I know that after my death you will become utterly corrupt, and turn aside from the way which I have commanded you, And evil will befall you in the latter days, . . .

Moving Into the Promised Land (transition to Joshua)

Deuteronomy 31:

24 So it was, when Moses had completed writing the words of this law in a book . . . 25 that Moses

Galatians 3:

24 Therefore the law was our tutor *to bring us* to Christ, that we might be justified by faith.
24 But after faith has come, we are no longer under a tutor.

Deuteronomy 32:

39 'Now see that I, *even* I, *am* He,
And *there is* no God besides Me;
I kill and I make alive;
I wound and I heal;
Nor *is there any* who can deliver from My Hand.

Deuteronomy 34:

9 Now Joshua the son of Nun was full of the spirit of wisdom, for Moses had laid his hands on him; so the children of Israel heeded him, and did as the LORD had commanded Moses.
10 But since then there has not arisen in Israel a prophet like Moses, whom the LORD knew face to face,
11 in all the signs and wonders which the LORD sent him to do in the land of Egypt, before Pharaoh, before all his servants, and in all his land,
12 and by all that mighty power and all the great terror which Moses performed in the sight of all Israel.

Deuteronomy 32:

20b . . .For they *are* a perverse generation,
Children in whom *is* no faith.

Joshua

Deuteronomy 34:

9 Now Joshua the son of Nun was full of the spirit of wisdom, for Moses had laid his hands on him; so the children of Israel heeded him, and did as the LORD had commanded Moses.

Joshua 4:

22 "then you shall let your children know, saying, 'Israel crossed over this Jordan on dry land';
23 "for the LORD your God dried up the waters of the Jordan before you until you had crossed over, as the LORD your God did to the Red Sea, which He dried up before us until we had crossed over,
24 "that all the peoples of the earth may know the hand of the LORD, that it is mighty, that you may fear the LORD your God forever."

Joshua 5:

12 Now the manna ceased on the day after they had eaten the produce of the land; and the children of Israel no longer had manna, but they ate the food of the land of Canaan that year.

Joshua 6: (Jericho)

20 So the people shouted when the priests blew the trumpets. And it happened when the people heard the sound of the trumpet, and the people shouted with a great shout, that the wall fell down flat. ....
21 And they utterly destroyed all that was in the city, both man and woman, young and old, ox and sheep and donkey, with the edge of the sword.
25 And Joshua spared Rahab the harlot, her father's household, and all that she had. So she dwells in Israel to this day, because she hid the messengers whom Joshua sent to spy out Jericho.

Joshua 10:

12 Then Joshua spoke to the LORD in the day when the LORD delivered up the Amorites before the children of Israel, and he said in the sight of Israel:

"Sun, stand still over Gibeon;
And Moon, in the Valley of Aijalon."
13 So the sun stood still,
And the moon stopped,
Till the people had revenge
Upon their enemies.

Is this not written in the Book of Jasher? So the sun stood still in the midst of heaven, and did not hasten to go down for about a whole day.
14 And there has been no day like that, before it or after it, that the LORD heeded the voice of a man; for the LORD fought for Israel.

Joshua 10:

40 So Joshua conquered all the land: the mountain, country and the South and the lowland and the wilderness slopes, and all their kings; he left none remaining, but utterly destroyed all that breathed, as the LORD God of Israel had commanded.

Joshua 11:

19 There was not a city that made peace with the children of Israel, except the Hivites, the inhabitants of Gibeon. All the others they took in battle.
20 For it was of the LORD to harden their hearts, that they should come against Israel in battle, that He might utterly destroy them, and that they might receive no mercy, but that He might destroy them, as the LORD had commanded Moses.
21 And at that time Joshua came and cut off the Anakim from the mountains; from Hebron, from Debir, from Anab, from all the mountains of Judah, and from all the mountains of Israel; Joshua utterly destroyed them with their cities.

Joshua 23:

14 "Behold, this day I am going the way of all the earth. And you know in all your hearts and in all your souls that not one thing has failed of all the good things which the LORD your God spoke concerning you. All have come to pass for you, and not one word of them has failed.

Joshua 24:

2 And Joshua said to all the people, "Thus says the LORD God of Israel: 'Your fathers, including Terah, the father of Abraham and the father of Nahor, dwelt on the other side of the River in old times; and they served other gods.
3 'Then I took your father Abraham from the other side of the River, led him throughout all the land of Canaan, and multiplied his descendants and gave him Isaac.
4 'To Isaac I gave Jacob and Esau. To Esau I gave the mountains of Seir to possess, but Jacob and his children went down to Egypt.
5 'Also I sent Moses and Aaron, and I plagued Egypt, according to what I did among them. Afterward I brought you out.
6 'Then I brought your fathers out of Egypt, and you came to the sea; and the Egyptians pursued your fathers with chariots and horsemen to the Red Sea.
7 'So they cried out to the LORD; and He put darkness between you and the Egyptians, brought the sea upon them, and covered them. And your eyes saw what I did in Egypt. Then you dwelt in the wilderness a long time.

Judges Period

Judges 2:

7 So the people served the LORD all the days of Joshua, and all the days of the elders who outlived Joshua, who had seen all the great works of the LORD which He had done for Israel.
10 When all that generation had been gathered to their fathers, another generation arose after them who did not know the LORD nor the work which He had done for Israel.
11 Then the children of Israel did evil in the sight of the LORD, and served the Baals;
12 and they forsook the LORD God of their fathers, who had brought them out of the land of Egypt; and they followed other gods from among the gods of the people who were all around them, and they bowed down to them; and they provoked the LORD to anger.
13 They forsook the LORD and served Baal and the Ashtoreths.
14 And the anger of the LORD was hot against Israel. So He delivered them into the hands of plunderers who despoiled them; and He sold them into the hands of their enemies all around, so that they could no longer stand before their enemies.
15 Wherever they went out, the hand of the LORD was against them for calamity, as the LORD had said, and as the LORD was sworn to them. And they were greatly distressed.
16 Then the LORD raised up judges who delivered them out of the hand of those who plundered them.
17 Yet they would not listen to their judges, but they played the harlot with other gods, and bowed down to them. They turned quickly from the way in which their fathers walked, in obeying the commandments of the LORD; they did not do so.
18 And when the LORD raised up judges for them, the LORD was with the judge and delivered them out of the hand of their enemies all the days of the judge; for the LORD was moved to pity by their groaning because of those who oppressed them and harassed them.

Judges 2 (cont)

19 And it came to pass, when the judge was dead, that they reverted and behaved more corruptly than their fathers, by following other gods, to serve them and bow down to them. They did not cease from their own doings nor from their stubborn way.
20 Then the anger of the LORD was hot against Israel; and He said, "Because this nation has transgressed My covenant which I commanded their fathers, and has not heeded My voice,
21 "I also will no longer drive out before them any of the nations which Joshua left when he died,
22 "so that through them I may test Israel, whether they will keep the ways of the LORD, to walk in them as their fathers kept them, or not."

Judges 21:

25 In those days there was no king in Israel; everyone did what was right in his own eyes.

Deuteronomy 23:

3 "An Ammonite or Moabite shall not enter the congregation of the LORD; even to the tenth generation none of his descendants shall enter the congregation of the LORD forever,

<(NOTE that the LAW did not limit God – His chosen line of David came only 3 generations from a Moabite!>

Ruth 4: (Ancestry of David and Jesus)

10 "Moreover, Ruth the Moabitess, the wife of Mahlon, I have acquired as my wife, to raise up the name of the dead on his inheritance, that the name of the dead may not be cut off from among his brethren and from the gate of his place. You are witnesses this day."
13 So Boaz took Ruth and she became his wife; and when he went in to her, the LORD gave her conception, and she bore a son.
16 Then Naomi took the child and laid him on her bosom, and became a nurse to him.
17 Also the neighbor women gave him a name, saying, "There is a son born to Naomi." And they called his name Obed. He is the father of Jesse, the father of David.

Samuel & The 1st King of the Jews - Saul

I Samuel 3:

1 Then the boy Samuel ministered to the LORD before Eli. And the word of the LORD was rare in those days; there was no widespread revelation.

I Samuel 8:

4 Then all the elders of Israel gathered together and came to Samuel at Ramah,
5 and said to him, "Look, you are old, and your sons do not walk in your ways. Now make for us a king to judge us like all the nations."
6 But the thing displease Samuel when they said, "Give us a king to judge us." So Samuel prayed to the LORD.
7 And the LORD said to Samuel, "Heed the voice of the people in all that they say to you; for they have not rejected you, but they have rejected Me, that I should not reign over them.

I Samuel 9:

2 And he had a son whose name was Saul, a choice and handsome young man. There was not a more handsome person than he among the children of Israel. From his shoulders upward he was taller than any of the people.

I Samuel 10:

24 And Samuel said to all the people, "Do you see him whom the LORD has chosen, that there is no one like him among all the people?" So all the people shouted and said, "Long live the king!"

I Samuel 15:

22 Then Samuel said:
"Has the LORD as great delight in burnt offerings and sacrifices,
As in obeying the voice of the LORD?
Behold, to obey is better than sacrifice,
And to heed than the fat of rams.
23 For rebellion is as the sin of witchcraft,
And stubbornness is as iniquity and idolatry.
Because you have rejected the word of the LORD,
He also has rejected you from being king."

35 And Samuel went no more to see Saul until the day of his death. Nevertheless Samuel mourned for Saul, and the LORD regretted that He had made Saul king over Israel.

I Samuel 27:

8 So Saul disguised himself and put on other clothes, and he went, and two men with him; and they came to the woman by night. And he said, "Please conduct a séance for me, and bring up for me the one I shall name to you."
9 Then the woman said to him, "Look, you know what Saul has done, how he has cut off the mediums and the spiritists from the land. Why then do you lay a snare for my life, to cause me to die?"
10 And Saul swore to her by the LORD, saying, "As the LORD lives, no punishment shall come upon you for this thing."
11 Then the woman said, "Whom shall I bring up for you?" And he said, "Bring up Samuel for me."

15 Now Samuel said to Saul, "Why have you disturbed me by bringing me up?" And Saul answered, "I am deeply distressed; for the Philistines make war against me, and God has departed from me and does not answer me anymore, neither by prophets nor by dreams. Therefore I have called you, that you may reveal to me what I should do."
16 Then Samuel said: "Why then do you ask me, seeing the LORD had departed from you and has become your enemy?
17 "And the LORD has done for Himself as He spoke by me. For the LORD has torn the kingdom out of your hand and given it to your neighbor, namely, David.
18 "Because you did not obey the voice of the LORD nor execute His fierce wrath upon Amalek, therefore the LORD has done this thing to you this day.
19 Moreover the LORD will also deliver Israel with you into the hand of the Philistines. And tomorrow you and your sons will be with me. The LORD will also deliver the army of Israel into the hand of the Philistines."

Deuteronomy 18:

10 "There shall not be found among you anyone who makes his son or daughter pass through the fire, or one who practices witchcraft, or a soothsayer, or one who interprets omens, or a sorcerer,
11 "or one who conjures spells, or a medium, or a spiritist, or one who calls up the dead.
12 "For all who do these things are an abomination to the LORD, and because of these abominations the LORD your God drives them out from before you.

A1 – B3 King David

I Samuel 16:

12 So he sent and brought him in. Now he was
ruddy, with bright eyes, and good-looking. And the
LORD said, "Arise, anoint him; for this is the one!"
13 Then Samuel took the horn of oil and anointed
him in the midst of his brothers; and the Spirit of
the LORD came upon David from that day
forward. So Samuel arose and went to Ramah.

7 But the LORD said to Samuel, "Do not look at
his appearance or at the height of his stature,
because I have refused him. For the LORD does
not see as man sees; for man looks at the outward
appearance, but the LORD looks at the heart."

II Samuel 7:

8 "Now therefore, thus shall you say to My
servant David, 'Thus says the LORD of hosts: "I
took you from the sheepfold, from following the
sheep, to be ruler over My people, over Israel.
9 "And I have been with you wherever you have
gone, and have cut off all your enemies from
before you, and have made you a great name, like
the name of the great men who are on the earth.

II Samuel 6:

16 And as the ark of the LORD came into the City
of David, Michal, Saul's daughter, looked
through a window and saw King David leaping
and whirling before the LORD; and she despised
him in her heart.

21 So David said to Michal, "It was before the
LORD, who chose me instead of your father and
all his house, to appoint me ruler the people of
the LORD, over Israel. Therefore I will play
music before the LORD.
22 "And I will be even more undignified than this,
and will be humble in my own sight.

Psalm 12:

1 Help, LORD , for the godly man ceases!
For the faithful disappear from among the sons
of men.
3 They speak idly everyone with his neighbor;
With flattering lips and a double heart the speak.
3 May the LORD cut off all flattering lips,
And the tongue that speaks proud things,
4 Who have said,
"With our tongue we will prevail;
Our lips are our own;
Who is Lord over us?"

< *Sounds like to today, doesn't it!* >

B3 King Solomon

II Samuel 12:

9 'Why have you despised the commandment of
the LORD, to do evil in His sight? You have
killed Uriah the Hittite with the sword; you have
taken his wife to be your wife, and have killed
him with the sword of the people of Ammon.
10 'Now therefore , the sword shall never depart
from your house, because you have despised me ,
and have taken the wife of Uriah to be your wife.'

24 Then David comforted Bathsheba his wife, and
went to her and lay with her, So bore a son, and
he called his name Solomon. And the LORD
loved him
25 And He sent word by the hand of Nathan the
prophet; so he 27 called his name Jedidiah, 28
because of the LORD.

(Solomon: Son of Bathsheba)

I Kings 2:

11 The period that David reigned over Israel was
forty years; seven years he reigned in Hebron,
and in Jerusalem he reigned thirty-three years.
12 Then Solomon sat on the throne of his father
David; and his kingdom was firmly established.

I Kings 3:

2 Meanwhile the people sacrificed at the high
places, because there was no house built for the
name of the LORD until those days.
3 And Solomon loved the LORD, walking in the
statutes of his father David, except that he
sacrificed and burned incense at the high
places.
5 At Gibeon the LORD appeared to Solomon in a
dream by night; and God said, "Ask! What shall
I give you?"

10 And the speech pleased the LORD, that
Solomon had asked this thing.
11 Then God said to him: "Because you have asked
this thing, and have not asked long life for
yourself, no have asked riches for yourself, no have
asked the life of your enemies, but have asked for
yourself understanding to discern justice,
12 "behold, I have done according to your words;
see, I have given you a wise and understanding
heart, so that there has not been anyone like you
before you, nor shall any like you arise after you.
13 "And I have also given you what you have not
asked: both riches and honor, so that there shall
not be anyone like you among the kings all your
days.

King Solomon

I Kings 3: (cont)

25 And the king said, "Divide the living child in two, and give half to one, and half to the other."
26 Then the woman whose son was living spoke to the king, for she yearned with compassion for her son; and she said, "O my lord, give her the living child, and by no means kill him!" But the other said, "Let him be neither mine nor yours, but divide him."
27 So the king answered and said, "Give the first woman the living child, and by no means kill him; she is his mother."

I Chronicles 22:

6 Then he called for his son Solomon, and charged him to build a house for the LORD God of Israel.
7 And David said to Solomon: "My son, as for me, it was in my mind to build a house to the name of the LORD my God;
8 "but the word of the LORD came to me, saying, 'You have shed much blood and have made great wars; you shall not build a house for My name, because you have shed much blood on the earth in My sight.

II Chronicles 7:

1 Now when Solomon had finished praying, fire came down from heaven and consumed the burnt offering and the sacrifices; and the glory of the LORD filled the temple.
2 And the priests could not enter the house of the LORD, because the glory of the LORD had filled the LORD's house.

11 Thus Solomon finished the house of the LORD and the king's house; and Solomon successfully accomplished all that came into his heart to make in the house of the LORD and in his own house.
12 Then the LORD appeared to Solomon by night, and said to him: "I have heard your prayer, and have chosen this place for Myself as a house of sacrifice.

14 "if My people who are called by My name will humble themselves, and pray and seek My face, and turn from their wicked ways, the I will hear from heaven, and will forgive their sin and heal their land.
15 "Now My eyes will be open and My ears attentive to prayer made in this place.

<Applies to our temple/bodies now!>
<see Pg. 88.A.1-2>

I Kings 10:

22 For the king had merchant ships at sea with the feet of Hiram. Once every three years the merchant ships came bringing gold, silver, ivory, apes, and monkeys.
23 So King Solomon surpassed all the kings of the earth in riches and wisdom.
24 And all the earth sought the presence of Solomon to hear his wisdom, which God had put in his heart.

Deuteronomy 17:

17 "Neither shall he multiply wives for himself, lest his heart turn away; nor shall he greatly multiply silver and gold for himself.
18 "Also it shall be, when he sits on the throne of his kingdom, that he shall write for himself a copy of this law in a book, from the one before the priests, the Levites.

I Kings 11:

2 from the nations of whom the LORD had said to the children of Israel, "you shall not intermarry with the, nor they with you. For surely they will turn away your hearts after their gods." Solomon clung to these in love.
3 And he had seven hundred wives, princesses, and three hundred concubines; and his wives turned his heart.
4 For it was so, when Solomon was old, that his wives turned his heart after other gods; and his heart was not loyal to the LORD his God, as was the heart of his father David.
5 For Solomon went after Ashtoreth the goddess of the Sidonians, and after Milcom the abomination of the Ammonites.
6 Solomon did evil in the sight of the LORD, and did not fully follow the LORD, as did his father David.
7 Then Solomon built a high place for Chemesh the abomination of Moab, on the hill that is east of Jerusalem, and for Molech the abomination of the people of Ammon.
8 And he did likewise for all his foreign wives, who burned incense and sacrificed to their gods.
9 So the LORD became angry with Solomon, because his heart had turned from the LORD God of Israel, who had appeared to him twice,

A. End of Solomon and Division of Israel

I Kings 11:

11 Therefore the LORD said to Solomon, "Because you have done this, and have not kept My covenant and My statutes, which I have commanded you, I will surely tear the kingdom away from you and give it to your servant.
12 "Nevertheless I will not do it in your days, for the sake of your father David; but I will tear it out of the hand of your son.
13 "However I will not tear away the whole kingdom, but I will give one tribe to your son for the sake of my servant David, and for the sake of Jerusalem which I have chosen."

II Chronicles 9:

30 Solomon reigned in Jerusalem over all Israel forty years.
31 Then Solomon rested with his fathers, and was buried in the City of David his father. And Rehoboam his son reigned in his place.

II Chronicles 10:

15 So the king did not listen to the people; for the turn of affairs was from God, that the LORD might fulfill His word, which He had spoken by the hand of Ahijah the Shilonite to Jeroboam the son of Nebat.
19 So Israel has been in rebellion against the house of David to this day.

II Chronicles 11:

5 So Rehoboam dwelt in Jerusalem, and built cities for defense in Judah.
12 Also in every city he put shields and spears, and made them very strong, having Judah and Benjamin on his side.
13 And from all their territories the priests and the Levites who were in all Israel took their stand with him.

II Chronicles 12:

1 Now it came to pass, when Rehoboam had established the kingdom and had strengthened himself, that he forsook the **law** of the LORD, and all Israel with him.
14 And he did evil, because he did not prepare his **heart** to seek the LORD.
9 So Shishak king of Egypt came up against Jerusalem, and took away the treasures of the house of the LORD and the treasures of the king's house; he took everything. He also carried away the gold shields which Solomon had made.

B. Elijah

I Kings 17:

21 And he stretched himself out on the child three times, and cried out to the LORD and said, " O LORD my God, I prey, let this child's **soul** come back to him."
22 Then the LORD heard the voice of Elijah; and the **soul** of the child came back to him, and he received.
23 And Elijah took the child and brought him down from the upper room into the house, and gave him to his mother. And Elijah said "See, your son lives!"
24 Then the woman said to Elijah, "Now by this I know that you are a man of God, and that the word of the LORD in your mouth is the **truth**."

<Relate this to Pg. 39.B.3.>

I Kings 18:

37 "Hear me, O LORD, hear me, that this people may know that You are the LORD God, and that You have turned their **hearts** back to You again."
38 Then the fire of the LORD fell and consumed the burnt sacrifice, and the wood and the stones and the dust, and it licked up the water that was in the trench.

I Kings 19:

14 So he said, "I have been very zealous for the LORD God of hosts; because the children of Israel have forsaken Your covenant, torn down your alters, and killed Your prophets with the sword. I alone am left; and they seek to take my life."
15 Then the LORD said to him: "Go, return on your way to the Wilderness of Damascus; and when you arrive, anoint Hazael as king over Syria.
16 "Also you shall anoint Jehu the son of Nimshi as king over Israel. And Elisha the son of Shaphat of Abel Meholah you shall anoint as prophet in your place.
17 "It shall be that whoever escapes the sword of Hazael, Jehu will kill; and whoever escapes from the sword of Jehu, Elisha will kill.
18 "Yet I have reserved seven thousand in Israel, all whose knees have not bowed to Baal, and every mouth that has not kissed him."

<God's Keeping Power>

A. Elijah and Elisha

II Kings 2

7 …while the two of them stood by the Jordan.
8 Now Elijah took his mantle, rolled it up, and struck the water; and it was divided this way and that, so that the two of them crossed over on dry ground.
9 And so it was, when they had crossed over, that Elijah said to Elisha, "Ask! What may I do for you, before I am taken away from you?" And Elisha said, "Please let a double portion* of your spirit be upon me."
10 So he said, "You have asked a hard thing. Nevertheless, if you see me when I am taken from you, it shall be so for you; but if not, it shall not be so."
11 Then it happened, as they continued on and talked, that suddenly a chariot of fire appeared with horses of fire, and separated the two of them; and Elijah went up by a whirlwind into heaven.
12 Now Elisha saw it, and he cried out, "My father, my father, the chariot of Israel and its horsemen!" So he saw him no more. And he took hold of his own clothes and tore them into two pieces.
13 He also took up the mantle of Elijah that had fallen from him, and went back and stood by the bank of the Jordan.
14 Then he took the mantle of Elijah that had fallen from him, and struck the water, and said, "Where is the LORD God of Elijah?" And when he also had struck the water, it was divided this way and that, and Elisha crossed over.

22 So the water remains healed to this day, according to the saying of Elisha which he spoke.
23 And he went up from there to Bethel; and as he was going up the road, some youths came from the city and mocked him, and said to him, "Go up, you baldhead! Go up you baldhead!"
24 So he turned around and looked at them, and pronounced a curse on them in the name of the LORD.

Deuteronomy 21:

17 But he shall acknowledge the son … *as* the firstborn by giving him a double portion* of all that he has, for he *is* the beginning of his strength; the right of the firstborn …

<: "Double Portion" means twice that given to other beneficiaries.>*

B. Elisha

II Kings 4:

32 And when Elisha came into the house, there was the child, lying dead on his bed.
33 He went in therefore, shut the door behind the two of them, and prayed to the LORD.
34 And he went up and lay on the child, and put his mouth on his mouth, his eyes on his eyes, and his hands on his hands; and he stretched himself out on the child, and the flesh of the child became warm.
35 He returned and walked back and forth in the house, and again went up and stretched himself out on him; then the child sneezed seven time, and the child opened his eyes.

II Kings 5:

10 And Elisha sent a messenger to him, saying, "Go and wash in the Jordan seven times, and your flesh shall be restored to you, and you shall be clean."
11 But Naaman became furious, and went away and said, "Indeed, I said to myself, 'He will surely come out to me, and stand and call on the name of the LORD his God, and wave his hand over the place, and heal the leprosy.'

13 And his servants came near and spoke to him, and said, "My father, if the prophet had told you to do something great, would you not have done it? How much more then, when he says to you, 'Wash, and be clean'?"

II Kings 6:

15 And when the servant of the man of God arose early and went out, there was an army, surrounding the city with horses and chariots. And his servant said to him, "Alas, my master! What shall we do?"
16 So he answered, "Do not fear, for those who are with us are more than those who are with them."
17 And Elisha prayed, and said, "LORD, I pray, open his eyes that he may see." Then the LORD opened the eyes of the young man, and he saw. And behold, the mountain was full of horses and chariots of fire all around Elisha.

A. Repopulation of Samaria with non-Jews after Israel carried off to Assyria.

II Kings 17:

18 Therefore the LORD was very angry with Israel, and removed them from His sight; there was none left but the tribe of Judah alone.

24 Then the king of Assyria brought people from Babylon, Cuthah, Ava, Hamath, and from Sepharvaim, and placed them in the cities of Samaria instead of the children of Israel; and they took possession of Samaria and dwelt in its cities.
25 And it was so, at the beginning of their dwelling there, that they did not fear the LORD; therefore the LORD sent lions among them, which killed some of them.
26 So they spoke to the king of Assyria, saying, "The nations whom you have removed and placed in the cities of Samaria do not know the rituals of the God of the land; therefore He has sent lions among them, and indeed, they are killing them because they do not know the rituals of the God of the land."

32 So they feared the LORD, and from every class they appointed for themselves priests of the high places, who sacrificed for them in the shrines of the high places. *
33 They feared the LORD, yet served their own gods – according to the rituals of the nations from among whom they were carried away.

** Relevant to religions today. Some truly fear the Lord but are influenced by surroundings and are unsaved. I can not help but comment on how this seems to be a metaphor for any who have been "moved" from outside, into the Kingdom of God, and fail by keeping their old "gods".*

Prophesy of Babylon Captivity

Jeremiah 23:

5 "Thus says the LORD, the God of Israel: 'Like these good figs, so will I acknowledge those who are carried away captive from Judah, whom I have sent out of this place for their own good, into the land of the Chaldeans.
6 For I will set My eyes on them for good, and I will bring them back to this land; I will build them and not pull them down, and I will plant them and not pluck them up.
7 Then I will give them a heart to know Me, that I am the LORD; and they shall be My people, and I will be their God, for they shall return to Me with their whole heart.

B. King Hezekiah

<handles "high places" right, but fails test, so Judea is doomed to captivity.>

II Kings 18:

1 Now it came to pass in the third year of Hoshea the son of Elah, king of Israel, that Hezekiah the son of Ahaz, king of Judah, began to reign.
2 He was twenty-five years old when he became king, and he reigned twenty-nine years in Jerusalem. His mother's name was Abi the daughter of Zechariah.
3 And he did what was right in the sight of the LORD, according to all that his father David had done.
4 He removed the high places and broke the sacred pillars, cut down the wooden images and broke in pieces the bronze serpent that Moses had made; for until those days the children of Israel burned incense to it, and called it Nehushtan.
5 He trusted in the LORD God of Israel, so that after him was none like him among all the kings of Judah, nor any who were before him.

II Chronicles 32:

30b Hezekiah prospered in all his works.
31 However, regarding the ambassadors of the princes of Babylon, whom they sent to him to inquire about the wonder that was done in the land, God withdrew from him, in order to test him, that He might know all that was in his heart.

Isaiah 39:

5 Then Isaiah said to Hezekiah, "Hear the word of the LORD of hosts:
6 'Behold, the days are coming when all that is in your house, and what your fathers have accumulated until this day, shall be carried to Babylon; nothing shall be left,' says the LORD.

Ezekiel 14:

13 "Son of man, when a land sins against Me by persistent unfaithfulness, I will stretch out My hand against it; I will cut off its supply of bread, send famine on it, and cut off man and beast from it.
14 "Though these three men, Noah, Daniel and Job, were in it, they would deliver only themselves by their righteousness," says the LORD God.

Jeremiah 15:

1 Then the LORD said to me, "*Even* if Moses and Samuel stood before Me, My mind *would* not *be* favorable toward this people.

Judah In Babylon

Shadrach, Meshach & Abed-Nego w/ Nebuchadnezzar || Daniels' vision of "a certain Man"

<Key Principle of Faith and Prayer>

Daniel 3:

15 "Now if you are ready at the time you hear the sound of the horn, flute, harp, lyre, and psaltery, in symphony with all kinds of music, and you fall down and worship the image which I have made, good! But if you do not worship, you shall be cast immediately into the midst of a burning fiery furnace. And who is the god who will deliver you from my hands?"

16 Shadrach, Meshach, and Abed-Nego answered and said to the king, "O Nebuchadnezzar, we have no need to answer you in this matter.

17 "If that is the case, our God whom we serve is able to deliver us from the burning fiery furnace, and He will deliver us from your hand, O king.

18 "But if not, let it be known to you, O king, that we do not serve your gods, nor will we worship the gold image which you have set up."

19 Then Nebuchadnezzar was full of fury, and the expression on his face changed toward Shadrach, Meschach, and Abed-Nego. Therefore he spoke and commanded that they heat the furnace seven times more than it was usually heated.

21 Then these men were bound in their coats, their trousers, their turbans, and their other garments, and were cast into the midst of the burning fiery furnace.

22 Therefore, because the king's command was urgent, and the furnace exceedingly hot, the flame of the fire killed those men who took up Shadrach, Meschach, and Abed-Nego.

23 And these three men, Shadrach, Meschach, and Abed-Nego, fell down bound into the midst of the burning fiery furnace.

24 Then King Nebuchadnezzar was astonished; and he rose in haste and spoke, saying to his counselors, "Did we not cast three men bound into the midst of the fire?" They answered and said to the king, "True, O king."

25 "Look!" he answered, "I see four men loose, walking in the midst of the fire; and they are not hurt, and the form of the fourth is like the Son of God."

26 Then Nebuchadnezzar went near the mouth of the burning fiery furnace and spoke, saying, "Shadrach, Meshach, and Abed-Nego, servants of the Most High God, come out, and come here." Then Shadrach, Meschach, and Abed-Nego came from the midst of the fire.

Daniel 4:

37 Now I, Nebuchadnezzar, praise and extol and honor the King of heaven, all of whose works are **truth**, and His ways justice. And those who walk in pride He is able to abase.

Daniel 10:

1 In the third year of Cyrus king of Persia a message was revealed to Daniel, whose name was called Belteshazzar. The message *was* true, but the appointed time *was* long; and he understood the message, and had understanding of the vision.

2 In those days I, Daniel, was mourning three full weeks.

3 I ate no pleasant food, no meat or wine came into my mouth, nor did I anoint myself at all, till three whole weeks were fulfilled.

4 Now on the twenty-fourth day of the first month, as I was by the side of the great river, that *is,* the Tigris,

5 I lifted my eyes and looked, and behold, a certain man clothed in linen, whose waist *was* girded with gold of Uphaz!

6 His body was like beryl, his face like the appearance of lightning, his eyes like torches of fire, his arms and feet like burnished bronze in color, and the sound of his words like the voice of a multitude.

7 And I, Daniel, alone saw the vision, for the men who were with me did not see the vision; but a great terror fell upon them, so that they fled to hide themselves.

11 And he said to me, "O Daniel, man greatly beloved, understand the words that I speak to you, and stand upright, for I have now been sent to you." While he was speaking this word to me, I stood trembling.

12 Then he said to me, "Do not fear, Daniel, for from the first day that you set your **heart** to understand, and to humble yourself before your God, your words were heard; and I have come because of your words.

13 "But the prince of the kingdom of Persia★ withstood me twenty-one days; and behold, **Michael**, one of the chief princes, came to help me, for I had been left alone there with the kings of Persia.

★ <"Prince ... of Persia" *is symbol for a high ranking fallen angel. It restrained answer to Daniel's prayer, until a higher ranking Angel (Michael) came to help.*>

<Continued on Pg 27B2 >

In Captivity

Daniel and the Lion's Den (Darius)

Daniel 6:

1 It pleased Darius to set over the kingdom one hundred and twenty satraps, to be over the whole kingdom;
2 and over these, three governors, of whom Daniel *was* one, that the satraps might give account to them, so that the king would suffer no loss.
3 Then this Daniel distinguished himself above the governors and satraps, because an excellent spirit *was* in him; and the king gave thought to setting him over the whole realm.
4 So the governors and satraps sought to find *some* charge against Daniel ...

10 Now when Daniel knew that the writing was signed, he went home. And in his upper room, with his windows open toward Jerusalem, he knelt down on his knees three times that day, and prayed and gave thanks before his God, as was his custom since early days.
11 Then these men assembled and found Daniel praying and making supplication before his God.
12 And they went before the king, and spoke concerning the king's decree: "Have you not signed a decree that every man who petitions any god or man within thirty days, except you, O king, shall be cast into the den of lions?" The king answered and said, "The thing is true, according to the law of the Medes and Persians, which does not alter."
13 So they answered and said before the king, "That Daniel, who is one of the captives from Judah, does not show due regard for you, O king, or for the decree that you have signed, but makes his petition three times a day."

16 So the king gave the command, and they brought Daniel and cast him into the den of lions. But the king spoke, saying to Daniel, "Your God, whom you serve continually, He will deliver you."
17 Then a stone was brought and laid on the mouth of the den, and the king sealed it with his own signet ring and with the signets of his lords, that the purpose concerning Daniel might not be changed.
18 Now the king went to his palace and spent the night fasting; and no musicians were brought before him. Also his sleep went from him.
19 Then the king arose very early in the morning and went in haste to the den of lions.

Daniel 6:

20 And when he came to the den, he cried out with a lamenting voice to Daniel. The king spoke, saying to Daniel, "Daniel, servant of the living God, has your God, whom you serve continually, been able to deliver you from the lions?"
21 Then Daniel said to the king, "O king, live forever!"
22 "My God has sent His angel and shut the lions' mouths, so they have not hurt me, because I was found innocent before Him; and also, O king, I have done no wrong before you."
23 Then the king was exceedingly glad for him, and commanded that they should take Daniel up out of the den. So Daniel was taken up out of the den, and no injury whatever was found on him, because he believed in his God.
25 Then King Darius wrote: . . .
26 I make a decree that in every dominion of my kingdom *men must* tremble and fear before the God of Daniel. . . .
28 So this Daniel prospered in the reign of Darius and in the reign of Cyrus the Persian.

Daniel's Vision *(Cont. from Pg 26B)*

"Scripture of Truth"

Messenger helped by Michael

Daniel 10:

20 Then he said, "Do you know why I have come to you? And now I must return to fight with the prince of Persia; and when I have gone forth, indeed the prince of Greece will come.
21 "But I will tell you what is noted in the Scripture of Truth. (No one upholds me against these, except Michael your prince. *

Daniel 11:

1 "Also in the first year of Darius the Mede, I, even I, stood up to confirm and strengthen him.)

****<Note: Michael, the Archangel, helped "certain man" most believe to have been the pre-incarnate "Angel of God"(Jesus- see also pg.26A1v25 & pg.26B2v11 & pg.27B1v22), and referenced an eternal "Scripture of Truth" of future events. Thus there are*

2 topics worthy of hard thinking:
1. the spirit realm power / dynamics, and
2. the idea of pre-destined life activity as being "written in a book" >

<Continued on Pg 28B2 (Daniel 11:1) >

Proven Prophecy

(Through the study of the metaphoric style of proven prophecy, we can better interpret other prophecies of future events.)

Daniel 2:

27 Daniel answered in the presence of the king,
and said, "The secret which the king has
demanded, the wise men, the astrologers, the
magicians, and the soothsayers cannot declare
to the king.
28 "But there is a God in heaven who reveals
secrets, and He has made known to King
Nebuchadnezzar what will be in the latter days.
Your dream, and the visions of your head upon
your bed, were these:
29 "As for you, O king, thoughts came to your
mind while on your bed, about what would
come to pass after this; and He who reveals
secrets has mad known to you what will be.
30 "But as for me, this secret has not been
revealed to me because I have more wisdom
than anyone living, but for our sakes who make
known the interpretation to the king, and that
you may know the thoughts of your heart.
31 "You, O king, were watching; and behold a
great image! This great image, whose splendor
was excellent, stood before you; and its form
was awesome.
36 "This is the dream. Now we will tell the
interpretation of it before the king.
37 "You, O king, are a king of kings. For the
God of heaven has given you a kingdom,
power, strength, and glory;
38 "and wherever the children of men dwell, or
the beasts of the field and the birds of the
heaven, He has given them into your hand, and
has made you ruler over them all – you are this
head of gold.
39 "But after you shall arise another kingdom
inferior to yours; then another, a third kingdom
of bronze, which shall rule over all the earth.
40 "And the fourth kingdom shall be as strong
as iron, inasmuch as iron breaks in pieces and
shatters all things; and like iron that crushes,
that kingdom will break in pieces and crush all
the others.
41 "Whereas you saw the feet and toes, partly of
potter's clay and partly of iron, the kingdom
shall be divided; yet the strength of the iron
shall be in it, just as you saw the iron mixed
with the ceramic clay.
42 "And as the toes of the feet were partly of
iron and partly of clay, so the kingdom shall be
partly strong and partly fragile.

Daniel 7:

2 Daniel spoke, saying, "I saw in my vision by
night, and behold, the four winds of heaven were
stirring up the Great Sea.
3 "And four great beasts came up from the sea,
each different from the other.
4 "The first was like a lion, and had eagle's wings.
I watched till its wings were plucked off; and it
was lifted up from the earth and made to stand on
two feet like a man, and a man's heart was given
to it.
5 "And suddenly another beast, a second, like a
bear. It was raised up on one side, and had three
ribs in its mouth between its teeth. And they said
thus to it: 'Arise, devour much flesh!'
6 "After this I looked, and there was another, like a
leopard, which had on its back four wings of a
bird. The beast also had four heads, and
dominion was given to it.

Daniel 11:

2 "And now I will tell you the truth: Behold, three
more kings will arise in Persia, and the fourth shall
be far richer than them all; by his strength, through
his riches, he shall stir up all against the realm of
Greece.
3 "Then a mighty king shall arise, who shall rule
with great dominion, and do according to his will.
4 "And when he has arisen, his kingdom shall be
broken up and divided toward the four winds of
heaven, but not among his posterity nor according
to his dominion with which he ruled; for his
kingdom shall be uprooted, even for others besides
these.
5 "Then the king of the South shall become strong,
as well as one of his princes; and he shall gain
power over him and have dominion. His
dominion shall be a great dominion.
6 "And at the end of some years they shall join
forces, for the daughter of the king of the South
shall go to the king of the North to make an
agreement; but she shall not retain the power of
her authority, and neither he nor his authority shall
stand; but she shall be given up, with those who
brought her, and with him who begot her, and
with him who strengthened her in those times.
7 "But from a branch of her roots one shall arise in
his place, who shall come with an army, enter the
fortress of the king of the North, and deal with
them and prevail. *(continued on next page)*

Prophetic Style - Continued

(All this can be compared to actual history!)

Daniel 11 (continued)

8 "And he shall also carry their gods captive to Egypt, with their princes and their precious articles of silver and gold; and he shall continue more years than the king of the North.
9 "Then the king of the North shall come to the kingdom of the king of the South, but shall return to his own land.
10 "However his sons shall stir up strife, and assemble a multitude of great forces; and one shall certainly come and overwhelm and pass through; then he shall return to his fortress and stir up strife.
11 "And the king of the South shall be moved with rage, and go out and fight with him, with the king of the North, who shall muster a great multitude; but the multitude shall be given into the hand of his enemy.
12 "When he has taken away the multitude, his **heart** will be lifted up; and he will cast down tens of thousands, but he will not prevail.
13 "For the king of the North will return and muster a multitude greater than the former, and shall certainly come at the end of some years with a great army and much equipment.
14 "And in those times many shall rise up against the king of the South; also certain violent men of your people shall exalt themselves in fulfillment of the vision, but they shall fall.
15 "So the king of the North shall come and build a siege mound, and take a fortified city; and the forces of the South shall not withstand him. Even his choice troops shall have no strength to resist.
16 "But he who comes against him shall do according to his own will, and no one shall stand against him. He shall stand in the Glorious Land with destruction in his power.
17 "He shall also set his face to enter with the strength of his whole kingdom, and upright ones with him; thus shall he do. And he shall give him the daughter of women to destroy it; but she shall not stand with him, or be for him.
18 "After this he shall turn his face to the coastlands, and shall take many. But a ruler shall bring the reproach against them to an end; and with the reproach removed, he shall turn back on him.
19 "Then he shall turn his face toward the fortress of his own land; but he shall stumble and fall, and not be found.

Daniel 11 (continued)

20 "There shall arise in his place one who imposes taxes on the glorious kingdom; but within a few days he shall be destroyed, but no in anger or in battle.
21 "And in his place shall arise a vile person, to whom they will not give the honor of royalty; but he shall come in peaceably, and seize the kingdom by intrigue.
22 "With the force of a flood they shall be swept away from before him and be broken, and also the prince of the covenant.
23 "And after the league is made with him he shall act deceitfully, for he shall come up and become strong with a small number of people.
24 "He shall enter peaceably, even into the richest places of the province; and he shall do what his fathers have not done, nor his forefathers: he shall disperse among them the plunder, spoil, and riches; and he shall devise his plans against the strongholds, but only for a time.
25 "He shall stir up his power and his courage against the king of the South with a great army. And the king of the South shall be stirred up to battle with a very great and mighty army; but he shall not stand, for they shall devise plans against him.
26 "Yes, those who eat of the portion of his delicacies shall destroy him; his army shall be swept away, and many shall fall down slain.
27 "Both these kings' **hearts** shall be bent on evil, and they shall speak lies at the same table; but it shall not prosper, for the end will still be at the appointed time.
28 "While returning to his land with great riches, his **heart** shall be moved against the holy covenant; so he shall do damage and return to his own land.
29 "At the appointed time he shall return and go toward the south; but it shall not be like the former or the latter.
30 "For ships from Cyprus shall come against him; therefore he shall be grieved, and return in rage against the holy covenant and do damage. So he shall return and show regard for those who forsake the holy covenant.
31 "And forces shall be mustered by him, and they shall defile the sanctuary fortress, then they shall take away the daily sacrifices and place there the abomination of desolation.
32 " Those who do wickedly against the covenant he shall corrupt with flattery; but the people who know their God shall be strong and carry out great exploits.

Return from Captivity

(Relevant to Daniel's Prophecy on Pg 57.A)

Isaiah 58:

12 Those from among you
Shall build the old waste places;
You shall raise up the foundations of many generations;
And you shall be called the Repairer of the Breach,
The Restorer of Streets to Dwell In.

Zechariah 1

12 Then the Angel of the LORD answered and said, "O LORD of hosts, how long will You not have mercy on Jerusalem and on the cities of Judah, against which You were angry these seventy years?"

Ezra 1:

1 Now in the first year of Cyrus king of Persia, that the word of the LORD spoken by the mouth of Jeremiah might be fulfilled, the LORD stirred up the spirit of Cyrus king of Persia, so that he made a proclamation throughout all his kingdom, and also put it in writing saying,

3 Who is there among you of all His people? May his God be with him! Now let him go up to Jerusalem, which is in Judah, and build the house of the LORD God of Israel (He is God), which is in Jerusalem.

7 King Cyrus also brought out the articles of the house of the LORD, which Nebuchadnezzar had taken from Jerusalem and put in the temple of his gods

Ezra 3:

1 And when the seventh month had come, and the children of Israel were in the cities, the people gathered together as one man to Jerusalem.

8 Now in the second month of the second year of their coming to the house of God at Jerusalem, Zerubbabel the son of Shealtiel, Jeshua the son of Jozadak, and the rest of their brethren the priests and the Levites, and all those who had come out of the captivity to Jerusalem, began work and appointed the Levites from twenty years old and above to oversee the work of the house of the LORD.

Ezra 4:

23 Now when the copy of King Artaxerxes' letter was read before Rehum, Shimshai the scribe, and their companions, they went up in haste to Jerusalem against the Jews, and by force of arms made them cease.
24 Thus the work of the house of God which is at Jerusalem ceased, and it was discontinued until the second year of the reign of Darius king of Persia.

Ezra 5:

5 But the eye of their God was upon the elders of the Jews, so that they could not make them cease till a report could go to Darius. Then a written answer was returned concerning this matter.

Ezra 6:

15 Now the temple was finished on the third day of the month of Adar, which was in the sixth year of the reign of King Darius.

Ezra 9: *

12 'Now therefore, do not give your daughters as wives for their sons, nor take their daughters to your sons; and never seek their peace or prosperity, that you may be strong and eat the good of the land, and leave it as an inheritance to your children forever.'

Ezra 10: *

2 And Shechaniah the son of Jehiel, one of the sons of Elam, spoke up and said to Ezra, "We have trespassed against our God, and have taken pagan wives from the peoples of the land; yet now there is hope in Israel in spite of this.
3 "Now therefore, let us make a covenant with our God to put away all these wives and those who have been born to them, according to the counsel of my master and of those who tremble at the commandment of our God; and let it be done according to the law.

** Mixing of racial blood is not of concern but marrying or other mixing outside our faith is strongly condemned for our own good!*

The Name of The LORD

is a review of His Works on Earth before mankind.

(To use His name in vain is to refer to Him without respect for the works associated with His name in the Bible.
To blaspheme His name is to try to add bad works to His name, or deny Him credit due Him.)

Nehemiah 9:

5b "Stand up and bless the LORD your God
Forever and ever!
"Blessed be Your glorious name,
Which is exalted above all blessing and praise!
6 You alone are the LORD;
You have made heaven,
The heaven of heavens, with all their host,
The earth and all things on it,
The seas and all that is in them,
And You preserve them all.
The host of heaven worships You.
7 "You are the LORD God.
Who chose Abram,
And brought him out of Ur of the Chaldees,
And gave him the name Abraham;
8 You found his heart faithful before you,
And made a covenant with him
To give the land of the Canaanites,
The Hittites, the Amorites,
The Perizzites, the Jebusites,
And the Girgashites –
To give it to his descendants.
You have performed Your words,
For You are righteous.
9 "You saw the affliction of our fathers in Egypt,
And heard their cry by the Red Sea.
10 You showed signs and wonders against Pharaoh,
Against all his servants,
And against all the people of his land.
For you knew that they acted proudly against them.
So you made a name for Yourself, as it is this day.
11 And You divided the sea before them,
So that they went through the midst of the sea on the dry land;
And their persecutors You threw into the deep,
As a stone into the mighty waters.
12 Moreover You led them by day with a cloudy pillar,
And by night with a pillar of fire,
To give them light on the road
Which they should travel
13 "You came down also no Mount Sinai,
And spoke with them from heaven,
And gave them just ordinances and true laws,
Good statutes and commandments.
14 You made know to them Your holy Sabbath,
And commanded them precepts, statues and laws,
By the hand of Moses Your servant.
15 You gave them bread from heaven for their hunger.
And brought them water out of the rock for their thirst,
And told them to go in to possess the land
Which You had sworn to give them.
16 "But they and our fathers acted proudly,
Hardened their necks,
And did not heed Your commandments.
17 They refused to obey,
And they were not mindful of Your wonders
That You did among them.
But they hardened their necks,
And in their rebellion
They appointed a leader
To return ger,
Abundant in kindness,
And did not forsake them.
18 "Even when they made a molded calf for themselves,
And said, 'This is your god
That brought you up out of Egypt,'
And worked great provocations,
19 Yet in Your manifold mercies
You did not forsake them in the wilderness.
The pillar of the cloud did not depart from them by day,
To lead them on the road;
Nor the pillar of fire by night,
To show them light,
And the way they should go.
20 You also gave Your good Spirit to instruct them,
And did not withhold Your manna from their mouth,
And gave them water for their thirst.
21 Forty years You sustained them in the wilderness,
So they lacked nothing;
Their clothes did not wear out
And their feet did not swell.

The Name of the LORD (continued)

Nehemiah 9: (continued)

22 "Moreover You gave them kingdoms and nations,
And divided them into districts.
So they took possession of the land of Sihon,
The land of the king of Heshbon,
And the land of Og king of Bashan.
23 You also multiplied their children as the stars of heaven,
And brought them into the land
Which You had told their fathers
To go in and possess.
24 So the people went in
And possessed the land;
You subdued before them the inhabitants of the land,
The Canaanites,
And gave them into their hands,
With their kings
And the people of the land,
That they might do with them as they would.
25 And they took strong cities and a rich land,
And possessed housed full of all goods,
Cisterns already dug, vineyards, olive groves,
And fruit trees in abundance.
So they ate and were filled and grew fat,
And delighted themselves in Your great goodness.
26 "Nevertheless they were disobedient
And rebelled against You,
Cast Your law behind their backs
And killed Your prophets, who testified against them
To turn them to Yourself;
And they worked great provocations.
27 Therefore You delivered them into the hand of their enemies,
Who oppressed them;
And in their time of trouble,
When they cried out to You,
You heard from heaven;
And according to Your abundant mercies
You gave them deliverers who saved them
From the hand of their enemies.
28 "But after they had rest,
They again did evil before You.
Therefore You left them in the hand of their enemies,
So that they had dominion over them;
Yet when they returned and cried out to You,
You heard from heaven;
And many times You delivered them according to Your mercies,
29 And testified against them,
That You might bring them back to Your law.
Yet they acted proudly,
And did not heed Your commandments,
But sinned against Your judgments,
'Which if a man does, he shall live by them.'
And they shrugged their shoulders,
Stiffened their necks,
And would not hear.
30 Yet for many years You had patience with them,
And testified against them by Your Spirit in Your prophets.
Yet they would not listen;
Therefore You gave them into the hand of the peoples of the lands.
31 Nevertheless in Your great mercy
You did not utterly consume them nor forsake them;
For You are God, gracious and merciful.
32 "Now therefore, our God,
The great, the mighty, and awesome God,
Who keeps covenant and mercy;
Do not let all the trouble seem small before You
That has come upon us,
Our kings and our princes,
Our priests and our prophets,
Our fathers and on all Your people,
From the days of the kings of Assyria until this day.
33 However You are just in all that has befallen us;
For You have dealt faithfully,
But we have done wickedly.
34 Neither our kings nor our princes,
Our priests nor our fathers,
Have kept Your law,
Nor heeded Your commandments and Your testimonies,
With which You testified against them.
35 For they have not served You in their kingdom,
Or in the many good things that You gave them,
Or in the large and rich land which You set before them;
Nor did they turn from their wicked works.

Prophecies of Messiah

Isaiah 63:

8 So He became their Savior.
9 In all their affliction He was afflicted,
And the Angel of His Presence saved them;

Psalm 30:

3 O LORD, You have brought my **soul** up from the grave;
You have kept me alive, that I should not go down to the pit.

Isaiah 52:

13 Behold, My Servant shall deal prudently,
He shall be exalted and extolled and be very high.
14 Just as many were astonished at you,
So His visage was marred more than any man,
And His form more than the sons of men;
15 So shall He sprinkle many nations.
Kings shall shut their mouths at Him;
For what had not been told them they shall see.
And what they had not heard they shall consider.

Isaiah 53:

1 Who has believed our report?
And to whom has the **arm** of the LORD been revealed?
2 For He shall grow up before Him as a tender plant,
And as a root out of dry ground.
He has not form or comeliness;
And when we see Him,
There is no beauty that we should desire Him.
3 He is despised and rejected by men,
A man of sorrows and acquainted with grief.
And we hid, as it were, our faces from Him;
He was despised, and we did not esteem Him.

4 Surely He has borne our griefs
And carried our sorrows;
Yet we esteemed Him stricken,
Smitten by God, and afflicted.
5 But He *was* wounded for our transgressions,
He was bruised for our iniquities;
The chastisement for our peace was upon Him,
And by His stripes we are healed.

Numbers 24:

17b A Star shall come out of Jacob;
A Scepter shall rise out of Israel,

Psalm 41:

4 I said, "LORD, be merciful to me;
Heal my **soul**, for I have sinned against You."

Isaiah 53: (continued)

6 All we like sheep have gone astray;
We have turned, every one, to his own way;
And the LORD has laid on Him the iniquity of us all.

7 He was oppressed and He was afflicted,
Yet He opened not His mouth;
He was led as a lamb to the slaughter,
And as a sheep before its shearers is silent,
So He opened not His mouth.
8 He was taken from prison and from judgment,
And who will declare His generation?
For He was cut off from the land of the living;
For the transgressions of My people He was stricken.
9 And they made His grave with the wicked –
But with the rich at His death,
Because He had done no violence,
Nor was any deceit in His mouth.

10 Yet it pleased the LORD to bruise Him;
He has put *Him* to grief.
When You make His **soul** an offering for sin,
He shall see *His* seed, He shall prolong *His* days,
And the pleasure of the LORD shall prosper in His hand.
11 He shall see the labor of His **soul**, *and* be satisfied.
By His knowledge My righteous Servant shall justify many,
For He shall bear their iniquities.
12 Therefore I will divide Him a portion with the great,
And He shall divide the spoil with the strong,
Because He poured out His **soul** unto death,
And He was numbered with the transgressors,
And He bore the sin of many,
And made intercession for the transgressors.

Prophecies of Messiah - continued

Genesis 49:

10 The scepter shall not depart from Judah,
Nor a lawgiver from between his feet,
Until Shiloh comes;
And to Him shall be the obedience of the people.

II Samuel 7:

5 "Go and tell My servant David, 'Thus says the
LORD: ...
12 "When your days are fulfilled and you rest
with your fathers, I will set up your seed after
you, who will come from your body, and I will
establish his kingdom.
13 He shall build a house for My name, and I
will establish the throne of his kingdom forever.
14 I will be his Father, and he shall be My son. If
he commits iniquity, I will chasten him with the
rod of men and with the blows of the sons of
men.
15 But My mercy shall not depart from him, as I
took it from Saul, whom I removed from before
you.
16 And your house and your kingdom shall be
established forever before you. Your throne shall
be established forever." ' "

Isaiah 11:

1 There shall come forth a Rod from the stem of Jesse,
And a Branch shall grow out of his roots.
2 The <u>Spirit of the LORD</u>
<u>shall rest upon Him,</u>
The <u>Spirit of wisdom</u>
<u>and understanding,</u>
The <u>Spirit of counsel and might,</u>
The <u>Spirit of knowledge</u>
<u>and of the fear of the LORD.</u>
3 His delight *is* in the fear of the LORD,
And He shall not judge by the sight of His eyes,
Nor decide by the hearing of His ears;
4 But with righteousness
He shall judge the poor,
And decide with equity for the meek of the earth;
He shall strike the earth with the rod of His mouth,
And with the breath of His lips He shall slay the wicked.
5 Righteousness shall be the belt of His loins,
And faithfulness the belt of His waist.

Psalm 45:

6 Your throne, O God, is forever and ever;
A scepter of righteousness is the scepter of Your kingdom.
7 You love righteousness and hate wickedness;
Therefore God, Your God, has anointed You

Psalm 110:

A Psalm of David.
1 The LORD said to my Lord,
"Sit at My right hand,
Till I make Your enemies Your footstool."
2 The LORD shall send the rod of Your strength out of Zion.
Rule in the midst of Your enemies!

Isaiah 9:

6 For unto us a Child is born,
Unto us a Son is given;
And the government will be upon His shoulder.
And His name will be called
Wonderful, Counselor, Mighty God,
Everlasting Father, Prince of Peace.
7 Of the increase of His government and peace
There will be no end,
Upon the throne of David and over His kingdom,
To order it and establish it with judgment and justice
From that time forward, even forever.
The zeal of the LORD of hosts will perform this.

Psalm 118:

22 The stone which the builders rejected
Has become the chief cornerstone.
23 This was the LORD's doing;
It is marvelous in our eyes.
24 This is the day the LORD has made;
We will rejoice and be glad in it.

Deuteronomy 18: <*(spoken to Moses)* >

18 "I will raise up for them a Prophet like you
from among their brethren, and will put My
words in His mouth, and He shall speak to them
all that I command Him.
19 'And it shall be that whoever will not hear My
words, which He speaks in My name, I will
require it of him.

Prophecies of Messiah - cont. (+Clues to When!)

Jonah 2:
6 I went down to the moorings of the mountains;
The earth with its bars closed behind me forever;
Yet You have brought up my life from the pit,
O LORD, my God.

Malachi 4:
2 But to you who fear My name
The Sun of Righteousness shall arise
With healing in His wings;

Isaiah 49:
5 "And now the LORD says,
Who formed Me from the womb to be His Servant,
To bring Jacob back to Him,
So that Israel is gathered to Him
(For I shall be glorious in the eyes of the LORD,
And My God shall be My strength),
6 Indeed He says,
'It is too small a thing that You should be My servant . . . ;
I will also give You as a light to the Gentiles,
That You should be My salvation to the ends of the earth.' "
9 That You may say to the prisoners, 'Go forth,'
To those who are in darkness, 'Show yourselves,'

Hosea 13:
14 "I will ransom them from the power of the grave;
I will redeem them from death.

Isaiah 12:
1 And in that day you will say:
" O LORD, I will praise You;
Though You were angry with me,
Your anger is turned away, and You comfort me.
2 Behold, God *is* my salvation,
I will trust and not be afraid;
'For YAH, the LORD, *is* my strength and song;
He also has become my salvation.'"
3 Therefore with joy you will draw water ***
From the wells of salvation. *<("Yeshua">*

Jeremiah 17: ****
13 O LORD, the hope of Israel,
All who forsake You shall be ashamed.
" Those who depart from Me
Shall be written in the earth,**
Because they have forsaken the LORD,
The fountain of living waters***."
** *< compare to Pg.38B7>*
*** >

Isaiah 28:
16 Therefore thus says the LORD God:
"Behold, I lay in Zion a stone for a foundation,
A tried stone, a precious cornerstone, a sure foundation;
Whoever believes will not act hastily.

Isaiah 62:
2 The Gentiles shall see your righteousness,
And all kings your glory.
You shall be called by a new name,
Which the mouth of the LORD will name.

Zechariah:
9 "Rejoice greatly, O daughter of Zion!
Shout, O daughter of Jerusalem!
Behold, your King is coming to you;
He is just and having salvation,
Lowly and riding on a donkey,
A colt, a foal of a donkey.

Isaiah 35:
5 Then the eyes of the blind shall be opened,
And the ears of the deaf shall be unstopped.
6 Then the lame shall leap like a deer,
And the tongue of the dumb sing.

Zechariah 14:
8 And it shall come to pass in that day, that living waters shall go out from Jerusalem

Genesis 33:
17 And Jacob journeyed to Succoth, built himself a house, and made booths for his livestock. Therefore the name of the place is called Succoth*.

* *<"Succoth"="Booths"=tabernacle" = Plural of "manger" in Luke 2:7 This means Christ was born during 7 day Feast of Tabernacles before the date of King Herod's death. Research!>*

Leviticus 23:
41 You shall keep it as a feast to the LORD for seven days in the year. *It shall be* a statute forever in your generations. You shall celebrate it in the seventh month.
42 You shall dwell in booths for seven days. All who are native Israelites shall dwell in booths*,

I Kings 8:
2 And all the men of Israel assembled themselves unto king Solomon at the feast, in the month Ethanim, which is the seventh month.

Prophecies of Messiah (continued)

Job 19:

25 For I know that my Redeemer lives,
And He shall stand at last on the earth;
26 And after my skin is destroyed, this I know,
That in★ my flesh I shall see God.

Psalm 110:

4 The LORD has sworn
And will not relent,
"You are a priest forever
According to the order of Melchizedek."

Psalm 22:

16 For dogs have surrounded Me;
The assembly of the wicked has enclosed Me.
They pierced My hands and My feet;
17 I can count all My bones.
They look and stare at Me.
18 They divide My garments among them,
And for My clothing they cast lots.

Psalm 69:

21 They also gave me gall for my food,
And for my thirst they gave me vinegar to drink.

Psalm 34:

19 Many are the afflictions of the righteous,
But the LORD delivers him out of them all.
20 He guards all his bones;
Not one of them is broken.

Psalm 16:

10 For You will not leave my soul in Sheol,
Nor will You allow Your Holy One to see
corruption.

Psalm 68:

18 You have ascended on high,
You have led captivity captive;
You have received gifts among men,
Even among the rebellious,
That the LORD God might dwell there.

Psalm 41:

9 Even my own familiar friend in whom I trusted,
Who ate my bread,
Has lifted up his heel against me.

Zechariah 12:

10 "And I will pour on the house of David and
on the inhabitants of Jerusalem the Spirit of
grace and supplication; then they will look on
Me whom they have pierced; they will mourn for
Him as one mourns for his only son, and grieve
for Him as one grieves for a firstborn.

Isaiah 60:

15 "Whereas you have been forsaken and hated,
So that no one went through you,
I will make you an eternal excellence,
A joy of many generations.
16 You shall drink dry the milk of the Gentiles,
And shall milk the breast of kings;
You shall know that I, the LORD, am your
Savior
And your Redeemer, the Mighty One of Jacob.

Galatians 3:

16 Now to Abraham and his Seed were the
promises made. He does not say, "And to
seeds," as of many, but as of one, "And to your
Seed," who is Christ.

Isaiah 42:

1 "Behold! My Servant whom I uphold,
My Elect One in whom My soul delights!
I have put My Spirit upon Him;
He will bring forth justice to the Gentiles.
2 He will not cry out, nor raise His voice,
Nor cause His voice to be heard in the street.
3 A bruised reed He will not break,
And smoking flax He will not quench;
He will bring forth justice for truth.
4 He will not fail nor be discouraged,
I will keep You and give You as a covenant to
the people,
As a light to the Gentiles,
7 To open blind eyes,
To bring out prisoners from the prison,
Those who sit in darkness from the prison
house.
8 I am the LORD, that is My name;
And My glory I will not give to another,
Nor My praise to graven images.

★< *Note: "in" should be "free from"* >

<The ministry of Christ on Earth should be understood in the context that He was the fulfillment of prophecies. Jesus was even baptized by John because of the importance of "signs" to the Jews. Jesus' message was "I am God." He used signs and scriptures and parables and metaphors to get the message across, yet still to be rejected.

Messiah Arrives (Clues to When!)

Isaiah 7:
14 "Therefore the LORD Himself will give you a sign: Behold, the virgin shall conceive and bear a Son, and shall call His name Immanuel.

Micah 5:
2 "But You, Bethlehem Ephrathah,
Though you are little among the thousands of Judah,
Yet out of you shall come forth to Me
The One to be ruler in Israel,
Whose goings forth have been from of old,
From everlasting."

Colossians 1:
15 He is the image of the invisible God, the firstborn over all creation,
16 For by Him all things were created that are in heaven and that are on earth, visible and invisible, whether thrones or dominions or principalities or powers. All things were created through Him and for Him.
17 And He is before all things, and in Him all things consist.

Luke 1: *<Clues when John the Baptist born!>*
5 There was in the days of Herod, the king of Judea, a certain priest named Zacharias, of the division of Abijah. His wife *was* of the daughters of Aaron, and her name *was* Elizabeth.
8 So it was, that while he was serving as priest before God in the order of his division,
9 according to the custom of the priesthood, his lot fell to burn incense when he went into the temple of the Lord.
10 And the whole multitude of the people was praying outside at the hour of incense.
11 Then an angel of the Lord appeared to him,
13 But the angel said to him, "Do not be afraid, Zacharias, for your prayer is heard; and your wife Elizabeth will bear you a son, and you shall call his name John.
14 And you will have joy and gladness, and many will rejoice at his birth.
15 For he will be great in the sight of the Lord, and shall drink neither wine nor strong drink. He will also be filled with the Holy Spirit, even from his mother's womb.
16 And he will turn many of the children of Israel to the Lord their God.
17 He will also go before Him in the spirit and power of Elijah,
19 And the angel answered and said to him, "I am Gabriel, who stands in the presence of God, and was sent to speak to you and bring you these glad tidings.

Luke 1: (cont.)
23 So it was, as soon as the days of his service were completed, that he departed to his own house.
24 Now after those days his wife Elizabeth conceived; and she hid herself five months, saying, . . .
26 Now in the sixth month the angel Gabriel was sent by God to a city of Galilee named Nazareth,
27 to a virgin betrothed to a man whose name was Joseph, of the house of David. The virgin's name was Mary.
28 And having come in, the angel said to her, "Rejoice, highly favored one, the Lord is with you; blessed are you among women!"
30 Then the angel said to her, "Do not be afraid, Mary, for you have found favor with God.
31 "And behold, you will conceive in your womb and bring forth a Son, and shall call His name Jesus.
32 "He will be great, and will be called the Son of the Highest; and the LORD God will give Him the throne of His father David.
33 "And He will reign over the house of Jacob forever, . . ."
34 Then Mary said to the angel, "How can this be, since I do not know a man?"
35 And the angel answered and said to her, "The Holy Spirit will come upon you , and the power of the Highest will overshadow you; therefore, also, that Holy One who is to be born will be called the Son of God.
36 "Now indeed, Elizabeth your relative has also conceived a son in her old age; and this is now the sixth month for her who was called barren.
37 "For with God nothing will be impossible." *<Cont. on Pg116B5>*

Luke 2:
3 So all went to be registered, everyone to his own city.
4 And Joseph also went up from Galilee, out of the city of Nazareth, into Judea, to the city of David, which is called Bethlehem, because he was of the house and lineage of David,
5 to be registered with Mary, his betrothed wife, who was with child.
6 So it was, that while they were there, the days were completed for her to be delivered.
7 And she brought forth here firstborn Son, and wrapped Him in swaddling cloths, and laid Him in a manger*, because there was no room for them in the inn.
* <see note Pg.35B6>

A. John the Baptizer

Malachi 3:

1 "Behold, I will send My messenger,
And he will prepare the way before Me.

Isaiah 40:

3 The voice of one crying in the wilderness:
"Prepare the way of the LORD;
Make straight in the desert
A highway for our God.

Mark 1:

4 John came baptizing in the wilderness and
preaching a baptism of repentance for the
remission of sins.
5 And all the land of Judea, and those from
Jerusalem, went out to him and were all baptized
by him in the Jordan River, confessing their sins.

John 1:

29 ..."Behold The Lamb of God who takes away
the sin of the world!
30 "This is He of whom I said, 'After me comes a
Man who is preferred before me, for He was
before me.'
31 "I did not know Him; but that He should be
revealed to Israel, therefore I came baptizing with
water."
32 And John bore witness, saying, "I saw the
Spirit descending from heaven like a dove, and
He remained upon Him.

Luke 3:

16 John answered, saying to them all, "I indeed
baptize you with water; but One mightier than I
is coming, whose sandal strap I am not worthy to
loose. He will baptize you with the Holy Spirit
and with fire.
17 "His winnowing fan is in His hand, and He
will thoroughly purge His threshing floor, and
gather the wheat into His barn, but the chaff He
will burn with unquenchable fire."

Matthew 17:

11 Then Jesus answered and said to them, "Elijah
truly is coming first and will restore all things.
12 "But I say to you that Elijah has come already,
and they did not know him but did to him
whatever they wished. Likewise the Son of Man
is also about to suffer at their hands."
13 Then the disciples understood that He spoke
to them of John the Baptist.

John 4:

1 Therefore, when the Lord knew that the
Pharisees had heard that Jesus made and baptized
more disciples than John 2 (though Jesus
Himself did not baptize, but His disciples),
3 He left Judea and departed again to Galilee

B. Signs from Jesus

John 2:

11 This beginning of signs Jesus did in Cana of
Galilee, and manifested His glory; and His
disciples believed in Him.

John 5:

20 "For the Father loves the Son, and shows Him
all things that He Himself does; and He will
show Him greater works than these, that you
may marvel.

John 5:

53 So the father knew that it was at the same hour
in which Jesus said to him, "Your son lives."
And he himself believed, and his whole
household.
54 This again is the second sign that Jesus did
when He had come out of Judea into Galilee.

Mark 8:

19 "When I broke the five loaves for the five
thousand, how many baskets full of fragments
did you take up?" They said to Him, "Twelve."
20 "And when I broke the seven for the four
thousand, how many large baskets full of
fragments did you take up?" And they said,
"Seven." 21 So He said to them, "How is it you
do not understand?"

John 6:

14 Then those men, when they had seen the sign
that Jesus did, said, "This is truly the Prophet
who is to come into the world."

26 Jesus answered them and said, "Most assuredly,
I say to you, you seek Me, not because you saw
the signs, but because you ate of the loaves and
were filled.
27 "Do not labor for the food which perishes, but
for the food which endures to everlasting life,
which the Son of Man will give you, because
God the Father has set His seal on Him."

John 10:

25 Jesus answered them, "I told you, and you do
not believe. The works that I do in My Father's
name, they bear witness of Me.

John 8:

7 So when they continued asking Him, He raised
Himself up and said to them, "He who is
without sin among you, let him throw a stone at
her first." 8 And again He stooped down and
wrote on the ground.

10 When Jesus had raised Himself up and saw no
one but the woman, He said to her, "Woman,
where are those accusers of yours? Has no one
condemned you?" 11 She said, "No one, Lord."

More Miraculous Signs *(See also page 110)*

Mark 6:

56 Wherever He entered, into villages, cities, or the country, they laid the sick in the marketplaces, and begged Him that they might just touch the border of His garment. And as many as touched Him were made well.

Matthew 8:

16 When evening had come, they brought to Him many who were demon-possessed. And He cast out the **spirits** with a word, and healed all who were sick,
17 that it might be fulfilled which was spoken by Isaiah the prophet, saying:

"He Himself took our infirmities
And bore our sicknesses."

Luke 11:

29 And while the crowds were thickly gathered together, He began to say, "This is an evil generation. It seeks a **sign**, and no **sign** will be given to it except the **sign** of Jonah the prophet.

John 7:

2 Now the Jews' Feast of Tabernacles was at hand.
31 And many of the people believed in Him, and said, "When the Christ comes, will He do more **signs** than these which this Man has done?"
37 On the last day, that great *day* of the feast, Jesus stood and cried out, saying, "If anyone thirsts, let him come to Me and drink.
38 He who believes in Me, as the Scripture has said, out of his heart will flow rivers of living water."
40 Therefore many from the crowd, when they heard this saying, said, "Truly this is the Prophet."
41 Others said, "This is the Christ."

John 9:

2 And His disciples asked Him, saying, "Rabbi, who sinned, this man or his parents, that he was born blind?"
3 Jesus answered, "Neither this man nor his parents sinned, but that the works of God should be revealed in him.
32 "Since the world began it has been unheard of that anyone opened the eyes of one who was born blind.
33 "If this Man were not from God, He could do nothing."

Lazarus raised from the dead

John 11:

4 When Jesus heard that, He said, "This sickness is not unto death, but for the glory of God, that the Son of God may be glorified through it."

35 Jesus wept. *
36 Then the Jews said, "See how He **loved** him!"

39 Jesus said, "Take away the stone." Martha, the sister of him who was dead, said to Him, "Lord, by this time there is a stench, for he has been dead four days."
40 Jesus said to her, "Did I not say to you that if you would believe you would see the glory of God?"

42 "And I know that You always hear Me, but because of the people who are standing by I said this, that they may believe that You sent Me."
43 Now when He had said these things, He cried with a loud voice, "Lazarus, come forth!"
44 And he who had died came out bound hand and foot with graveclothes, and his face was wrapped with a cloth. Jesus said to them, "Loose him, and let him go."

John 12:

9 Then a great many of the Jews knew that He was there; and they came, not for Jesus' sake only, but that they might also see Lazarus, whom He had raised from the dead.
10 But the chief priests took counsel that they might also put Lazarus to death,
11 because on account of him many of the Jews went away and believed in Jesus.

John 12

16 His disciples did not understand these things at first; but when Jesus was glorified, then they remembered that these things were written about Him and that they had done these things to Him.
17 Therefore the people, who were with Him when He called Lazarus out of his tomb and raised him from the dead, bore witness.
18 For this reason, the people also met Him, because they heard that He had done this **sign**.
(Pg. 23.B.1 v. 24 makes this a sign.)

**Note "human" feelings of Jesus. Also shortest verse in Bible.*

A. Christ's rejection and crucifixion

John 12:
37 But although He had done so many **signs** before them, they did not believe in Him,
38 that the word of Isaiah the prophet might be fulfilled, which he spoke:

> *"LORD, who has believed our report?*
> *And to whom has the* **arm** *of the LORD*
> *been revealed?"*

42 Nevertheless even among the rulers many believed in Him, but because of the Pharisees they did not confess Him, lest they should be put out of the synagogue.

Mark 14:
10 Then Judas Iscariot, one of the twelve, went to the chief priests to betray Him to them.

34 Then He said to them, "My **soul** is exceedingly sorrowful, even to death. Stay here and watch."

Mark 15:
22 And they brought Him to the place Golgotha, which is translated, Place of a Skull.
23 Then they gave Him wine mingled with myrrh to drink, but He did not take it.
24 And when they crucified Him, they divided His garments, casting lots for them to determine what every man should take.
25 Now it was the third hour, and they crucified Him.
26 And the inscription of His accusation was written above:
THE KING OF THE JEWS.
27 With Him they also crucified two robbers, one on His right and the other on His left.
28 So the Scripture was fulfilled which says, "And He was numbered with the transgressors."

John 19:
28 After this, Jesus, knowing that all things were now accomplished, that the Scripture might be fulfilled, said, "I thirst!"
29 Now a vessel full of sour wine was sitting there; and they filled a sponge with sour wine, put it on hyssop, and put it to His mouth.
30 So when Jesus had received the sour wine, He said, "It is finished!" And bowing His head, He gave up His **spirit**.

John 20:
21 So Jesus said to them again, "Peace to you! As the Father has sent Me, I also send you."
22 And when He had said this, He breathed on *them,* and said to them, "Receive the Holy Spirit.

B. 1. Christ's death and resurrection
B. 2. Great commission to the Apostles

John 19:
31 Therefore, because it was the Preparation Day, that the bodies should not remain on the cross on the Sabbath (for that Sabbath was a high day), the Jews asked Pilate that their legs might be broken, and that they might be taken away.

33 But when they came to Jesus and saw that He was already dead, they did not break His legs.
34 But one of the soldiers pierced His side with a spear, and immediately blood and water came out.
35 And he who has seen has testified, and his testimony is true; and he knows that he is telling the **truth**, so that you may believe.
36 For these things were done that the Scriptures should be fulfilled,
"Not one of His bones shall be broken."
37 And again another Scripture says,
"They shall look on Him whom they pierced."

Mark 16:
15 And He said to them, "Go into all the world and preach the gospel to every creature.
<see Pg. 96.B.4. for fulfillment>
16 "He who believes and is baptized will be saved; but he who does not believe will be condemned.
17 "And these **signs** will follow those who believe: In **My name** they will cast out demons; they will speak with new tongues;
18 "they will take up serpents; and if they drink anything deadly, it will b no means hurt them; they will lay hands on the sick, and they will recover."
19 So then, after the Lord had spoken to them, He was received up into heaven, and sat down at the right hand of God.
20 And they went out and preached everywhere, the Lord working with them and confirming the word through the accompanying **signs**. Amen.

<Purpose of signs>

Acts 26:
26 "For the king, before whom I also speak freely, knows these things; for I am convinced that none of these things escapes his attention, since this thing was not done in a corner.

John 18:
37 ... For this cause I was born, and for this cause I have come into the world, that I should bear witness to the **truth**. Everyone who is of the **truth** hears My voice

The Spirit Comes at Pentecost

Hebrews 2:

3 how shall we escape if we neglect so great a
salvation, which at the first began to be spoken
by the Lord, and was confirmed to us by those
who heard Him.
4 God also bearing witness both with signs and
wonders, with various miracles, and gifts of the
Holy Spirit, according to His own will?

!

Original Pentecost: Moses at Mt. Horeb.

Hebrews 12:

18 ...that mountain that may not be touched and
that burned with fire, and to blackness and
darkness and tempest,
19 And the sound of a trumpet and the voice of
words, so that those who heard it begged that the
word should not be spoken to them anymore.
21 And so terrifying was the sight that Moses said
"I am exceedingly afraid and trembling."

Acts 1:

14 These all continued with one accord in prayer
and supplication, with the women and Mary the
mother of Jesus, and with His brothers.

Acts 2:

1 Now when the Day of Pentecost had fully
come, they were all with one accord in one place.
2 And suddenly there came a sound from heaven,
as of a rushing mighty wind, and it filled the
whole house where they were sitting.
3 Then there appeared to them divided tongues,
as of fire, and one sat upon each of them.
4 And they were all filled with the Holy Spirit
and began to speak with other tongues, as the
Spirit gave them utterance.
5 Now there were dwelling in Jerusalem Jews,
devout men, from every nation under heaven.
6 And when this sound occurred, the multitude
came together, and were confused, because
everyone heard them speak in his own language.
7 Then they were all amazed and marveled, saying
to one another, "Look, are not all these who
speak Galileans?"
8 "And how is it that we hear, each in our own
language in which we were born?
9 "Parthians and Medes and Elamites, those
dwelling in Mesopotamia, Judea and Cappadocia,
Pontus and Asia,
10 "Phrygia and Pamphylia, Egypt and the parts
of Libya adjoining Cyrene, visitors from Rome,
both Jews and proselytes,

The Acts of the Apostles were also dominated by "signs" because of the prophecies and the necessity to help the Church take root in a hostile environment.

Acts 2: (continued)

11 "Cretans and Arabs – we hear them speaking
in our own tongues the wonderful works of
God."
12 So they were all amazed and perplexed, saying
to one another, "Whatever could this mean?"
13 Others mocking said, "They are full of new
wine."
14 But Peter, standing up with the eleven, raised
his voice and said to them, "Men of Judea and all
who dwell in Jerusalem, let this be known to you,
and heed my words.
15 "For these are not drunk, as you suppose, since
it is only the third hour of the day.
16 "But this is what was spoken by the prophet
Joel:
17 *'And it shall come to pass in the last days,*
says God,
That I will pour out My Spirit *on all flesh;*
Your sons and daughters shall prophesy,
Your young men shall see visions,
Your old men shall dream dreams.

Isaiah 28:

9 "Whom will he teach knowledge?
And whom will he make to understand the
message?
Those just weaned from milk?
Those just drawn from the breasts?
10 For precept must be upon precept, precept
upon precept,
Line upon line, line upon line,
Here a little, there a little."
11 For with stammering lips and another tongue
He will speak to this people.

Joel 2:

28 "And it shall come to pass afterward
That I will pour out My Spirit on all flesh;
Your sons and your daughters shall prophesy,
Your old men shall dream dreams,
Your young men shall see visions;
29 And also on My menservants and on My
maidservants
I will pour out My Spirit in those days.

Early Church

Acts 2:

22 "Men of Israel, hear these words: Jesus of Nazareth, a Man attested by God to you by miracles, wonders, and signs which God did through Him in your midst, as you yourselves also know –

40 And with many other words he testified and exhorted them, saying, "Be saved from this perverse generation."
41 Then those who gladly received his word were baptized; and that day about three thousand
souls were added *to them.* 42 And they continued
steadfastly in the apostles' doctrine and fellowship, in the breaking of bread, and in prayers.
43 Then fear came upon every soul, and many wonders and signs were done through the apostles.
44 Now all who believed were together, and had all things in common,
45 and sold their possessions and goods, and divided them among all, as anyone had need.

Acts 4:

32 Now the multitude of those who believed were of one heart and one soul; neither did anyone say that any of the things he possessed was his own, but they had all things in common.
33 And with great power the apostles gave witness to the resurrection of the Lord Jesus. ...

Acts 5:

1 But a certain man named Ananias, with Sapphira his wife, sold a possession.
2 And he kept back *part* of the proceeds. ...
3 But Peter said, "Ananias, why has Satan filled your heart to lie to the Holy Spirit ...
4 ...Why have you conceived this thing in your heart? You have not lied to men but to God."
5 Then Ananias, hearing these words, fell down and breathed his last.
8 ... Now it was about three hours later when his wife came in, not knowing what had happened.
9 Then Peter said to her, "How is it that you have agreed together to test the Spirit of the Lord? Look, the feet of those who have buried your husband *are* at the door, and they will carry you out."
10 Then immediately she fell down at his feet and breathed her last. ...

(Note boldness of Apostles. Not just anyone performed sign miracles. Only the Apostles.)

Acts 5:

11 So great fear came upon all the church and upon all who heard these things.
12 And through the hands of the apostles many signs and wonders were done among the people. And they were all with one accord in Solomon's Porch.
13 Yet none of the rest dared join them, but the people esteemed them highly.
15 so that they brought the sick out into the streets and laid *them* on beds and couches, that at least the shadow of Peter passing by might fall on some of them.

Acts 6:

2 Then the twelve summoned the multitude of the disciples and said, "It is not desirable that we should leave the word of God and serve tables.
3 "Therefore, brethren, seek out from among you seven men of good reputation, full of the Holy Spirit and wisdom, whom we may appoint over this business;
4 "but we will give ourselves continually to prayer and to the ministry of the word."
5 And the saying pleased the whole multitude. And they chose Stephen, a man full of faith and the Holy Spirit, and Philip, Prochorus, Nicanor, Timon, Parmenas, and Nicolas, a proselyte from Antioch,
6 whom they set before the apostles; and when they had prayed, they laid hands on them.

8 And Stephen, full of faith and power, did great wonders and signs among the people.

(Peter had the "keys" or ceremonial authority to give the Spirit to the nations.)

Matthew 16:

18 "And I also say to you that you are Peter, and on this rock I will build My church, and the gates of Hades shall not prevail against it.
19 "And I will give you the keys of the kingdom of heaven, and whatever you bind on earth will be bound in heaven, and whatever you loose on earth will be loosed in heaven."

A. Peter uses the "keys" to give the Spirit to Samaria and then the Gentiles. (Relate to pg 46.A.2)

Acts 8:

13 Then Simon himself also believed; and when he was baptized he continued with Philip, and was amazed, seeing the miracles and signs which were done.
14 Now when the apostles who were at Jerusalem heard that Samaria had received the word of God, they sent Peter and John to them.
15 who, when they had come down, prayed for them that they might receive the Holy Spirit.
16 For as yet He had fallen upon none of them. They had only been baptized in the name of the Lord Jesus.
17 Then they laid hands on them, and they received the Holy Spirit.
18 Now when Simon saw that through they laying on of the apostles' hands the Holy Spirit was given, he offered them money.

Acts 10:

25 As Peter was coming in, Cornelius met him and fell down at his feet and worshiped him.
26 But Peter lifted him up, saying, "Stand up; I myself am also a man."
27 And as he talked with him, he went in and found many who had come together.
28 Then he said to them, "You know how unlawful it is for a Jewish man to keep company with or go to one of another nation. But God has shown me that I should not call any man common or unclean.

44 While Peter was still speaking these words, the Holy Spirit fell upon all those who heard the word.*
45 And those of the circumcision who believed were astonished, as many as came with Peter, because the gift of the Holy Spirit had been poured out on the Gentiles also.
46 For they heard them speak with tongues and magnify God. Then Peter answered,
47 "Can anyone forbid water, that these should not be baptized who have received the Holy Spirit just as we have?"
48 And he commanded them to be baptized in the name of the Lord. Then they asked him to stay a few days.

* *Note they were baptized in the Spirit before water.*

B. Paul: the Apostle to the Gentiles

Acts 9:

15 But the Lord said to him, "Go, for he is a chosen vessel of Mine to bear My name before Gentiles, kings, and the children of Israel.
16 "For I will show him how many things he must suffer for My name's sake."
17 And Ananias went his way and entered the house; and laying his hands on him he said, "Brother Saul, the Lord Jesus who appeared to you on the road as you came, has sent me that you may receive your sight and be filled with the Holy Spirit."

Acts 11:

20 But some of them were men from Cyprus and Cyrene, who, when they had come to Antioch, spoke to the Hellenists, preaching the Lord Jesus.
21 And the hand of the Lord was with them, and a great number believed and turned to the Lord.
22 Then news of these things came to the ears of the church in Jerusalem, and they sent out Barnabas to go as far as Antioch.

24 For he was a good man, full of the Holy Spirit and of faith. And a great many people were added to the Lord.
25 Then Barnabas departed for Tarsus to seek Saul.
26 And when he had found him, he brought him to Antioch. So it was that for a whole year they assembled with the church and taught a great many people. And the disciples were first called Christians in Antioch.

Acts 12:

2 As they ministered to the Lord and fasted, the Holy Spirit said, "Now separate to Me Barnabas and Saul for the work to which I have called them."
3 Then, having fasted and prayed, and laid hands on them, they sent them away.

More Boldness of the Church Through Signs

I Timothy 5:
22 Do not lay hands on anyone hastily, nor share in other people's sins; keep yourself pure.

(Note that the "Laying on of hands" means almost the same as blood brothers' rite to Indians.)

Acts 14:
3 Therefore they stayed there a long time, speaking boldly in the Lord, who was bearing witness to the word of His grace, granting signs and wonders to be done by their hands.

Acts 4:
29 "Now, Lord, look on their threats, and grant to Your servants that with all boldness they may speak Your word,
30 "by stretching out Your hand to heal, and that signs and wonders may be done through the name of Your holy Servant Jesus."

Acts 15:
8 "So God, who knows the heart, acknowledged them, by giving them the Holy Spirit just as He did to us,
9 "and made no distinction between us and them, purifying their hearts by faith.
10 "Now therefore, why do you test God by putting a yoke on the neck of the disciples which neither our fathers nor we were able to bear?
11 "But we believe that through the grace of the Lord Jesus Christ we shall be saved in the same manner as they."
12 Then all the multitude kept silent and listened to Barnabas and Paul declaring how many miracles and wonders God had worked through them among the Gentiles.

Acts 21:
18 On the following day Paul went in with us to James, and all the elders were present.
19 When he had greeted them, he told in detail those things which God had done among the Gentiles through his ministry.*

**Note that by this late Paul did not perform miracles in Jerusalem, but only told about them. Miracles seem to be restricted to new territories.*

Acts 19:
1 And it happened, while Apollos was at Corinth, that Paul, having passed through the upper regions, came to Ephesus. And finding some disciples
2 he said to them, "Did you receive the Holy Spirit when you believed?" And they said to him, "We have not so much as heard whether there is a Holy Spirit."
3 And he said to them, "Into what then were you baptized?" So they said, "Into John's baptism."
6 And when Paul had laid hands on them, the Holy Spirit came upon them, and they spoke with tongues and prophesied.
8 And he went into the synagogue and spoke boldly for three months, reasoning and persuading concerning the things of the kingdom of God.
11 Now God worked unusual miracles by the hands of Paul, *
12 so that even handkerchiefs or aprons were brought from his body to the sick, and the diseases left them and the evil spirits went out of them.
13 Then some of the itinerant Jewish exorcists took it upon themselves to call the name of the Lord Jesus over those who had evil spirits, saying, "We adjure you by the Jesus whom Paul preaches."
15 And the evil spirit answered and said, "Jesus I know, and Paul I know, but who are you?" **
16 Then the man in whom the evil spirit was leaped on them, overpowered them, and prevailed against them, so that they fled out of that house naked and wounded.
17 This became known both to **all** Jews and Greeks dwelling in Ephesus; and fear fell on them all, and the name of the Lord Jesus was magnified.
20 So the word of the Lord was growing mightily and prevailing.

** Probably greater than even Jesus' style (as He prophesied). Note also how the healing gift was not common.*

*** Note the understanding of the concept of Authority - the evil spirit expected the exorcist to realize he was no authority to use those names .*

A. 1-2 Typical Signs
A. 3-6 To help us understand "...the name..."
A. 7 "baptized for the dead?"

Acts 9:

34 And Peter said to him, "Aeneas, Jesus the Christ heals you. Arise and make your bed." Then he arose immediately.
35 So all who dwelt at Lydda and Sharon saw him and turned to the Lord.

40 But Peter put them all out, and knelt down and prayed. And turning to the body he said, "Tabitha, arise." And she opened her eyes, and when she saw Peter she sat up.
41 Then he gave her his hand and lifted her up; and when he had called the saints and widows, he presented her alive.
42 And it became known throughout all Joppa, and many believed on the Lord.

Acts 4:

10 Let it be known to you all, and to all the people of Israel, that by the name of Jesus Christ of Nazareth, whom you crucified, whom God raised from the dead, by Him this man stands here before you.

Acts 10:

43 "To Him all the prophets witness that, through His name, whoever believes in Him will receive remission of sins."
<compare to Pg 45. B.2!>

Acts 3:

16 "And His name, through faith in His name, has made this man strong, whom you see and know. Yes, the faith which comes through Him has given him this perfect soundness in the presence of you all.

Acts 26:

9 "Indeed, I myself thought I must do many things contrary to the name of Jesus of Nazareth.
10 "This I also did in Jerusalem, and many of the saints I shut up in prison.

I Corinthians 15:

29 Otherwise, what will they do who are baptized for the dead, if the dead do not rise at all? Why then are they baptized for the dead?
30 And why do we stand in jeopardy every hour?
31 I affirm, by the boasting in you which I have in Christ Jesus our Lord, I die daily.
32 ...If *the* dead do not rise, *"Let us eat and drink, for tomorrow we die!"* < Isaiah 22:13 >

B. 1-3
<u>Baptism into "the name"</u>

(enables calling on the name, saying "put my name in your name.")

B. 4-6 <u>One Baptism</u>, by the Spirit

Matthew 28:

19 "Go therefore and make disciples of all the nations, baptizing them in the name of the Father and of the Son and of the Holy Spirit."

Acts 2:

38 Than Peter said to them, "Repent, and let every one of you be baptized in the name of Jesus Christ★ for the remission of sins; and you shall receive the gift of the Holy Spirit."

<compare to Pg. 45.A.4 and to Pg. 38.A.3>

★<Note: Treat this as a compound name: "Jesus-Christ-for-the-remission-of-sins." (Water baptism then had the meaning of symbolizing the yielding of one's identity into another larger identity.) >

Acts 22:

16 "And now why are you waiting? Arise and be baptized, and wash away your sins, calling on the name of the Lord."

< Note: A comma separates the two distinct actions: "be baptized" and "wash". "Calling" is grammatically associated with "wash" as a "How" adverb phrase.>

Ephesians 4:

4 There is one body and one Spirit, just as you were called in one hope of your calling;
5 one Lord, one faith, one baptism;
6 one God and Father of all, who is above all, and through all, and in you all.
<See also Pg. 43.A.2. and Pg. 44.B.1a>

I Corinthians 12:

13 For by one Spirit we were all baptized into one body – whether Jews or Greeks, whether slaves or free – and have all been made to drink into one Spirit.

Acts 11:

16 "Then I remembered the word of the Lord, how He said, 'John indeed baptized with water, but you shall be baptized with the Holy Spirit.'

The Symbolism of Baptism

Colossians 2:

12 buried with Him in baptism, in which you also were raised with Him through faith in the working of God, who raised Him from the dead.

< An example of God's promise to get the saving message to any who seek the Lord.>

Acts 8:

27 So he arose and went. And behold, a man of Ethiopia, a eunuch of great authority under Candace the queen of the Ethiopians, who had charge of all her treasury, and had come to Jerusalem to worship,

28 was returning. And sitting in his chariot, he was reading Isaiah the prophet.

29 Then the Spirit said to Philip, "Go near and overtake this chariot."

35 Then Philip opened his mouth, and beginning at this Scripture, preached Jesus to him.

36 Now as they went down the road, they came to some water. And the eunuch said, "See, here is water. What hinders me from being baptized?"

37 Then Philip said, "If you believe with all your heart, you may." And he answered and said, "I believe that Jesus Christ is the Son of God."

38 So he commanded the chariot to stand still. And both Philip and the eunuch went down into the water, and he baptized him.

39 Now when they came up out of the water, the Spirit of the Lord caught Philip away, so that the eunuch saw him no more; and he went on his way rejoicing.

<Note: the Ethiopian believed before the Spirit was given to the Gentiles. See Pg. 43.A.2.
(The "mystery of the Church" that was not yet taught meant that Spirit baptism went beyond the identifying of one with the Name of Jesus but actually joins one into the Body of Christ with a unifying Spirit that makes our flesh part of His body.)>

Romans 6:

2 Certainly not! How shall we who died to sin live any longer in it?

3 Or do you not know that as many of us as were baptized into Christ Jesus were baptized into His death?

4 Therefore we were buried with Him through baptism into death, that just as Christ was raised from the dead by the glory of the Father, even so we also should walk in newness of life.

5 For if we have been united together in the likeness of His death, certainly we also shall be in the likeness of His resurrection.

I Peter 3:

20 who formerly were disobedient, when once the longsuffering of God waited in the days of Noah, while the ark was being prepared, in which a few, that is, eight souls, were saved through water.

21 There is also an antitype which now saves us, namely baptism (not the removal of the filth of the flesh, but the answer of a good conscience toward God), through the resurrection of Jesus Christ.

Matthew 20:

22 But Jesus answered and said, "You do not know what you ask. Are you able to drink the cup that I am about to drink, and be baptized with the baptism that I am baptized with?" They said to Him, "We are able."

23 So He said to them, "You will indeed drink My cup, and be baptized with the baptism that I am baptized with; but to sit on **My right hand** and on My left is not Mine to give, but it is for those for whom it is prepared by My Father."

I Corinthians 10:

1 Moreover, brethren, I do not want you to be unaware that all our fathers were under the cloud, all passed through the sea.

2 all were baptized into Moses in the cloud and in the sea,

3 all ate the same spiritual food,

4 and all drank the same spiritual drink. For they drank of that spiritual Rock that followed them, and that Rock was Christ.

Paul

Pages 47 & 48 focus on the life and style of Paul.
Paul was an example saint worth imitating.

I Corinthians 11:1

Imitate me, just as I imitate Christ.

Acts 18:

4 And he reasoned in the synagogue every
Sabbath, and persuaded both Jews and Greeks.

II Corinthians 11:

5 For I consider that I am not at all inferior to
the most eminent apostles.
6 Even though I am untrained in speech, yet I am
not in knowledge. But we have been thoroughly
made manifest among you in all things.
7 Did I commit sin in abasing myself that you
might be exalted, because I preached the gospel
of God to you free of charge?
8 I robbed other churches, taking wages from
them to minister to you.
9 And when I was present with you, and in need,
I was a burden to no one, for what was lacking to
me the brethren who came from Macedonia
supplied. And in everything I kept myself from
being burdensome to you, and so I will keep
myself.
10 As the truth of Christ is in me, no one shall
stop me from this boasting in the regions of
Achaia.

II Corinthians 12:

1 It is doubtless not profitable for me to boast. I
will come to visions and revelations of the Lord:
2 I know a man in Christ who fourteen years ago
– whether in the body I do not know, or whether
out of the body I do not know, God knows –
such a one was caught up to the third heaven.
3 And I know such a man – whether in the body
or out of the body I do not know, God knows –
4 how he was caught up into Paradise and heard
inexpressible words, which it is not lawful for a
man to utter.
5 Of such a one I will boast; yet of myself I will
not boast, except in my infirmities.

II Thessalonians 2:

1 . . . , we ask you, 2 not to be soon shaken in
mind or troubled, either by spirit or by word or
by letter, as if from us, as though the day of
Christ had come.

Romans 15:

18 For I will dare not to speak of any of those
things which Christ has not accomplished
through me, in word and deed, to make the
Gentiles obedient –
19 in mighty signs and wonders, by the power of
the Spirit of God, so that from Jerusalem and
round about to Illyricum I have fully preached
the gospel of Christ.
20 And so I have made it my aim to preach the
gospel, not where Christ was named, lest I should
build on another man's foundation.

I Corinthians 9:

20 and to the Jews I became as a Jew, that I might
win Jews; to those who are under the law, as
under the law, that I might win those who are
under the law;
21 to those who are without law, as without law
(not being without law toward God, but under
law toward Christ), that I might win those who
are without law;
22 to the weak I became as weak, that I might win
the weak. I have become all things to all men,
that I might by all means save some.

Philippians 4:

9 The things which you learned and received and
heard and saw in me, these do, and the God of
peace will be with you.

I Corinthians 9:

4 Do we have no right to eat and drink?
5 Do we have no right to take along a believing
wife, as do also the other apostles, the brothers
of the Lord, and Cephas?
6 Or is it only Barnabas and I who have no right
to refrain from working?
7 Who ever goes to war at his own expense?
Who plants a vineyard and does not eat of its
fruit? Or who tends a flock and does not drink
of the milk of the flock?
8 Do I say these things as a mere man? Or does
not the law say the same also?
9 For it is written in the law of Moses, "You
shall not muzzle an ox while it treads out the
grain." Is it oxen God is concerned about?
10 Ore does He say it altogether for our sakes?
For our sakes, no doubt, this is written, that he
who plows should plow in hope, and he who
threshes in hope should be partaker of his
hope.

Paul

A. miraculous strength and physical weakness.

the Last Apostle? (B1,2) Timothy, (not an apostle).

<see also Pg. 44B>

II Corinthians 12:

11 I have become a fool in boasting; you have compelled me. For I ought to have been commended you; for in nothing was I behind the most eminent apostles, though I am nothing.

12 Truly the signs of an apostle were accomplished among you with all perseverance, in signs and wonders and mighty deeds.

Galatians 4:

13 You know that because of physical infirmity I preached the gospel to you at the first.

14 And my trial which was in my flesh you did not despise or reject, but you received me as an angel of God, even as Christ Jesus.

II Corinthians 10:

10 "For his letters," they say, "are weighty and powerful, but his bodily presence is weak, and his speech contemptible."

II Corinthians 12:

7 And lest I should be exalted above measure by the abundance of the revelations, a thorn in the flesh was given to me, a messenger of Satan to buffet me, lest I be exalted above measure.

8 Concerning this thing I pleaded with the Lord three times that it might depart from me.

9 And He said to me, "My grace is sufficient for you, for My strength is made perfect in weakness." Therefore most gladly I will rather boast in my infirmities, that the power of Christ may rest upon me.

10 Therefore I take pleasure in infirmities, in reproaches, in needs, in persecution, in distresses, for Christ's sake. For when I am weak, then I am strong.

I Corinthians 2:

3 I was with you in weakness, in fear, and in much trembling.

4 And my speech and my preaching *were* not with persuasive words of human wisdom, but in demonstration of the Spirit and of power,

5 That your faith should not be in the wisdom of men but in the power of God.

1 Corinthians 15:

8 Then last of all He was seen by me also, as by one born out of due time.

9 For I am the least of the apostles, who am not worthy to be called an apostle, because I persecuted the church of God.

I Corinthians 4:

9 For I think that God has displayed us, the apostles, last, as men condemned to death; for we have been made a spectacle to the world, both to angels and to men.

10 We are fools for Christ's sake, but you are wise in Christ! We are weak, but you are strong! You are distinguished, but we are dishonored!

11 Even to the present hour we both hunger and thirst, and we are poorly clothed, and beaten, and homeless.

I Thessalonians 1:

5 For our gospel did not come to you in word only, but also in power, and in the Holy Spirit and in much assurance, as you know what kind of men we were among you for your sake.

6 And you became followers of us and of the Lord, having received the word in much affliction, with joy of the Holy Spirit,

7 so that you became examples to all in Macedonia and Achaia who believe.

8 For from you the word of the Lord has sounded forth, not only in Macedonia and Achaia, but also in every place. Your faith toward God has gone out, so that we do not need to say anything.

II Timothy 4:

5 But you be watchful in all things, endure afflictions, do the work of an evangelist, fulfill your ministry.

6 For I am already being poured out as a drink offering, and the time of my departure is at hand.

7 I have fought the good fight, I have finished the race, I have kept the faith.

Instructions to the New Body of Christ

< *Also see Pg. 41, 42 for context of Tongues and other Signs*
and see Pg. 11.A.2 (Heb. 1:1,2) and Pg. 107.A.4, B.1 >

I Corinthians 1:

21 For since, in the wisdom of God, the world through wisdom did not know God, it pleased God through the foolishness of the message preached to save those who believe.
22 For Jews request a sign, and Greeks seek after wisdom;
23 but we preach Christ crucified, to the Jews a stumbling block and to the Greeks foolishness.

I Corinthians 12:

3 Therefore I make known to you that no one speaking by the Spirit of God calls Jesus accursed, and no one can say that Jesus is Lord except by the Holy Spirit.
4 Now there are diversities of gifts, but the same Spirit.
5 There are differences of ministries, but the same Lord.
6 And there are diversities of activities, but it is the same God who works all in all.
7 But the manifestation of the Spirit is given to each one for the profit of all:
8 for to one is given the word of wisdom through the Spirit, to another the word of knowledge through the same Spirit,
9 to another faith by the same Spirit, to another gifts of healings by the same Spirit,
10 to another the working of miracles, to another prophecy, to another discerning of spirits, to another different kinds of tongues, to another the interpretation of tongues.
11 But one and the same Spirit works all these things, distributing them to each one individually as He wills.

I Corinthians 12: <*See also Pg. 108* >

28 And God has appointed these in the church: first apostles, second prophets, third teachers, after that miracles, then gifts of healing, helps, administrations, varieties of tongues.
29 *Are* all apostles? *Are* all prophets? *Are* all teachers? *Are* all workers of miracles?
30 Do all have gifts of healings? Do all speak with tongues? Do all interpret?
31 But earnestly desire the best gifts.
And yet I show you a more excellent way.

I Corinthians 13:

8 Love never fails. But whether there are prophecies, they will fail; whether there are tongues, they will cease; whether there is knowledge, it will vanish away.
9 For we know in part and we prophesy in part.
10 But when that which is perfect has come, then that which is in part will be done away.
11 When I was a child, I spoke as a child, I understood as a child, I thought as a child; but when I became a man, I put away childish things.
12 For now we see in a mirror, dimly, but then face to face. Now I know in part, but then I shall know just as I also am known.

<See also Pg. 20.A.1 to see that God has not always continuously dispensed signs and prophecy in one consistent pattern!>
<Also Pg. 97.B.4>

I Timothy 6:

20 O Timothy! Guard what was committed to your trust, avoiding the profane and vain babblings and contradictions of what is falsely called knowledge –
21 by professing it, some have strayed concerning the faith. Grace be with you. Amen.

II Timothy 2:

16 But shun profane and vain babblings, for they will increase to more ungodliness.
17 And their message will spread like cancer. Hymanaeus and Philetus are of this sort,
18 who have strayed concerning the truth, saying that the resurrection is already past; and they overthrow the faith of some.

Ephesians 2:

20 having been built on the foundation of the apostles and prophets, Jesus Christ Himself being the chief corner*stone,*
21 in whom the whole building, being fitted together, grows into a holy temple in the Lord,
22 in whom you also are being built together for a dwelling place of God in the Spirit.

"Tongues"

<Note: See Pg. 71.B.3 (I Cor. 5 1,2) to note the extent of the spiritual deformity at the Church in Corinth at the time of Paul's letter to them. >

I Corinthians 14:

1 Pursue love, and desire spiritual gifts,
but especially that you may prophesy.
2 For he who speaks in a tongue does not
speak to men but to God, for no one
understands him; however, in the spirit he
speaks mysteries.
3 But he who prophesies speaks edification
and exhortation and comfort to men.
4 He who speaks in a tongue edifies himself,
but he who prophesies edifies the church.
5 I wish you all spoke with tongues, but
even more that you prophesied; for he who
prophesies is greater than he who speaks with
tongues, unless indeed he interprets, that the
church may receive edification.
6 But now, brethren, if I come to you speaking
with tongues, what shall I profit you unless I
speak to you either by revelation, by knowledge,
by prophesying, or by teaching?
7 Even things without life, whether flute or
harp, when they make a sound, unless they
make a distinction in the sounds, how will it be
known what is piped or played?
8 For if the trumpet makes an uncertain sound,
who will prepare himself for battle?
9 So likewise you, unless you utter by the
tongues words easy to understand, how will it
be known what is spoken?
10 There are, it may be, so many kinds of
languages in the world, and none of them is
without significance.
11 Therefore, I do not know the meaning of the
language, I shall be foreigner to him who speaks,
and he who speaks will be a foreigner to me.
12 Even so you, since you are zealous for
spiritual gifts, let it be for the edification
of the church that you seek to excel.
13 Therefore let him who speaks in a
tongue pray that he may interpret.
14 For if I pray in a tongue, my spirit
prays, but my understanding is unfruitful.

*<This is an overly debated subject.
I just have to point out 2 things:
1. A "Gift" is not a gift if taken back.
2. These passages are only clear only in stating "tongues" is less useful and desirable than other gifts, and that not everyone will have it. >*

I Corinthians 14: (continued)

15 What is the result then? I will pray with the
spirit, and I will also pray with the
understanding. I will sing with the spirit,
and I will also sing with the understanding.

19 yet in the church I would rather speak five
words with my understanding, that I may
teach others also, than ten thousand words in
a tongue.
20 Brethren, do not be children in
understanding; however, in malice be babes, but
in understanding be mature.
21 In the law, it is written:

> *" With men of other tongues*
> *and other lips*
> *I will speak to this people;*
> *And yet, for all that,*
> *they will not hear Me,"*

says the Lord.
22 Therefore, tongues are for a sign, not to
those who believe but to unbelievers; but
prophesying is not for unbelievers but for
those who believe.
23 Therefore if the whole church comes together in
one place, and all speak with tongues, and there
comes in those who are uninformed or unbelievers,
will they not say that you are out of your mind?
24 But if all prophesy, and an unbeliever or
uninformed person comes in, he is convinced by
all, he is judged by all.
25 And thus the secrets of his heart are revealed;
and so, falling down on his face, he will worship
God and report that God is truly among you.
26 How is it then, brethren? Whenever you come
together, each of you has a psalm, has a teaching,
has a tongue, has a revelation, has an interpretation.
Let all things be done for edification.
27 If anyone speaks in a tongue, let there be two or
at the most three, each in turn, and let one interpret.
28 But if there is no interpreter, let him keep silent
in church, and let him speak to himself and to
God.

Ephesians 4:

7 But to each one of us grace was given
according to the measure of Christ's gift.
8 Therefore He says:

> "When He ascended on high,
> He led captivity captive,
> And gave gifts to men."

Warnings of False Doctrines
and Imitations of Signs and Prophecies

<*See also Pg. 89.B.6, Pg. 97.B.1, 2, 4 and Pg. 98.A.2-5 and Pg. 82 & Pg. 80.B.2-3*>

Jeremiah 48:

10 Cursed is he who does
the work of the LORD deceitfully.

II Corinthians 11:

13 For such are false apostles, deceitful workers, transforming themselves into apostles of Christ.
14 And no wonder! For Satan himself transforms himself into an angel of light.
15 Therefore it is no great thing if his ministers also transform themselves into ministers of righteousness, whose end will be according to their works.

Hebrews 13:

8 Jesus Christ is the same yesterday, today and forever.
9 Do not be carried about with various and strange doctrines. For it is good that the heart be established by grace, not with foods which have not profited those who have been occupied with them.

II Thessalonians 2:

5 Do you not remember that when I was still with you I told you these things?
6 For the mystery of lawlessness is already at work; only He who now restrains will do so until He is taken out of the way.
7 And then the lawless one will be revealed, whom the Lord will consume with the breath of His mouth and destroy with the brightness of His coming.
9 The coming of the lawless one is according to the work of Satan, with all power, signs, and lying wonders,
10 and with all unrighteous deception among those who perish, because they did not receive the love of the truth, that they might be saved.
11 And for this reason, God will send them strong delusion, that they should believe the lie,
12 that they all may be condemned who did not believe the truth but had pleasure in unrighteousness.

Jeremiah 23:

26 How long will *this* be in the heart of the prophets who prophesy lies? Indeed *they are* prophets of the deceit of their own heart,
27 who try to make My people forget My name by their dreams which everyone tells his neighbor, as their fathers forgot My name for Baal.

Philippians 2:

21 For all seek their own, not the things of Christ Jesus.

Ezekiel 13:

3 Thus says the LORD God: "Woe to the foolish prophets, who follow their own spirit and have seen nothing!"
6 They have envisioned futility and false divination, saying, 'Thus says the LORD!' But the LORD has not sent them; yet they hope that the word may be confirmed.

Matthew 7:

21 "Not everyone who says to Me, 'Lord, Lord', shall enter the kingdom of heaven, but he who does the will of My Father in heaven.
22 "Many will say to Me in that day, 'Lord, Lord, have we not prophesied in Your name, cast out demons in Your name, and done many wonders in Your name?"
23 "And then I will declare to them, 'I never knew you; depart from Me, you who practice lawlessness!'

Deuteronomy 13:

1 "If there arises among you a prophet or a dreamer of dreams, and he gives you a sign or a wonder,
2 "and the sign or the wonder of which he spoke to you comes to pass, saying, 'Let us go after other gods which you have not known, and let us serve them,'
3 "you shall not listen to the words of that prophet or that dreamer of dreams, for the LORD your God is testing you to know whether you love the LORD your God with all your heart and with all your soul.

Deuteronomy 18:

20 "But the prophet who presumes to speak a word in My name, which I have not commanded him to speak, or who speaks in the name of other gods, that prophet shall die.'
21 "And if you say in your heart, 'How shall we know the word which the LORD has not spoken?" –
22 "when a prophet speaks in the name of the LORD, if the thing does not happen or come to pass, that is the thing which the LORD has not spoken; the prophet has spoken it presumptuously; you shall not be afraid of him.

Examples of Demonism and Imitators of God's Work

II Timothy 3:
13 But evil men and impostors will grow worse and worse, deceiving and being deceived.

Numbers 24:
1 Now when Balaam saw that it pleased the LORD to bless Israel, he did not go as at other times, to seek to use sorcery, but he set his face toward the wilderness.

Mark 13:
21 "Then if anyone says to you, 'Look, here *is* the Christ!' or, 'Look, *He is* there!' do not believe it.
22 "For false christs and false prophets will rise and show signs and wonders to deceive, if possible, the elect. !

Matthew 24:
23 "Then if anyone says to you, 'Look, here *is* the Christ!' or 'There!' do not believe *it.*
24 "For false christs and false prophets will arise and show great signs and wonders, so as to deceive, if possible, even the elect.

I Timothy 4:
1 Now the Spirit expressly says that in latter times some will depart from the faith, giving heed to deceiving spirits and doctrines of demons,
2 speaking lies in hypocrisy, having their own conscience seared with a hot iron,
3 forbidding to marry, and commanding to abstain from foods which God created to be received with thanksgiving by those who believe and know the truth.

<Demonic powers could imitate many of Moses' miracles. >

Exodus 7:
22 Then the magicians of Egypt did so with their enchantments; and Pharaoh's heart grew hard, and he did not heed them, as the LORD had said.

Exodus 8:
6 So Aaron stretched out his hand over the waters of Egypt, and the frogs cam up and covered the land of Egypt.
7 And the magicians did so with their enchantments, and brought up frogs on the land of Egypt.
18 Now the magicians so worked with their enchantments to bring forth lice, but they could not. So there were lice on man and beast.
19 Then the magicians said to Pharaoh, "This is the finger of God."

Isaiah 8:
19 And when they say to you, "Seek those who are mediums and wizards, who whisper and mutter," should not a people seek their God? Should they seek the dead on behalf of the living? *<("No!" implied)>*

Isaiah 49:
25 Who frustrates the signs of the babblers,
And drives diviners mad;

Leviticus 19:
31 'Give no regard to mediums and familiar spirits; do not seek after them, to be defiled by them: I am the LORD your God.

Zechariah 13:
3 It shall come to pass *that* if anyone still prophesies, then his father and mother who begot him will say to him, 'You shall not live, because you have spoken lies in the name of the LORD.' And his father and mother who begot him shall thrust him through when he prophesies.
4 "And it shall be in that day *that* every prophet will be ashamed of his vision when he prophesies; they will not wear a robe of coarse hair to deceive.
5 But he will say, 'I *am* no prophet, I *am* a farmer; for a man taught me to keep cattle from my youth.'

Satan/Lucifer

So, "Who's behind all this?" And "What's to come?"
This brings us to the point of needing to know more about Satan.

<See also Pg. 58.B, Pg. 63.B, Pg. 64.A.3 and Pg. 115.A.4.>

Ezekiel 28:

12 "Son of man, take up a lamentation for the king of Tyre, and say to him, 'Thus says the LORD God:

"You were the seal of perfection,
Full of wisdom and perfect in beauty.
13 You were in Eden, the garden of God;
Every precious stone was your covering:
The sardius, topaz, and diamond,
Beryl, onyx, and jasper,
Sapphire, turquoise, and emerald with gold.
The workmanship of your timbrels and pipes
Was prepared for you on the day you were created.

14 "You were the anointed cherub who covers;
I established you;
You were on the holy mountain of God;
You walked back and forth in the midst of fiery stones.
15 You were perfect in your ways from the day you were created,
Till iniquity was found in you.

16 "By the abundance of your trading
You became filled with violence within,
And you sinned;
Therefore I cast you as a profane thing
Out of the mountain of God;
And I destroyed you,
O covering cherub,
From the midst of the fiery stones.

17 "Your **heart** was lifted up because of your beauty;
You corrupted your wisdom for the sake of your splendor;
I cast you to the ground,
I laid you before kings,
That they might gaze at you.

Hebrews 2:

14 Inasmuch then as the children have partaken of flesh and blood, He Himself likewise shared in the same, that through death He might destroy <u>him who had the power of death, that is, the devil</u>,
15 and release those who through fear of death were all their lifetime subject to bondage.

Ezekiel 28: continued

18 "You defiled your sanctuaries
By the multitude of your iniquities,
By the iniquity of your trading;
Therefore I brought fire from your midst;
It devoured you,
And I turned you to ashes upon the earth
In the sight of all who saw you.
19 All who knew you among the peoples are astonished at you;
You have become a horror,
And shall be no more forever." ' "

Isaiah 14:

12 "How you are fallen from heaven,
O <u>Lucifer</u>, son of the morning! **!**
How you are cut down to the ground,
You who weakened the nations!
13 For you have said in your **heart**:
'I will ascend to heaven,
I will exalt my throne above the stars of God;
I will also sit on the mount of the congregation
On the farthest sides of the north;
14 I will ascend above the heights of the clouds,
I will be like the Most High.' **!!!**
15 Yet you shall be brought down to Sheol,
To the lowest depths of the Pit.

16 "Those who see you will gaze at you,
And consider you, saying:
'Is this the man who made the earth tremble,
Who shook kingdoms,
17 Who made the world as a wilderness
And destroyed its cities,
Who did not open the house of his prisoners?'

John 14:

30 "I will no longer talk with you much, for <u>the ruler of this world</u> is coming, and he has nothing in Me.

Satan/Lucifer (The Accuser)

<See also Pg. 27.B.2>

Revelation 12:

10 Then I heard a loud voice saying in heaven, "Now salvation, and strength, and the kingdom of our God, and the power of His Christ have come, for the accuser of our brethren, who accused them before our God day and night, has been cast down.

11 "And they overcame him by the blood of the Lamb and by the word of their testimony, and they did not love their lives to the death.

Jude:

9 Yet Michael the archangel, in contending with the devil, when he disputed about the body of Moses, dared not bring against him a reviling accusation, but said, "The Lord rebuke you!"

Job 1:

6 Now there was a day when the sons of God came to present themselves before the LORD, and Satan also came among them.

7 And the LORD said to Satan, "From where do you come?" So Satan answered the LORD and said, "From going to and fro on the earth, and from walking back and forth on it."

8 Then the LORD said to Satan, "Have you considered My servant Job, that there is none like him on the earth, a blameless and upright man, one who fears God and shuns evil?"

9 So Satan answered the LORD and said, "Does Job fear God for nothing?

10 "Have You not made a hedge around him, around his household, and around all that he has on every side? You have blessed the work of his hands, and his possessions have increased in the land.

11 "But now, stretch out Your hand and touch all that he has, and he will surely curse You to Your face!"

12 So the LORD said to Satan, "Behold, all that he has is in your power; only do not lay a hand on his person." Then Satan went out from the presence of the LORD.

Luke 10:

17 Then the seventy returned with joy, saying, :Lord, even the demons are subject to us in Your name,"

18 And He said to them, "I saw Satan fall Like lightning from heaven.".

21 In that hour Jesus rejoiced in the Spirit and said, "I thank You Father, Lord of heaven and earth, that You have hidden these things from the wise and prudent and revealed them to babes. . . .

< Job was one of God's favorite men. See Pg. 25.B.4.>

Job 2:

1 Again there was a day when the sons of God came to present themselves before the LORD, and Satan came also among them to present himself before the LORD.

2 And the LORD said to Satan, "From where do you come?" So Satan answered the LORD and said, "From going to and fro on the earth, and from walking back and forth on it."

3 Then the LORD said to Satan, "Have you considered My servant Job, that there is none like him on earth, a blameless and upright man, one who fears God and shuns evil? And still he holds fast to his integrity, although you incited Me against him, to destroy him without cause."

4 So Satan answered the LORD and said, "Skin for skin! Yes, all that a man has he will give for his life.

5 "But stretch out Your hand now, and touch his bone and his flesh, and he will surely curse You to Your face!"

6 So the LORD said to Satan, "Behold, he is in your hand, but spare his life."

7 Then Satan went out from the presence of the LORD, and struck Job with painful boils from the sole of his foot to the crown of his head.

Looking Ahead to Last Days:
End Without Warning

Mark 13:

10 "And the gospel must first be preached to all the nations.

<See Pg. 96.B.4 (Romans 16:26) !>

Matthew 24:

6 "And you will hear of wars and rumors of wars. See that you are not troubled; for all these things must come to pass, but the end is not yet.
7 "For nation will rise against nation, and kingdom against kingdom. And there will be famines, pestilence, and earthquakes in various places.
8 "All these are the beginning of sorrows.
9 "Then they will deliver you up to tribulation and kill you, and you will be hated by all nations for My name's sake.
10 "And then many will be offended, will betray one another, and will hate one another.
11 "Then many false prophets will rise and deceive many.
12 "And because lawlessness will abound, the love of many will grow cold.
13 "But he who endures to the end shall be saved.
14 "And this gospel of the kingdom will be preached in all the world as a witness to all the nations, and then the end will come.
15 "Therefore when you see the 'abomination of desolation,' spoken of by Daniel the prophet, standing in the holy place" (whoever reads, let him understand),
16 "then let those who are in Judea flee to the mountains.
17 "Let him who is on the housetop not come down to take anything out of his house.
18 "And let him who is in the field not go back to get his clothes.

36 "But of that day and hour no one knows, not even the angels of heaven, but My Father only.
37 But as the days of Noah *were,* so also will the coming of the Son of Man be.
38 ...they were eating and drinking, marrying and giving in marriage, until the day that Noah entered the ark,
39 " ...<see pg 120B5>..., so also will the coming of the Son of Man be.

Matthew 24:

43 "But know this, that if the master of the house had known what hour the thief would come, he would have watched and not allowed his house to be broken into.
44 "Therefore you also be ready, for the Son of Man is coming at an hour when you do not expect Him.

Mark 13:

32 "But of that day and hour no one knows, neither the angels in heaven, nor the Son, but only the Father.
33 "Take heed, watch and pray; for you do not know when the time is.
34 "It is like a man going to a far country, who left his house and gave authority to his servants, and to each his work, and commanded the doorkeeper to watch.
35 "Watch therefore, for you do not know when the master of the house is coming – in the evening, at midnight, at the crowing of the rooster, or in the morning –
36 "lest, coming suddenly, he find you sleeping.
37 "And what I say to you, I say to all: Watch!"

II Timothy 3:

1 But know this, that in the last days perilous times will come:
2 For men will be lovers of themselves, lovers of money, boasters, proud, blasphemers, disobedient to parents, unthankful, unholy,
3 unloving, unforgiving, slanderers, without self-control, brutal, despisers of good,
4 traitors, headstrong, haughty, lovers of pleasure rather than lovers of God,
5 having a form of godliness but denying its power. And from such people turn away!
6 For of this sort are those who creep into households and make captives of gullible women loaded down with sins, led away by various lusts,
7 always learning and never able to come to the knowledge of the truth.

I John 4:

3 and every spirit that does not confess that Jesus Christ has come in the flesh is not of God. And this is the *spirit* of the Antichrist, which you have heard was coming, and is now already in the world.

The "Rapture of the Church"

< Do your own research! Check meaning of word translated as "Rapture", >

<See Pg. 52.A.3-5 and Pg57B1>

I Thessalonians 5:

1 But concerning the times and the seasons, brethren, you have no need that I should write to you.
2 For you yourselves know perfectly that the day of the LORD so comes as a thief in the night.
3 For when they say, "Peace and safety!" then sudden destruction comes upon them, as labor pains upon a pregnant woman. And they shall not escape.
4 But you, brethren, are not in darkness, so that this Day should overtake you as a thief.
5 You are all sons of light and sons of the day. We are not of the night nor of darkness.
6 Therefore let us not sleep, as others do, but let us watch and be sober.

I Corinthians 15:

50 Now this I say, brethren, that flesh and blood cannot inherit the kingdom of God; nor does corruption inherit incorruption.
51 Behold, I tell you a mystery: We shall not all sleep, but we shall all be changed –
52 in a moment, in the twinkling of an eye, at the last trumpet. For the trumpet will sound, and the dead will be raised incorruptible, and we shall be changed.
53 For this corruptible must put on incorruption, and this mortal must put on immortality.

Revelation 3:

9 "Indeed I will make those of the synagogue of Satan, who say they are Jews and are not, but lie – indeed I will make them come and worship before your feet, and to know that I have loved you.
10 "Because you have kept My command to persevere, I also will keep you from the hour of trial, which shall come upon the whole world, to test those who dwell on earth.

Act 1:

11 ,,,"Men of Galilee, why do you stand gazing at the heavens? This *same* Jesus, who was taken from you into heaven, will come in like manner as you saw Him go into heaven".

Mark 12: (of the dead)

26 "But concerning the dead, that they rise, have you not read in the book of Moses, in the burning bush passage, how God spoke to him, saying, 'I am the God of Abraham, the God of Isaac, and God of Jacob'?
27 "He is not the God of the dead, but the God of the living. You are therefore greatly mistaken."

Jude

14 Now Enoch, the seventh from Adam, prophesied about these men also, saying, "Behold, the Lord comes with ten thousand of His saints,
15 "to execute judgment on all, to convict all who are ungodly among them of all their ungodly deeds which they have committed in an ungodly way, and of all the harsh things which ungodly sinners have spoken against Him."

I Thessalonians 4:

13 But I do not want you to be ignorant, brethren, concerning those who have fallen asleep, lest you sorrow as others who have no hope.
14 For if we believe that Jesus died and rose again, even so God will bring with Him those who sleep in Jesus.
15 For this we say to you by the word of the Lord, that we who are alive and remain until the coming of the Lord will be no means precede those who are asleep.
16 For the Lord Himself will descend from heaven with a shout, with the voice of an archangel, and with the trumpet of God. And the dead in Christ will rise first.
17 Then we who are alive and remain shall be caught up together with them in the clouds to meet the Lord in the air. And thus we shall always be with the Lord.
18 Therefore comfort one another with these words.

Daniel's Outline of Times

Daniel 9:

24 "Seventy weeks are determined
For your people and for your holy city,
To finish the transgression,
To make an end of sins,
To make reconciliation for iniquity,
To bring in everlasting righteousness,
To seal up vision and prophecy,
And to anoint the Most Holy.
25 "Know therefore and understand,
That from the going forth of the command
To restore and build Jerusalem
Until Messiah the Prince,
There shall be seven weeks and sixty-two weeks;
The street shall be built again, and the wall,
Even in troublesome times.
26 "And after the sixty-two weeks
Messiah shall be cut off, but not for Himself;
And the people of the prince who is to come
Shall destroy the city and the sanctuary.
The end of it shall be with a flood,
And till the end of the war desolations are determined.
27 Then he shall confirm a covenant with many for one week;
But in the middle of the week
He shall bring an end to sacrifice and offering.
And on the wing of abominations shall be one who makes desolate,
Even until the consummation, which is determined,
Is poured out on the desolate."

Isaiah 28:

18 Your covenant with death will be annulled,
And your agreement with Sheol will not stand;
When the overflowing scourge passes through,
Then you will be trampled down by it.

The Last "Week" of Daniel (each Week = 7 years)

Mark 13:

19 "For in those days there will be tribulation, such as has not been from the beginning of creation which God created until this time, nor ever shall be.
20 "And unless the Lord had shortened those days, no flesh would be saved; but for the elect's sake, whom He chose, He shortened the days.

Daniel 12:

4 "But you, Daniel, shut up the words, and seal the book until the time of the end; many shall run to and fro, and knowledge shall increase."
5 Then I, Daniel, looked; and there stood two others, one on this riverbank and the other on that riverbank.
6 And one said to the man clothed in linen, who was above the waters of the river, "How long shall the fulfillment of these wonders be?"
7 Then I heard the man clothed in linen, who was above the waters of the river, when he held up his right hand and his left hand to heaven, and swore by Him who lives forever, that it shall be for a time, times, and a half a time; and when the power of the holy people has been completely shattered, all these things shall be finished.
8 Although I heard, I did not understand. Then I said, "My lord, what shall be the end of these things?"
9 And he said, "Go your way, Daniel, for the words are closed up and sealed till the time of the end.
10 "Many shall be purified, made white, and refined, but the wicked shall do wickedly; and none of the wicked shall understand, but the wise shall understand.
11 "And from the time that the daily sacrifice is taken away, and the abomination of desolation is set up, there shall be one thousand two hundred and ninety days.
12 "Blessed is he who waits, and comes to the one thousand three hundred and thirty-five days.
13 "But you, go your way till the end; for you shall rest, and will arise to your inheritance at the end of the days."

Tribulation Prophecy

Daniel 7:

7 "After this I saw in the night visions, and behold, a fourth beast, dreadful and terrible, exceedingly strong. It had huge iron teeth; it was devouring, breaking in pieces, and trampling the residue with its feet. It was different from all the beasts that were before it, and it had ten horns.

8 "I was considering the horns, and there was another horn, a little one, coming up among them, before whom three of the first horns were plucked out by the roots. And there, in this horn, were eyes like the eyes of a man, and a mouth speaking pompous words.

11 "I watched then because of the sound of the pompous words which the horn was speaking; I watched till the beast was slain, and its body destroyed and given to the burning flame.

12 "As for the rest of the beasts, they had their dominion taken away, yet their lives were prolonged for a season and a time.

13 "I was watching in the night visions,
And behold, One like the Son of Man,
Coming with the clouds of heaven!
He came to the Ancient of Days,
And they brought Him near before Him.
14 Then to Him was given dominion and glory and a kingdom,
That all peoples, nations, and languages should serve Him.
His dominion is an everlasting dominion,
Which shall not pass away,
And His kingdom the one
Which shall not be destroyed.

Revelation 17:

10 There are also seven kings. Five have fallen, one is, and the other has not yet come. And when he comes, he must continue a short time.

11 "And the beast that was, and is not, is himself also the eighth, and is of the seven, and is going to perdition.

12 "And the ten horns which you saw are ten kings who have received no kingdom as yet, but they receive authority for one hour as kings with the beast.

13 "These are of one mind, and they will give their power and authority to the beast.

Revelation 12:

1 Now a great sign appeared in heaven; a woman clothed with the sun, with the moon under her feet, and on her head a garland of twelve stars.

2 Then being with child, she cried out in labor and in pain to give birth.

3 And another sign appeared in heaven: behold, a great, fiery red dragon having seven heads and ten horns, and seven diadems on his heads.

4 His tail drew a third of the stars of heaven* and threw them to the earth. And the dragon stood before the woman who was ready to give birth, to devour her Child as soon as it was born.

5 And she bore a male Child who was to rule all nations with a rod of iron. And her Child was caught up to God and to His throne.

6 Then the woman fled into the wilderness, where she has a place prepared by God, that they should feed her there one thousand two hundred and sixty days.

7 And war broke out in heaven: Michael and his angels fought against the dragon; and the dragon and his angels* fought,

8 but they did not prevail, nor was a place found for them in heaven any longer.

9 So the great dragon was cast out, that serpent of old, called the Devil and Satan, who deceives the whole world; he was cast to the earth, and his angels* were cast out with him.

12 "Therefore rejoice, O heavens, and you who dwell in them! Woe to the inhabitants of the earth and the sea! For the devil has come down to you, having great wrath, because he knows that he has a short time."

13 Now when the dragon saw that he had been cast to the earth, he persecuted the woman who gave birth to the male Child.

14 But the woman was given two wings of a great eagle, that she might fly into the wilderness to her place, where she is nourished for a time and times and half a time, from the presence of the serpent.

17 And the dragon was enraged with the woman, and he went to make war with the rest of her offspring, who keep the commandments of God and have the testimony of Jesus Christ.

* *Other fallen angels.*

Tribulation Prophecy

(at start of second half of Pg. B.2)

Mark 13:

14 “But when you see the ‘abomination of desolation’, spoken of by Daniel the prophet, standing where it ought not” (let the reader understand), “then let those who are in Judea flee to the mountains.

Revelation 13:

1 Then I stood on the sand of the sea. And I saw a beast rising up out of the sea, having seven heads and ten horns, and on his horns ten crowns, and on his heads a blasphemous name.

2 Now the beast which I saw was like a leopard, his feet were like the feet of a bear, and his mouth like the mouth of a lion. And the dragon gave him his power, his throne, and great authority.

3 I saw one of his heads as if it had been mortally wounded, and his deadly wound was healed. And all the world marveled and followed the beast.

4 So they worshiped the dragon who gave authority to the beast; and they worshiped the beast, saying, “Who is like the beast? Who is able to make war with him?”

5 And he was given a mouth speaking great things and blasphemies, and he was given authority to continue for forty-two months.

6 Then he opened his mouth in blasphemy against God, to blaspheme His name, His tabernacle, and those who dwell in heaven.

7 And it was granted to him to make war with the saints and to overcome them. And authority was given him over every tribe, tongue, and nation.

8 And all who dwell on the earth will worship him, whose names have not been written in the Book of Life of the Lamb slain from the foundation of the world.

9 If anyone has an ear, let him hear.

10 He who leads into captivity shall go into captivity; he who kills with the sword must be killed with the sword. Here is the patience and the **faith** of the saints.

Revelation 13: *(continued)*

11 Then I saw another beast coming up out of the earth, and he had two horns like a lamb and spoke like a dragon.

12 And he exercises all the authority of the first beast in his presence and causes the earth and those who dwell in it to worship the first beast, whose deadly wound was healed.

13 He performs great **signs**, so that he even makes fire come down from heaven on the earth in the sight of men. **!**

14 And he deceives those who dwell on the earth by those **signs** which he was granted to do in the sight of the beast, telling those who dwell on the earth to make an image to the beast who was wounded by the sword and lived.

15 He was granted power to give breath to the image of the beast, that the image of the beast should both speak and cause as many as would not worship the image of the beast to be killed.

16 And he causes all, both small and great, rich and poor, free and slave, to receive a mark on their right hand or on their foreheads,

17 and that no one may buy or sell except one who has the mark of the **name** of the beast, or the number of his name.

18 Here is wisdom. Let him who has understanding calculate the number of the beast, for it is the number of a man: His number is <u>666</u>.

Revelation 7:

4 And I heard the number of those who were sealed. One hundred and forty-four thousand of all the tribes of the children of Israel were sealed:

Revelation 14:

3 And they sang as it were a new song before the throne, before the four living creatures, and the elders; and no one could learn that song except the hundred and forty-four thousand who were redeemed from the earth.

4 These are the ones who were not defiled with women, for they are virgins. These are the ones who follow the Lamb wherever He goes. These were redeemed from among men, being first-fruits to God and to the Lamb.

The End of the First Half of the Seven Years
And then, Prophesy of Timing "of Jacob's Troubles" **

Malachi 4:

5 Behold, I will send you Elijah the prophet
Before the coming of the great and dreadful day of the LORD.

Revelation 11:

2 "But leave out the court which is outside the temple, and do not measure it, for it has been given to the Gentiles. And they will tread the holy city under foot for forty-two months.
3 And I will give power to my witnesses, and they will prophesy one thousand two hundred and sixty days, clothed in sackcloth."
6 These have power to shut heaven, so that no rain falls in the days of their prophecy; and they have power over waters to turn them to blood, and to strike the earth with all plagues, as often as they desire.
7 Now when they finish their testimony, the beast that ascends out of the bottomless pit will make war against them, overcome them, and kill them.

11 Now after three and a half days the breath of life from God entered them, and they stood on their feet, and great fear fell on those who saw them.
12 And they heard a loud voice from heaven saying to them, "Come up here." And they ascended to heaven in a cloud, and their enemies saw them.

II Thessalonians 2:

3 Let no one deceive you by any means; for that Day will not come unless the falling away comes first, and the man of sin* is revealed, the son of perdition,
4 who opposes and exalts himself above all that is called God or that is worshiped, so that he sits as God in the temple of God, showing himself that he is God.

* *aka "Lawlessness"*
aka "anti-christ"

** ***"Jacob's Troubles"*** *continue thru Pg. 62B2. Note that Babylon City will be literal Capital of the World! >*

Revelation 14:

6 Then I saw another angel flying in the midst of heaven, having the everlasting gospel to preach to those who dwell on the earth – to every nation, tribe, tongue, and people –
7 saying with a loud voice, "Fear God and give glory to Him, for the hour of His judgment has come; and worship Him who made heaven and earth, the sea and springs of water."

10 "he himself shall also drink of the wine of the wrath of God, which is poured out full strength into the cup of His indignation. And he shall be tormented with fire and brimstone in the presence of the holy angels and in the presence of the Lamb.
11 "And the smoke of the torment ascends forever and ever; and they have no rest day or night, who worship the beast and his image, and whoever receives the mark of his name."

13 Then I heard a voice from heaven saying to me, "Write: 'Blessed are the dead who die in the Lord from now on.'"

Revelation 6:

7 When He opened the fourth seal, I heard the voice of the fourth living creature saying, "Come and see."
8 And I looked, and behold, a pale horse. And the name of him who sat on it was Death, and Hades followed with him. And power was given to them over a fourth of the earth, to kill with sword, with hunger, with death, and by the beasts of the earth.

Daniel 12:

1 "At that time Michael shall stand up,
The great prince who stands watch over the sons of your people;
And there shall be a time of trouble,
Such as never was since there was a nation,
Even to that time.
And at that time your people shall be delivered,
Every one who is found written in the book.
6 ..., "How long shall the fulfillment of these wonders *be?*"
10 Many shall be purified, made white, and refined, but the wicked shall do wickedly; and none of the wicked shall understand, but the wise shall understand.
11 "And from the time *that* the daily *sacrifice* is taken away, and the abomination of desolation is set up, *there shall be* one thousand two hundred and ninety days.
12 Blessed *is* he who waits, and comes to the one thousand three hundred and thirty-five days.

The Extent of the Troubles

Zechariah 13:

8 Says the LORD,
"That two thirds in it shall be cut off and die,
But one third shall be left in it:
9 I will bring the one third through the fire,
Will refine them as silver is refined,
And test them as gold is tested.
They will call on My name,
And I will answer them.
I will say, 'This is My people';
And each one will say, 'The LORD is my God.'"

Zechariah 14:

1 Behold, the day of the LORD is coming.
And your spoil will be divided in your midst.
2 For I will gather all the nations to battle against Jerusalem;
The city shall be taken,
The houses rifled,
And the women ravished.
Half of the city shall go into captivity,
But the remnant of the people shall not be cut off from the city.

Revelation 8:

7 The first angel sounded: And hail and fire followed, mingled with blood, and they were thrown to the earth; and a third of the trees were burned up, and all green grass was burned up.

9 and a third of the living creatures in the sea died, and a third of the ships were destroyed.

11 and the name of the star is Wormwood; and a third of the waters became wormwood; and many men died from the water, because it was made bitter.

12 Then the fourth angel sounded: And a third of the sun was struck, a third of the moon, and a third of the stars, so that a third of them darkened; and a third of the day did not shine.

Revelation 9:

4 They were commanded not to harm the grass of the earth, or any green thing, or any tree, but only those men who do not have the seal of God on their foreheads.
5 And they were not given authority to kill them, but to torment them for five months. And their torment was like the torment of a scorpion when it strikes a man.

Revelation 16:

11 And they blasphemed the God of heaven because of their pains and their sores, and did not repent of their deeds.

Revelation 9:

6 In those days men will seek death and will not find it; they will desire to die, and death will flee from them.

14 saying to the sixth angel who had the trumpet, "Release the four angels who are bound at the great river Euphrates."
15 So the four angels, who had been prepared for the hour and day and month and year, were released to kill a third of mankind.
16 Now the number of the army of the horsemen was two hundred million, and I heard the number of them.
18 By these three plagues a third of mankind was killed – by the fire and the smoke and the brimstone which came out of their mouths.
20 But the rest of mankind, who were not killed by these plagues, did not repent of the works of their hands, that they should not worship demons, and idols of gold, silver, brass, stone, and wood, which can neither see nor hear nor walk;
21 and they did not repent of their murders or their sorceries or their sexual immorality or their thefts.

Mystery, Babylon

Revelation 17:

1 Then one of the seven angels who had the seven bowls came and talked with me, saying to me, "Come, I will show you the judgment of the great harlot who sits on many waters,
2 with whom the kings of the earth committed fornication, and the inhabitants of the earth were made drunk with the wine of her fornication."
3 So he carried me away in the Spirit into the wilderness. And I saw a woman sitting on a scarlet beast *which was* full of names of blasphemy, having seven heads and ten horns.
4 The woman was arrayed in purple and scarlet, and adorned with gold and precious stones and pearls, having in her hand a golden cup full of abominations and the filthiness of her fornication.
5 And on her forehead a name *was* written:

MYSTERY, BABYLON THE GREAT,
THE MOTHER OF HARLOTS AND OF
THE ABOMINATIONS OF THE EARTH.

6 I saw the woman, drunk with the blood of the saints and with the blood of the martyrs of Jesus. And when I saw her, I marveled with great amazement.

The End of the Tribulation

Revelation 16:

12 Then the sixth angel poured out his bowl on the great river Euphrates, and its water was dried up, so that the way of the kings from the east might be prepared.
13 And I saw three unclean spirits like frogs coming out of the mouth of the dragon, out of the mouth of the beast, and out of the mouth of the false prophet.
14 For they are spirits of demons, performing signs, which go out to the kings of the earth and of the whole world, to gather them to the battle of that great day of God Almighty.
15 "Behold, I am coming as a thief. Blessed is he who watches, and keeps his garments, lest he walk naked and they see his shame."
16 And they gathered them together to the place called in Hebrew, Armageddon.

Revelation 19:

11 Then I saw heaven opened, and behold, a white horse. And He who sat on him was called Faithful and True, and in righteousness He judges and makes war.
12 His eyes were like a flame of fire, and on His head were many crowns. He had a name written that no one knew except Himself.
13 He was clothed with a robe dipped in blood, and His name is called The Word of God.
14 And the armies in heaven, clothed in fine linen, white and clean, followed Him on white horses.
15 Now out of His mouth goes a sharp sword, that with it He should strike the nations. And He Himself will rule them with a rod of iron. He Himself treads the winepress of the fierceness and wrath of Almighty God.
19 And I saw the beast, the kings of the earth, and their armies, gathered together to make war against Him who sat on the horse and against His army.
20 Then the beast was captured, and with him the false prophet who worked signs in his presence, by which he deceived those who received the **mark of the beast** and those who worshiped his image. These two were cast alive into the lake of fire burning with brimstone.
21 And the rest were killed with the sword which proceeded from the mouth of Him who sat on the horse. And all the birds were filled with their flesh.

Zechariah 14:

3 Then the LORD will go forth
And fight against those nations,
As He fights in the day of the battle.
4 And in that day His feet will stand on the
Mount of Olives,
Which faces Jerusalem on the east.
And the Mount of Olives will be split in two,
From east to west,
Making a very large valley;
Half of the mountain shall move toward the
north
And half of it toward the south.
5 Then you shall flee through My mountain
valley,
For the mountain valley shall reach to Azal.
Yes, you shall flee
As you fled from the earthquake
In the days of Uzziah king of Judah.
Thus the LORD my God will come,
And all the saints with You.

6 It shall come to pass in that day
That there will be no light;
The lights will diminish.
7 It shall be one day
Which is known to the LORD –
Neither day nor night.
But at evening time it shall happen
That it will be light.

12 And this shall be the plague with which the
LORD will strike all the people who
fought against Jerusalem:
Their flesh shall dissolve while they stand
on their feet
Their eyes shall dissolve in their sockets.

Jeremiah 30:

7 Alas! For that day is great,
So that none is like it;
And it is the time of Jacob's trouble,
But he shall be saved out of it.

Revelation 17: **(Babylon's end.)**

15 Then he said to me, "The waters which you saw, where the harlot sits, are peoples, multitudes, nations, and tongues.
16 And the ten horns which you saw on the beast, these will hate the harlot, make her desolate and naked, eat her flesh and burn her with fire.
17 For God has put it into their hearts to fulfill His purpose, to be of one mind, and to give their kingdom to the beast, until the words of God are fulfilled. < "woman"*=Babylon on Pg61B3*>
18 And the woman whom you saw is that great city which reigns over the kings of the earth."

The Second Coming of Jesus

Matthew 24:

27 "For as the lightning comes from the east
and flashes to the west, so also will the
coming of the Son of Man be.
29 "Immediately after the tribulation of those
days the sun will be darkened, and the moon will
not give its light; the stars will fall from heaven,
and the powers of the heavens will be shaken.
30 "Then the sign of the Son of Man will appear
in heaven, and then all the tribes of the earth will
mourn, and they will see the Son of Man coming
on the clouds of heaven with power and great
glory.
31 "And He will send His angels with a
great sound of a trumpet, and they will
gather together His elect from the four
winds, from one end of heaven to the other.

Revelation 16:

17 Then the seventh angel poured out his
bowl into the air, and a loud voice came out
of the temple of heaven, from the throne,
saying, "It is done!"
18 And there were noises and thunderings and
lightnings; and there was a great earthquake, such
a mighty and great earthquake as had not
occurred since men were on the earth.
19 Now the great city was divided into three
parts, and the cities of the nations fell. And
great Babylon was remembered before God, to
give her the cup of the wine of the fierceness of
His wrath.
20 Then every island fled away, and the
mountains were not found.
21 And great hail from heaven fell upon men, every
hailstone about the weight of a talent. And men
blasphemed God because of the plague of the hail,
since that plague was exceedingly great.

Isaiah 13:

9 Behold, the day of the LORD comes,
Cruel, with both wrath and fierce anger,
To lay the land desolate;
And He will destroy its sinners from it.
10 For the stars of heaven and their constellations
Will not give their light;
The sun will be darkened in its going forth,
And the moon will not cause its light to shine.
11 "I will punish the world for *its* evil,
And the wicked for their iniquity;
I will halt the arrogance of the proud,
And will lay low the haughtiness of the terrible.
12 I will make a mortal more rare than fine gold,
A man more than the golden wedge of Ophir.

Isaiah 13:

13 Therefore I will shake the heavens,
And the earth will move out of her place,
In the wrath of the LORD of hosts
And in the day of His fierce anger.

Revelation 18:

20 "Rejoice over her, O heaven, and you holy
apostles and prophets, for God has avenged you
on her!"
21 Then a mighty angel took up a stone like a
great millstone and threw it into the sea, saying,
"Thus with violence the great city Babylon
shall be thrown down, and shall not be
found anymore."

Satan Bound 1000 Years

Revelation 20:

1 Then I saw an angel coming down from
heaven, having the key to the bottomless pit and
a great chain in his hand.
2 He laid hold of the dragon, that serpent of
old, who is the Devil and Satan, and bound
him for a thousand years;
3 and he cast him into the bottomless pit, and
shut him up, and set a seal on hi m, so that he
should deceive the nations no more till the
thousand years were finished. But after these
things he must be released for a little while.
4 And I saw thrones, and they sat on them, and
judgment was committed to them. And I saw the
souls of those who had been beheaded for their
witness to Jesus and for the word of God, who
had not worshiped the beast or his image, and
had not received his mark on their foreheads or
on their hands. And they lived and reigned
with Christ for a thousand years.
5 But the rest of the dead did not live again
until the thousand years were finished. This
is the first resurrection.
6 Blessed and holy is he who has part in the first
resurrection. Over such the second death has no
power, but they shall be priests of God and of
Christ, and shall reign with Him a thousand years.
7 Now when the thousand years have expired,
Satan will be released from his prison
8 and will go out to deceive the nations which
are in the four corners of the earth, Gog and
Magog, to gather them together to battle, whose
number is as the sand of the sea.

The End of the 1,000 Year Reign "The Day of the LORD"

Revelation 14:

16 So He who sat on the cloud thrust in His sickle on the earth, and the earth was reaped.

Ezekiel 38:

3 "and say, 'Thus says the LORD God: "Behold, I am against you, O Gog, the prince of Rosh, Meshech, and Tubal.

8 "After many days you will be visited. In the latter years you will come into the land of those brought back from the sword and gathered from many people on the mountains of Israel, which had long been desolate; they were brought out of the nations, and now all of them dwell safely.

15 "Then you will come from your place out of the far north, you and many peoples with you, all of them riding on horses, a great company and a mighty army.
16 "You will come up against My people Israel like a cloud, to cover the land. It will be in the latter days that I will bring you against My land, so that the nations may know me, when I am hallowed in you, O Gog, before their eyes."

Revelation 20:

9 They went up on the breadth of the earth and surrounded the camp of the saints and the beloved city. And fire came down from God out of heaven and devoured them.
10 And the devil, who deceived them, was cast into the lake of fire and brimstone where the beast and the false prophet are. And they will be tormented day and night forever and ever.

Revelation 10:

4 Now when the seven thunders uttered their voices, I was about to write; but I heard a voice from heaven saying to me, "Seal up the things which the seven thunders uttered, and do not write them."

7 but in the days of the sounding of the seventh angel, when he is about to sound, the mystery of God would be finished, as He declared to His servants the prophets.

Ezekiel 38:

19 "For in My jealousy and in the fire of My wrath I have spoken: 'Surely in that day there shall be a great earthquake in the land of Israel,
20 'so that the fish of the sea, the birds of the heavens, the beasts of the field, all creeping things that creep on the earth, and all men who are on the face of the earth shall shake in My presence. The mountains shall be thrown down, the steep places shall fall, and every wall shall fall to the ground.'
21 "I will call for a sword against Gog throughout all My mountains," says the LORD God. "Every man's sword will be against his brother.
22 "And I will bring him to judgment with pestilence and bloodshed; I will rain down on him, on his troops, and on the many peoples who are with him, flooding rain, great hailstones, fire, and brimstone.
23 "Thus I will magnify Myself and sanctify Myself, and I will be known in the eyes of many nations. Then they shall know that I am the LORD."'

Revelation 6:

12 I looked when He opened the sixth seal, and behold, there was a great earthquake; and the sun became black as sackcloth of hair, and the moon became like blood.
13 And the stars of heaven fell to the earth, as a fig tree drops its late figs when it is shaken by a mighty wind.
14 Then the sky receded as a scroll when it is rolled up, and every mountain and island was moved out of its place.
17 "For the great day of His wrath has come, and who is able to stand?"

II Peter 3:

10 But the day of the LORD will come as a thief in the night, in which the heavens will pass away with a great noise, and the elements will melt with fervent heat; both the earth and the works that are in it will be burned up.

Revelation 22:

12 "And behold, I am coming quickly, and my reward is with Me, to give to every one according to his work."

End of the Old Earth

Ezekiel 39:

6 "And I will send fire on Magog and on those who live in security in the coastlands. Then they shall know that I am the LORD.
7 "So I will make My holy name known in the midst of My people Israel, and I will not let them profane My holy name anymore. Then the nations shall know that I am the LORD, the Holy One in Israel.

Isaiah 34:

4 All the host of heaven shall be dissolved,
And the heavens shall be rolled up like a scroll;
All their host shall fall down
As the leaf falls from the vine,
And as fruit falling from a fig tree.

Daniel 2:

44 "And in the days of these kings the God of heaven will set up a kingdom which shall never be destroyed; and the kingdom shall not be left to other people; it shall break in pieces and consume all these kingdoms, and it shall stand forever.

Daniel 12:

2 And many of those who sleep in the dust of the earth shall awake,
Some to everlasting life,
Some to shame and everlasting contempt.
3 Those who are wise shall shine
Like the brightness of the firmament,
And those who turn many to righteousness*
Like the stars forever and ever.

** reward for evangelism**

John 5:

28 "Do not marvel at this; for the hour is coming in which all who are in the graves will hear His voice
29 "and come forth – those who have done good, to the resurrection of life, and those who have done evil, to the resurrection of condemnation.

Hebrews 12:

26 whose voice then shook the earth; but now He has promised, saying, "Yet once more I shake not only the earth, but also heaven."
27 Now this, "Yet once more," indicates the removal of those things that are being shaken. As of things that are made. That the things which cannot be shaken may remain.
28 Therefore, since we are receiving a kingdom which cannot be shaken, let us have grace, by which we may serve God acceptably with reverence and godly fear.

Final Judgment

Revelation 20:

11 Then I saw a great white throne and Him who sat on it, from whose face the earth and the heaven fled away. And there was found no place for them.
12 And I saw the dead, small and great, standing before God, and books were opened. And another book was opened, which is the Book of Life. And the dead were judged according to their works, by the things which were written in the books.
13 The sea gave up the dead who were in it, and Death and Hades delivered up the dead who were in them. And they were judged, each one according to his works.
14 Then Death and Hades were cast into the lake of fire. This is the second death.
15 And anyone not found written in the Book of Life was cast into the lake of fire.

Revelation 7:

9 After these things I looked, and behold, a great multitude which no one could number, of all nations, tribes, people, and tongues, standing before the throne and before the Lamb, clothed with white robes, with palm branches in their hands,
14 And I said to him, "Sir, you know." So he said to me, "These are the ones who come out of the great tribulation, and washed their robes and made them white in the blood of the Lamb.
15 "Therefore they are before the throne of God, and serve Him day and night in His temple. And He who sits on the throne will dwell among them.

New Universe

Revelation 21:

1 And I saw a new heaven and a new earth, for the first heaven and the first earth had passed away. Also there was no more sea.
2 Then I, John, saw the holy city, New Jerusalem, coming down out of heaven from God, prepared as a bride adorned for her husband.
3 And I heard a loud voice from heaven saying, "Behold, the tabernacle of God is with men, and He will dwell with them, and they shall be His people, and God Himself will be with them *and be* their God.

Eternity

Jewish + Church

Amos 9:

15 I will plant then in their land,
And no longer will they be pulled up
From the land I have given them,"
Says the LORD your God..

Jeremiah 30:

9 But they shall serve the LORD their God,
And David their king,
Whom I will raise up for them.

Ezekiel 37:

11 Then He said to me, "Son of man, these bones are the whole house of Israel. They indeed say, 'Our bones are dry, our hope is lost, and we ourselves are cut off!'

12 "Therefore prophesy and say to them, 'Thus says the LORD God: "Behold, O My people, I will open your graves and cause you to come up from your graves, and bring you into the land of Israel.

13 "Then you shall know that I am the LORD, when I have opened your graves, O My people, and brought you up from your graves.

14 "I will put My Spirit in you, and you shall live.

22 "and I will make them one nation in the land. On the mountains of Israel; and one king shall be king over them all; they shall no longer be divided into two kingdoms again.

24 "David My servant shall be king over them, and they shall have one shepherd; they shall also walk in My judgments and observe My statutes, and do them.

25 "Then they shall dwell in the land that I have given to Jacob My servant, where your fathers dwelt; and they shall dwell there, they, their children, and their children's children, forever; and My servant David shall be their prince forever.

26 "Moreover I will make a covenant of peace with them, and it shall be an everlasting covenant with them; I will establish them and multiply them, and I will set My sanctuary in their midst forevermore.

27 "My tabernacle also shall be with them; indeed I will be their God, and they shall be My people.

Revelation 21:

4 "And God will wipe away every tear from their eyes; there shall be no more death, nor sorrow, nor crying, and there shall be no more pain, for the former things have passed away."

5 Then He who sat on the throne said, "Behold, I make all things new." And He said to me, "Write, for these words are true and faithful."

Isaiah 62:

5 For as a young man marries a virgin,
So shall your sons marry you;
And as the bridegroom rejoices over the bride,
So shall your God rejoice over you.

Isaiah 66:

22 "For as the new heavens and the new earth
Which I will make shall remain before Me,"
says the LORD,
"So shall your descendants and your name
remain.

23 And it shall come to pass
That from one New Moon to another,
And from one Sabbath to another,
All flesh shall come to worship before Me,"
says the LORD.

24 "And they shall go forth and look
Upon the corpses of the men
Who have transgressed against Me.
For their worm does not die,
And their fire is not quenched.
They shall be an abhorrence to all flesh."

Zechariah 14:

16 And it shall come to pass *that* everyone who is left of all the nations which came against Jerusalem shall go up from year to year to worship the King, the LORD of hosts, and to keep the Feast of Tabernacles.

New Jerusalem

Zechariah 13:

1 "In that day a fountain shall be opened for the house of David and for the inhabitants of Jerusalem, for sin and for uncleanness.
2 "It shall be in that day," says the LORD of hosts, "*that* I will cut off the names of the idols from the land, and they shall no longer be remembered. I will also cause the prophets and the unclean spirit to depart from the land."

Revelation 22:

3 And there shall be no more curse, but the throne of God and of the Lamb shall be in it, and His servants shall serve Him.
4 They shall see His face, and His name shall be on their foreheads.
5 And there shall be no night there: They need no lamp nor light of the sun, for the Lord God gives them light. And they shall reign forever and ever.

Zechariah 12:

8 And it shall come to pass in that day, that living waters shall go out from Jerusalem: half of them toward the eastern sea, and half of them toward the western sea; in summer and in winter shall it be.
9 And the LORD shall be King over all the earth; in that day shall the LORD be One, and His name one.
10 All the land shall be turned as the Arabah, from Geba to Rimmon south of Jerusalem; and she shall be lifted up, and inhabited in her place, from Benjamin's gate unto the place of the first gate, unto the corner gate, and from the tower of Hananel unto the king's winepresses.
11 And men shall dwell therein, and there shall be no more extermination; but Jerusalem shall dwell safely.

Revelation 21:

9 Then one of the seven angels who had the seven bowls filled with the seven last plagues came to me and talked with me, saying, "Come, I will show you the bride, the Lamb's wife."
10 And he carried me away in the Spirit to a great and high mountain, and showed me the great city, the holy Jerusalem, descending out of heaven from God,
11 having the glory of God. Her light *was* like a most precious stone, like a jasper stone, clear as crystal.
12 Also she had a great and high wall with twelve gates, and twelve angels at the gates, and names written on them, which are *the names* of the twelve tribes of the children of Israel:

Revelation 21:

13 three gates on the east, three gates on the north, three gates on the south, and three gates on the west.
14 Now the wall of the city had twelve foundations, and on them were the names of the twelve apostles of the Lamb.

16 And the city is laid out as a square, and its length is as great as its breadth. And he measured the city with the reed: twelve thousand furlongs. Its length, breadth, and height are equal.
17 Then he measured its wall: one hundred and forty-four cubits, according to the measure of a man, that is, of an angel.
18 And the construction of its wall was of jasper; and the city was pure gold, like clear glass.
19 And the foundations of the wall of the city were adorned with all kinds of precious stones: the first foundation was jasper, the second sapphire, the third chalcedony, the fourth emerald,
20 the fifth sardonyx, the sixth sardius, the seventh chrysolite, the eighth beryl, the ninth topaz, the tenth chrysoprase, the eleventh jacinth, and the twelfth amethyst.
21 And the twelve gates were twelve pearls: each individual gate was of one pearl. And the street of the city was pure gold, like transparent glass.
22 But I saw no temple in it, for the LORD God Almighty and the Lamb are its temple.
23 And the city had no need for the sun or of the moon to shine in it, for the glory of God illuminated it, and the Lamb is its light.
24 And the nations of those who are saved shall walk in its light, and the kings of the earth bring their glory and honor into it.
25 Its gates shall not be shut at all by day (there shall be no night there).

Jeremiah 31:

33 "But this is the covenant that I will make with the house of Israel: After those days, says the LORD, I will put My law in their minds, and write it on their hearts; and I will be their God, and they shall be My people.
34 "No more shall every man teach his neighbor, and every man his brother, saying, 'Know the LORD,' for they all shall know Me, from the least of them to the greatest of them," says the LORD. "For I will forgive their iniquity, and their sin I will remember no more."

New Temple, etc.

Ezekiel 36:

25 "Then I will sprinkle clean water on you, and you shall be clean; I will cleanse you from all your filthiness and from all your idols.
26 "I will give you a new heart and put a new spirit within you; I will take the heart of stone out of your flesh and give you a heart of flesh.
27 "I will put My Spirit within you and cause you to walk in My statutes, and you will keep My judgments and do them.

Ezekiel 39:

25 "Therefore thus says the LORD God: 'Now I will bring back the captives of Jacob, and have mercy on the whole house of Israel; and I will be jealous for My holy name.

29 'And I will not hide My face from them anymore; for I shall have poured out My Spirit on the house of Israel,' says the LORD God."

Ezekiel 43:

7 And He said to me, "Son of man, this is the place of My throne and the place of the soles of My feet, where I will dwell in the midst of the children of Israel forever. No more shall the house of Israel defile My holy name, they nor their kings, by their harlotry or with the carcasses of their kings on their high places.

10 "Son of man, describe the temple to the house of Israel, that they may be ashamed of their iniquities; and let them measure the pattern.
11 "And if they are ashamed of all that they have done, make known to them the design of the temple and its arrangement, its exits and its entrances, its entire design and all its ordinances, all its forms and all its laws. Write it down in their sight, so that they may keep its whole design and all its ordinances, and perform them.

Ezekiel 44:

9 'Thus says the LORD God: "No foreigner, uncircumcised in heart or uncircumcised in flesh, shall enter My sanctuary, including any foreigner who is among the children of Israel."

Ezekiel 47:

1 Then he brought me back to the door of the temple; and there was water, flowing from under the threshold of the temple toward the east, for the front of the temple faced east; the water was flowing from under the right side of the temple, south of the altar.

9 "And it shall be that every living thing that moves, wherever the rivers go, will live. There will be a very great multitude of fish, because these waters go there; for they will be healed, and everything will live wherever the river goes.

11 "But its swamps and marshes will not be healed; they will be given over to salt.
12 "Along the bank of the river, on this side and that, will grow all kinds of trees used for food; their leaves will not wither, and their fruit will not fail. They will bear fruit every month, because their water flows from the sanctuary. Their fruit will be for food, and their leaves for medicine.

21 "Thus you shall divide this land among yourselves according to the tribes of Israel.
22 "It shall be that you will divide it by lot as an inheritance for yourselves, and for the strangers who sojourn among you and who bear children among you. They shall be to you as native-born among the children of Israel; they shall have an inheritance with you among the tribes of Israel.
23 "And it shall be that in whatever tribe the stranger sojourns, there you shall give him his inheritance," says the LORD God.

End of Section I - Chronological Overview of Characters and Events of the Bible

Remember! That section was just a starter. Many famous stories are omitted. You can and should continue to build your own chronological study.

EXAMPLES OF OTHER SUBJECTS TO EXPLORE:

1. Life of Job (Book of Job)
2. Life of Noah (Genesis 6-10) *<Note: Pg. 25.B.4 (Ez.14:14) for why.>*
3. Tower of Babel (Genesis 11:1-9)

The "Center" of the Bible:

Psalm 117:

Let All Peoples Praise the LORD

Let All Peoples Praise the LORD
1 Praise the LORD, all you Gentiles!
Laud Him, all you peoples!
2 For His merciful kindness is great toward us,
And the truth of the LORD *endures* forever.
Praise the LORD!

Trivia tidbits: In the Old King James Version, there are 594 chapters before and after ***Psalm 117*** *(some say* ***118****). Add these numbers up and you get 1188. The praise* ***Psalm 117*** *is the shortest chapter of the Bible, and* ***Psalm 119*** *is the longest, and is about the "Word" of God. Between them,* ***Psalm 118*** *is like <u>an example prayer of life</u>*

Psalm 118:

1 Oh, give thanks to the LORD for *He is* good!
For His mercy *endures* forever.
14 The LORD *is* my strength and song,
And He has become my salvation.
29 Oh, give thanks to the LORD for *He is* good!
For His mercy *endures* forever.

<Psalm 118:14 is same as Exodus 15:2>

Psalm 118: (cont.)

Praise to God for His Everlasting Mercy
8 *It is* better to trust in the LORD
Than to put confidence in man.
9 *It is* better to trust in the LORD
Than to put confidence in princes.

A (The?) Central Theme of the Bible:

I Chronicles 16:

David's Song of Thanksgiving

23 Sing to the LORD, all the earth;
Proclaim the good news of His salvation
from day to day.
24 Declare His glory among the nations,
His wonders among all the peoples.

29 Give to the LORD the glory due His name;
Bring an offering, and come before Him.
Oh, worship the LORD in the beauty of
holiness!

34 Oh, give thanks to the LORD, for He is good!
For His mercy endures forever.

I Corinthians 4:

20 <u>For the kingdom of God is not in word but in power.</u>
21 What do you want? Shall I come to you with a rod, or <u>in love and a spirit of gentleness</u>?

Psalm 9:

16 The LORD is known by the judgment He
executes;
The wicked is snared in the work of his
own hands.
Meditation Selah

II Chronicles 16:

9 "For the eyes of the LORD run to and fro throughout the whole earth, to show Himself strong on behalf of those whose heart is loyal to Him.

Psalm 30:

4 Sing praise to the LORD, You saints of His,
And give thanks at the remembrance of His
holy name.
5 For His anger is but for a moment,
His favor is for life;
Weeping may endure for a night,
But joy comes in the morning.

SECTION TWO

1. Sequential Topical Studies

Understanding of the truths of the passages in each column and page, helps to build the foundation for understanding the truths on all pages that follow.

2. Special Topic Highlights
(Randomly organized)

Miscellaneous reference passages on topics not (fully) developed in rest of B.M.B. because they either did not fit on the appropriate page or were not considered necessary to the logical progression of the doctrinal development. (i.e. stuff I think is cool or worth reading, but could not fit into the main pages of the BMB.)

Sin

Ecclesiastes 7:

20 For there is not a just man on earth who does good And does not sin. *

Romans 3:

23 for all have sinned and fall short of the glory of God.

Genesis 8:

21 And the LORD smelled a soothing aroma. Then the LORD said in His heart, "I will never again curse the ground for man's sake, although the imagination of man's heart is evil from his youth.

Matthew 19:

16 Now behold, one came and said to Him, "Good Teacher, what good thing shall I do that I may have eternal life?"
17 So He said to him, "Why do you call Me good? No one is good but One, that is, God. But if you want to enter into life, keep the commandments."

Psalm 53: (and Psalm 14)

1 The fool has said in his heart,
"There is no God."
They are corrupt, and have done abominable iniquity;
There is none who does good.
2 God looks down from heaven upon the children of men,
To see if there are any who understand, who seek God.
3 Every one of them has turned aside;
They have together become corrupt;
There is none who does good,
No, not one.

!

Matthew 19:

21 Jesus said to Him, "If you want to be perfect, go, sell what you have and give to the poor, and you will have treasure in heaven; and come, follow Me."
22 But when the young man heard that saying, he went away sorrowful, for he had great possessions.
23 Then Jesus said to His disciples, "Assuredly, I say to you that it is hard for a rich man to enter the kingdom of heaven.
24 "And again I say to you, it is easier for a camel to go through the eye of a needle than for a rich man to enter the kingdom of God."
25 When His disciples heard it, they were exceedingly amazed, saying, "Who then can be saved?"

Matthew 19:

26 But Jesus looked at *them* and said to them, "With men this is impossible,
<u>but with God all things are possible."</u>

Isaiah 47:

10 "For you have trusted in your wickedness;
You have said, 'No one sees me';
Your wisdom and your knowledge have warped you;
And you have said in your heart,
'I am, and there is no one else besides me.'

Romans 1:

24 Therefore God also gave them up to uncleanness, in the lusts of their hearts, to dishonor their bodies among themselves,
25 who exchanged the truth of God for the lie, and worshiped and served the creature rather than the Creator, who is blessed forever. Amen.
26 For this reason God gave them up to vile passions. For even their women exchanged the natural use for what is against nature.
27 Likewise also the men, leaving the natural use of the woman, burned in their lust for one another, men with men committing what is shameful, and receiving in themselves the penalty of their error which was due.
28 And even as they did not like to retain God in their knowledge, God gave them over to a debased mind, to do those things which are not fitting;
29 being filled with all unrighteousness, sexual immorality, wickedness, covetousness, maliciousness, full of envy, marcher, strife, deceit, evil-mindedness; they are whisperers,
30 backbiters, haters of God, violent, proud, boasters, inventors of evil things, disobedient to parents,
31 undiscerning, untrustworthy, unloving, unforgiving, unmerciful;
32 who, knowing the righteous judgment of God, that they who practice such things are worthy of death, not only do the same but also approve of those who practice them.

I Corinthians 5:

5 It is actually reported that there is sexual immorality among you, and such sexual immorality as is not eve named among the Gentiles – that a man has his father's wife!
2 And you are puffed up, and have not rather mourned, that he who has done this deed might be taken away from among you.

* *<See a definition of sin: Pg.84.B.2:23>*

A.1, 2 Sin
A.3 Sin & Condemnation

John 15:
22 "If I had not come and spoken to them, they
would have no sin, but now they have no excuse
for their sin.
23 "He who hates Me hates My Father also.
24 "If I had not done among them the works
which no one else did, they would have no sin; but
now they have seen and also hated both Me and
My Father.
25 "But this happened that the word might be
fulfilled which is written in their law, 'They hated
Me without a cause.'

Mark 7:
20 And He said, "What comes out of a man, that
defiles a man. *<SeePg.81B3>*
21 "For from within, out of the heart of men,
proceed evil thoughts, adulteries, fornications,
murders,
22 "thefts, covetousness, wickedness, deceit,
licentiousness, an evil eye, blasphemy, pride,
foolishness.
23 "All these evil things come from within and
defile a man."

II Peter 2:
4 For if God did not spare the angels who
sinned, but cast them down to hell and delivered
them into chains of darkness, to be reserved for
judgment;
5 and did not spare the ancient world, but saved
Noah, one of eight people, a preacher of
righteousness, bringing in the flood on the world
of the ungodly;
6 and turning the cities of Sodom and Gomorrah
into ashes, condemned them to destruction,
making them an example to those who afterward
would live ungodly;
7 and delivered righteous Lot*, who was
oppressed with the filthy conduct of the wicked
8 (for that righteous man, dwelling among them,
tormented his righteous soul from day to day by
seeing and hearing their lawless deeds) –
9 then the LORD knows how to deliver the godly
out of temptations and to reserve the unjust under
punishment for the day of judgment,
10 and especially those who walk according to the
flesh in the lust of uncleanness and despise
authority. They are presumptuous, self-willed;
they are not afraid to speak evil of dignitaries,
11 whereas angels, who are greater in power and
might, do not bring a reviling accusation against
them before the LORD.

* *example of unsanctified believer*

B. Sin and the Law

Romans 2:
11 For there is no partiality with God.
12 For as many as have sinned without the law will
also perish without the law, and as many as have
sinned in the law will be judged by the law.

James 2:
9 but if you show partiality, you commit sin, and
are convicted by the law as transgressors.
10 For whoever shall keep the whole law, and
yet stumble in one point, he is guilty of all.

Numbers 16:
28 'So the priest shall make atonement for the
person who sins unintentionally, when he sins
unintentionally before the LORD, to make
atonement for him; and it shall be forgiven him.
29 'You shall have one law for him who sins
unintentionally, both for him who is native-born
among the children of Israel and for the stranger
who sojourns among them.
30 'But the person who does anything
presumptuously, whether he is native-born or a
stranger, that one brings reproach on the LORD,
and he shall be cut off from among his people.
31 'Because he has despised the word of the LORD,
and has broken His commandment, that person
shall be completely cut off; his guilt shall be upon
him.'"

Leviticus 5:
17 "If a person sins, and commits any of these
things which are forbidden to be done by the
commandments of the LORD, though he does not
know it, yet he is guilty and shall bear his iniquity.

I Timothy 1:
8 But we know that the law is good if one uses it
lawfully,
9 knowing this: that the law is not made for a
righteous person, but for the lawless and
insubordinate, for the ungodly and for sinners, for
the unholy and profane, for murderers of fathers
and murderers of mothers, for manslayers,

Matthew 6:
27 "You have heard that it was said to those of old,
'You shall not commit adultery.'
28 "But I say to you that whoever looks at a
woman to lust for her has already committed
adultery with her in his heart.

The Consequences of Sin

A.1. Daily Separation from God
A. 2-4 Eternal death (Hell)
A.5 Inherited sin from Adam

Romans 6:

23 For the wages of sin is death, but the gift of God is eternal life in Christ Jesus our Lord.

Mark 9:

44 "where 'their worm does not die and the fire is not quenched.'

45 "And if your foot makes you sin, cut it off. It is better for you to enter life lame, than having two feet, to be cast into hell, into the fire that shall never be quenched –

46 "where 'their worm does not die and the fire is not quenched.'

47 "And if your eye makes you sin, pluck it out. It is better for you to enter the kingdom of God with one eye, than having two eyes, to be cast into hell fire –

48 "where 'their worm does not die and the fire is not quenched.' *<see also Pg. 65.B.1>*

I Thessalonians 1:

8 on those who do not obey the gospel of our Lord Jesus Christ.

9 These shall be punished with everlasting destruction from the presence of the Lord and from the glory of His power.

Matthew 25:

41 "Then He will also say to those on the left hand, 'Depart from Me, you cursed, into the everlasting fire prepared for the devil and his angels:

Romans 5:

12 Therefore, just as through one man sin entered into the world, and death through sin, and thus death spread to all men, because all sinned –

13 (For until the law sin was in the world, but sin is not imputed when there is no law.

14 Nevertheless death reigned from Adam to Moses, even over those who had not sinned according to the likeness of the transgression of Adam, who is a type of Him who was to come.

Leviticus 17:

11 'For the life of the flesh is in the blood, and I have given it to you upon the altar to make atonement for your souls; for it is the blood that makes atonement for the soul.'

B. Christ's Death: "Atoned" for our sin

Romans 5:

19 For as by one man's disobedience many were made sinners, so also by one Man's obedience many will be made righteous.*

6 For when we were still without strength, in due time Christ died for the ungodly.

7 For scarcely for a righteous man will one die; yet perhaps for a good man someone would even dare to die.

8 But God demonstrates His own love toward us, in that while we were still sinners, Christ died for us.

I Corinthians 15:

20 But now Christ is risen from the dead, and has become the firstfruits of those who have fallen asleep.

21 For since by man came death, by Man also came the resurrection of the dead.

22 For as in Adam all die, even so in Christ all shall be made alive.

23 But each one in his own order: Christ the first-fruits, afterward those who are Christ's at His coming.

Ephesians 4:

9 (Now this, "*He ascended*" – what does it mean but that He also first descended into the lower parts of the earth?

10 He who descended is also the One who ascended far above all the heavens, that He might fill all things.)

John 3:

36 "He who believes in the Son has everlasting life; and he who does not believe the Son shall not see life, but the wrath of God abides on him."

19 "And this is the condemnation, that the light has come into the world, and men loved darkness rather than light, because there deeds were evil.

20 "For everyone practicing evil hates the light and does not come to the light, lest his deeds should be exposed.

21 "But he who does the truth comes to the light, that his deeds may by clearly seen, that they have been done in God."

**<Ponder, if Adam had refused the forbidden fruit, and had said, "let me die as payment for my wife's sin." Might that love in faith have been rewarded by God's raising him from the dead, and accepting his sacrifice for all Mankind's sins?>*

Salvation Through Christ

(If we believe that Jesus is who He said He is, and accomplished what He said He did, then we have hope in His Name through faith in His mercy.)

Acts 16:

"Sirs, what must I do to be saved?"

31 So they said, "Believe on the Lord Jesus Christ, and you will be saved, you and your household."

32 Then they spoke the word of the Lord to him and to all who were in his house.

Romans 10:

9 that if you confess with your mouth the Lord Jesus and believe in your heart that God has raised Him from the dead, you will be saved. !

10 For with the heart one believes to righteousness, and with the mouth confession is made to salvation.

11 For the Scripture says, "Whoever believes on Him will not be put to shame."

Acts 4:

12 "Nor is there salvation in any other, for there is no other name under heaven given among men by which we must be saved." !

John 11:

25 Jesus said to her, "I am the resurrection and the life. He who believes in Me, though he may die, he shall live. !

Titus 3:

5 not by works of righteousness which we may have done, but according to His mercy He saved us, through the washing of regeneration and renewing of the Holy Spirit,

6 whom He poured out on us abundantly through Jesus Christ our Savior.

I Timothy 1:

12 And I thank Christ Jesus our Lord who has enabled me, because He counted me faithful, putting me into the ministry,

13 although I was formerly a blasphemer, a persecutor, and an insolent man; but I obtained mercy because I did it ignorantly in unbelief.

14 And the grace of our Lord was exceedingly abundant, with faith and love which are in Christ Jesus.

15 This is a faithful saying and worthy of all acceptance, that Christ Jesus came into the world to save sinners, of whom I am chief.

John 3:

3 Jesus answered and said to him, "Most assuredly, I say to you, unless one is born again, he cannot see the kingdom of God."

4 Nicodemus said to Him, "How can a man be born when he is old? Can he enter a second time into his mother's womb and be born?"

5 Jesus answered, "Most assuredly, I say to you, unless one is born of water and the Spirit, he cannot enter the kingdom of God.

6 "That which is born of the flesh is flesh, and that which is born of the Spirit is spirit.

7 "Do not marvel that I said to you, 'You must be born again.'

8 "The wind blows where it wishes, and you hear the sound of it, but cannot tell where it comes from and where it goes. So is everyone who is born of the Spirit."

9 Nicodemus answered and said to Him, "How can these things be?"

10 Jesus answered and said to him, "Are you the teacher of Israel, and do not know these things?

11 "Most assuredly, I say to you, We speak what We know and testify what We have seen, and you do not receive Our witness.

12 "If I have told you earthly things and you do not believe, how will you believe if I tell you heavenly things?

13 "No one has ascended to heaven but He who came down from heaven, that is, the Son of Man who is in heaven.

14 "And if Moses lifted up the serpent in the wilderness, even so must the Son of Man be lifted up,

15 "that whoever believes in Him should not perish but have eternal life.

16 "For God so loved the world that He gave His only begotten Son, that whoever believes in Him should not perish but have everlasting life. !

17 "For God did not send His Son into the world to condemn the world, but that the world through Him might be saved.

18 "He who believes in Him is not condemned; but he who does not believe is condemned already, because he has not believed in the name of the only begotten Son of God.

Predestination / Election
(of Saints by God to Eternal Life)
(opposite of salvation through spontaneous accomplishments during our own lifetimes)

John 6:

44 "No one can come to Me unless the Father who sent Me draws him; and I will raise him up at the last day.

Ephesians 3:

8 To me, who am less than the least of all the saints, this grace was given, that I should preach among the Gentiles the unsearchable riches of Christ,
9 and to make all people see what is the fellowship of the mystery, which from the beginning of the ages has been hidden in God who created all things through Jesus Christ;
10 to the intent that now the manifold wisdom of God might be made known by the church to the principalities and powers in the heavenly places,
11 according to the eternal purpose which He accomplished in Christ Jesus our Lord,
12 in whom we have boldness and access with confidence through faith in Him.

Ephesians 1:

4 just as He chose us in Him before the foundation of the world, that we should be holy and without blame before Him in love,
5 having predestined us to adoption as sons by Jesus Christ to Himself, according to the good pleasure of His will,
6 to the praise of the glory of His grace, by which He has made us accepted in the Beloved.
7 In Him we have redemption through His blood, the forgiveness of sins, according the riches of His grace
8 which He made to abound toward us in all wisdom and prudence,
9 having made known to us the mystery of His will, according to His good pleasure which He purposed in Himself,
10 that in the dispensation of the fullness of the times He might gather together in one all things in Christ, both which are in heaven and which are on earth – in Him,
11 in whom also we have obtained an inheritance, being predestined according to the purpose of Him who works all things according to the counsel of His will.

Ecclesiastes 9:

11 I returned and saw under the sun that –
The race is not to the swift,
Nor the battle to the strong,
Nor bread to the wise,
Nor riches to men of understanding,
Nor favor to men of skill;
But time and chance happen to them all.

II Thessalonians 2:

13 But we are bound to give thanks to God always for you, brethren beloved by the Lord, because God from the beginning chose you for salvation through sanctification by the Spirit and belief in the truth.

I Peter 1:

20 He indeed was foreordained before the foundation of the world, but was manifest in these last times for you
21 who through Him believe in God, who raised Him from the dead and gave Him glory, so that your faith and hope are in God.

II Corinthians 4:

3 But even if our gospel is veiled, it is veiled to those who are perishing,
4 whose minds the god of this age has blinded, who do not believe, lest the light of the gospel of the glory of Christ, who is the image of God, should shine on them.

Acts 13:

48 Now when the Gentiles heard this, they were glad and glorified the word of the Lord. And as many as had been appointed to eternal life believed.

Romans 8:

28 And we know that all things work together for good to those who love God, to those who are called according to His purpose.
29 For whom He foreknew, He also predestined to be conformed to the image of His Son, that He might be the firstborn among many brethren.
30 Moreover whom He predestined, these He also called; whom He called, these He also justified; and whom He justified, these He also glorified.

<See also Pg.80A1, Pg 9B2, Pg 77B2>

Predestination / Election – cont.

Ecclesiastes 3:

14 I know that whatever God does,
It shall be forever,
Nothing can be added to it,
And nothing taken from it.
God does it, that men should fear before Him.
15 That which is has already been,
And what is to be has already been;
And God requires an account of what is past.

Romans 9:

11 (for the children not yet being born, nor
having done any good or evil, that the purpose of
God according to **election** might stand, not of
works but of Him who calls),
12 it was said to her, "The older shall serve the
younger."
13 As it is written, "Jacob I have **loved**, but Esau
I have hated."
14 What shall we say then? Is there
unrighteousness with God? Certainly not!
15 For He says to Moses, I will have mercy
on whomever I will have mercy, and I will
have compassion on whomever I will have
compassion."
16 So then it is not of him who wills, nor of
him who runs, but of God who shows
mercy.
17 For the Scripture says to Pharaoh, "Even
for this same purpose I have raised you up,
that I might show My power in you, and
that **My name** might be declared in all the
earth."
18 Therefore <u>He has mercy on whom He
wills, and whom He wills He hardens</u>.
19 You will say to me then, "Why does He still
find fault? For who has resisted His will?"
20 But indeed, O man, who are you to reply
against God? Will the thing formed say to
him who formed it, "Why have you made
me like this?"
21 Does not the potter have power over the
clay, from the same lump to make one vessel
for honor and another for dishonor?
22 What if God, wanting to show His wrath
and to make His power known, endured
with much longsuffering the vessels of wrath
prepared for destruction,
23 and that He might make known the riches
of His glory on the vessels of mercy, which
He had prepared beforehand for glory,
24 even us whom He called, not of the Jews only,
but also of the Gentiles?

Ecclesiastes 3:

11 He has made everything beautiful in its
time. Also He has put eternity in their
hearts, except that no one can find out the
work that God does from beginning to end.

Romans 11:

25 For I do not desire, brethren, that you should
be ignorant of this **mystery**, lest you should be
wise in your own opinion, that hardening in part
has happened to Israel until the fullness of the
Gentiles has come in.
26 And so all Israel will be saved, as it is
written:
"The Deliverer will come out of Zion,
And He will turn away ungodliness from
Jacob;
27 For this is My covenant with them,
When I take away their sins."
28 Concerning the gospel they are enemies for
your sake, but concerning the **election** they are
beloved for the sake of the fathers.
29 For the **gifts** and the calling of God
are irrevocable. **!**
30 For as you were once disobedient to God, yet
have now obtained mercy through their
disobedience,
31 even so these also have now been disobedient,
that through the mercy shown you they also may
obtain mercy.
32 For God has committed them all to
disobedience, that He might have mercy on
all.

Deuteronomy 4:

37 "And because He **loved** your fathers,
therefore He chose their descendants after them;
and He brought you out of Egypt with His
Presence, with His mighty power.

Matthew 13:

10 And the disciples came and said to Him,
"Why do You speak to them in parables?"
11 He answered and said to them, "Because it
has been given to you to know the **!**
mysteries of the kingdom of heaven, but
to them it has not been given.
12 "For whoever has, to him more will be
given, and he will have abundance; but
whoever does not have, even what he has
will be taken away from him.

A. Salvation Through Faith

Romans 4:

13 For the promise that he would be the heir of the world was not to Abraham or to his seed through the law, but through the righteousness of faith.
14 For if those who are of the law are heirs, faith is made void and the promise made of no effect.
15 because the law brings about wrath; for where there is no law there is no transgression.
16 Therefore it is of faith that it might be according to grace, so that the promise might be sure to all the seed, not only to those who are of the law, but also to those who are of the faith of Abraham, who is the father of us all
17 (as it is written, "I have made you a father of many nations.") in the presence of Him whom he believed, even God, who give life to the dead and calls those things which do not exist as though they did;
18 who, contrary to hope, in hope believed, so that he became the father of many nations, according to what was spoken, "So shall your descendants be."
19 And not being weak in faith, he did not consider his own body, already dead (since he was about a hundred years old), and the deadness of Sarah's womb.
20 He did not waver at the promise of God through unbelief, but was strengthened in faith, giving glory to God, *
21 and being fully convinced that what He had promised He was also able to perform.
22 And therefore, "it was accounted to him for righteousness."
23 Now it was not written for his sake alone that it was imputed to him,
24 but also for us. It shall be imputed to us who believe in Him who raised up Jesus our Lord from the dead,
25 who was delivered up because of our offenses, and was raised because of our justification.

Hebrews 11:

4 By faith Abel offered to God a more excellent sacrifice than Cain, through which he obtained witness that he was righteous, God testifying to his gifts; and through it he being dead still speaks.
5 By faith Enoch was translated so that he did not see death, "and was not found because God had translated him", for before his translation he had this testimony, that he pleased God.

** Definition of Faith (also Pg 105.B.1; 104.A.)*

B. Completed; Assurance

Hebrews 11:

13 These all died in faith, not having received the promises, but having seen them afar off were assured of them, embraced them, and confessed that they were strangers and pilgrims on the earth.

Hebrews 4:

1 Therefore, since a promise remains of entering His rest, let us fear lest any of you seem to have come short of it.
2 For indeed the gospel was preached to us as well as to them; but the word which they heard did not profit them, not being mixed with faith in those who heard it.
3 For we who have believed do enter that rest, as He has said:

"So I swore in My wrath,
They shall not enter My rest."

although the works were finished from the foundation of the world.
4 For He has spoken in a certain place of the seventh day in this way: "And God rested on the seventh day from all His works";
5 and again in this place: "They shall not enter My rest."
6 Since therefore it remains that some must enter it, and those to whom it was first preached did not enter because of disobedience,
7 again, He designates a certain day, saying in David, "Today," after such a long time, as it has been said:

"Today, if you will hear His voice,
Do not harden your hearts."

8 For if Joshua had given them rest, then He would not afterward spoken of another day.
9 There remains therefore a rest for the people of God.
10 For he who has entered His rest has himself also ceased from his works as God did from His.
11 Let us therefore be diligent to enter that rest, lest anyone fall after the same example of disobedience.

I Peter 1:

23 having been born again, not of corruptible seed but incorruptible, through the word of God which lives and abides forever.

Permanent Assurance of Salvation

You can't lose it since you can't earn it! *(See also Pg. 86.B.5 and Pg. 79.B.2; 97.A.2)*

Hebrews 12:

28 Therefore, since we are receiving a
kingdom which cannot be shaken, let us
have grace, by which we may serve God
acceptably with reverence and godly fear.
29 For our God is a consuming fire.

Romans 8:

31 What then shall we say to these things? If
God is for us, who can be against us?
32 He who did not spare His own Son, but
delivered Him up for us all, how shall He
not with Him also freely give us all things?
38 For I am persuaded that neither !
death nor life, nor angels nor
principalities nor powers, nor things
present nor things to come,
39 nor height, nor depth, nor any other
created thing, shall be able to separate us
from the love of God which is in Christ
Jesus our Lord.

John 10:

27 "My sheep hear My voice, and I know them,
and they follow Me.
28 "And I give them eternal life, and they shall
never perish; neither shall anyone snatch them
out of My hand.
29 "My Father, who has given them to Me, is
greater than all; and no one is able to snatch
them out of My Father's hand.
30 "I and My Father are one."

I Corinthians 5:

4 In the name of our Lord Jesus Christ, when
you are gathered together, along with my spirit,
with the power of our Lord Jesus Christ,
5 deliver such a one to Satan for the
destruction of the flesh, that his spirit may
be saved in the day of the LORD Jesus.
6 Your glorying is not good. Do you not know
that a little leaven leavens the whole lump?

Ephesians 1:

13 In Him you also trusted, after you heard the
word of truth, the gospel of your salvation; in
whom also, having believed, you were sealed
with the Holy Spirit of promise.

II Corinthians 1:

21 Now He who establishes us with you in
Christ and has anointed us is God.
22 who also has sealed us and given us the
Spirit in our hearts as a deposit.

I John 5:

18 We know that whoever is born of God does not
sin; but he who has been born of God keeps
himself, and the wicked one does not touch him.

II Timothy 2:

For if we died with Him,
We shall also live with Him.
12 If we endure,
We shall also reign with Him.
If we deny Him,
He also will deny us.
13 If we are faithless,
He remains faithful;
He cannot deny Himself.

I Peter 1:

4 to an inheritance incorruptible* and undefiled
and that does not fade away, reserved in heaven for
you,
5 who are kept by the power of God through faith
for salvation ready to be revealed in the last time.
* *<per Pg117A4 >*

Romans 8:

1 There is therefore now no
condemnation to those who are in Christ !
Jesus, who do not walk according to the
flesh, but according to the Spirit.
2 For the law of the Spirit of life in Christ Jesus
has made me free from the law of sin and death.
3 For what the law could not do in that it was
weak through the flesh, God did by sending His
own Son in the likeness of sinful flesh, on account
of sin: He condemned sin in the flesh,
4 that the righteous requirement of the law might
be fulfilled in us who do not walk according to the
flesh but according to the Spirit.

I Corinthians 15:

54 So when this corruptible has put on
incorruption, and this mortal has put on
immortality, then shall be brought to pass the
saying that is written, "Death is swallowed up in
victory."
55 "O Death, where is your sting?
O Hades, where is your victory?"
56 The sting of death is sin, and the strength of sin
is the law.
57 But thanks be to God, who gives us the victory
through our Lord Jesus Christ.
58 Therefore, my beloved brethren, be steadfast,
immovable, always abounding in the work of the
Lord, knowing that your labor is not in vain in the
Lord.

The Saving Hope *<See also Pg. 95.B.4>*

I John 5:

19 We love Him because He first loved us.

I John 3:

1 Behold what manner of love the Father has bestowed on us, that we should be called children of God! Therefore the world does not know us, because it did not know Him.

2 Beloved, now we are children of God; and it has not yet been revealed what we shall be, but we know that when He is revealed, we shall be like Him, for we shall see Him as He is.

3 And everyone who has this hope in Him purifies himself, just as He is pure.

I Peter 1:

13 Therefore gird up the loins of your mind, be sober, and rest your hope fully upon the grace that is to be brought to you at the revelation of Jesus Christ.

Hebrews 7:

19 for the law made nothing perfect; on the other hand, there is the bringing in of a better hope, through which we draw near to God.

I Thessalonians 5:

8 But let us who are of the day be sober, putting on the breastplate of faith and love, and as a helmet the hope of salvation.

Colossians 1:

23 if indeed you continue in the faith, grounded and steadfast, and are not moved away from the hope of the gospel which you heard, which was preached to every creature under heaven, of which I, Paul, became a minister.

Galatians 5:

5 For we through the Spirit eagerly wait for the hope of righteousness by faith.

Romans 8:

22 For we know that the whole creation groans and labors with birth pangs together until now.

23 And not only they, but we also who have the firstfruits of the Spirit, even we ourselves groan within ourselves, eagerly waiting for the adoption, the redemption of our body.

24 For we were saved in this hope, but hope that is seen is not hope; for why does one still hope for what he sees?

25 But if we hope for what we do not see, then we eagerly wait for it with perseverance.

I John 4:

16 And we have known and believed the love that God has for us. God is love, and he who abides in love abides in God and God in him.

17 Love has been perfected among us in this: that we may have boldness in the day of judgment; because as He is, so are we in this world.

18 There is no fear in love; but perfect love casts out fear, because fear involves torment. But he who fears has not been made perfect in love.

Romans 5:

1 Therefore, having been justified by faith, we have peace with God through our Lord Jesus Christ.

2 through whom also we have access by faith into this grace in which we stand, and rejoice in hope of the glory of God.

3 And not only that, but we also glory in tribulations, knowing that tribulation produces perseverance;

4 and perseverance, character; and character, hope.

5 Now hope does not disappoint, because the love of God has been poured out in our hearts by the Holy Spirit who was given to us.

Hebrews 6:

10 For God is not unjust to forget your work and labor of love which you have shown toward His name, in that you have ministered to the saints, and do minister.

11 And we desire that each one of you show the same diligence to the full assurance of hope until the end.

Grace

A. The Gift of Salvation <see Pg. 77.B.2>

Ephesians 2:
8 For by grace you have been saved through faith, and that not of yourselves; it is the gift of God,
9 not of works, lest anyone should boast.
10 For we are His workmanship, created in Christ Jesus for good works, which God prepared beforehand that we should walk in them.

Romans 5:
15 But the free gift is not like the offense. For if by the one man's offense many died, much more the grace of God and the gift by the grace of the one Man, Jesus Christ, abounded to many.

II Corinthians 8:
9 For you know the grace of our Lord Jesus Christ, that though He was rich, yet for your sakes He became poor, that you through His poverty might become rich.

Romans 3:
27 Where is boasting then? It is excluded. By what law? Of works? No, but by the law of faith.
28 Therefore we conclude that a man is justified by faith apart from the deeds of the law.

Galatians 2:
21 "I do not set aside the grace of God; for if righteousness comes through the law, then Christ died in vain."

Galatians 4:
9 But now after you have known God, or rather are known by God, how is it that you turn again to the weak and beggarly elements, to which you desire again to be in bondage?
10 You observe days and months and seasons and years.
11 I am afraid for you, lest I have labored for you in vain.

Galatians 3:
2 This only I want to learn from you: Did you receive the Spirit by the works of the law, or by the hearing of faith?
3 Are you so foolish? Having begun in the Spirit, are you now being made perfect by the flesh?

Romans 11:
6 And if by grace, then it is no longer of works; otherwise grace is no longer grace. But if it is of works, it is no longer grace; otherwise work is no longer work.

B. The Law of Liberty

Galatians 5:
4 You have become estranged from Christ, you who attempt to be justified by law; you have fallen from grace.

12 For all the law is fulfilled in one word, even in this: "You shall love your neighbor as yourself."

Colossians 2:
20 Therefore, if you died with Christ from the basic principles of the world, why, as though living in the world, do you subject yourselves to regulations –
21 "Do not touch, do not taste, do not handle,"
22 which all concern things which perish with the using – according to the commandments and doctrines of men?
23 These things indeed have an appearance of wisdom in self-imposed religion, false humility, and neglect of the body, but are of no value against indulgence of the flesh. **!**

II Corinthians 11:
3 But I fear, lest somehow, as the serpent deceived Eve by his craftiness, so your minds may be corrupted from the simplicity that is in Christ. *(What)*
4 For if he who comes preaches another Jesus whom we have not preached, or if you receive a different spirit which you have not received, or a different gospel which you have not accepted, you may well put up with it. *(Why)* **!**

Mark 10:
25 "It is easier for a camel to go through the eye of a needle than for a rich man to enter the kingdom of God."
26 And they were astonished beyond measure, saying among themselves, "Who then can be saved?"
27 But looking at them, Jesus said, "With men it is impossible, but not with God; for with God all things are possible."

Acts 15:
28 For it seemed good to the Holy Spirit, and to us, to lay upon you no greater burden than these necessary things:
29 that you abstain from things offered to idols, from blood, from things strangles, and from sexual immorality. If you keep yourselves from these, you will do well. Farewell.

James 1:
25 But he who looks into the perfect law of liberty continues in it, and is not a forgetful hearer but a doer of the work, this one will be blessed in what he does.

Good Works (resulting from faith)

< Ponder this! "Good works" (i.e.Righteousness) is to "Faith" as Heat is to Energy – the unavoidable byproduct of useage. >

Titus 2:

11 For the grace of God that brings salvation has appeared to all men,
12 teaching us that, denying ungodliness and worldly lusts, we should live soberly, righteously, and godly in the present age.

Romans 6:

12 Therefore do not let sin reign in your mortal body, that you should obey it in its lusts.
13 And do not present your members as instruments of unrighteousness to sin, but present yourselves to God as being alive from the dead, and your members as instruments of righteousness to God.
14 For sin shall not have dominion over you, for you are not under law but under grace.
15 What then? Shall we sin because we are not under law but under grace? Certainly not!
16 Do you not know that to whom you present yourselves slaves to obey, you are that one's slaves whom you obey, whether of sin to death, or of obedience to righteousness?

James 2:

17 Thus also faith by itself, if it does not have works, is dead.
18 But someone will say, "You have faith, and I have works." Show me your faith without your works, and I will show you my faith by my works.
19 You believe that there is one God. You do well. Even the demons believe – and tremble! **!**
20 But do you want to know, O foolish man, that faith without works is dead?
21 Was not Abraham our father justified by works when he offered Isaac his son on the altar?
22 Do you see that faith was working together with his works, and by works faith was made perfect? *(complete)* **!**
23 And the Scripture was fulfilled which says, "Abraham believed God, and it was accounted to him for righteousness." And he was called the friend of God.
24 You seen then that a man is justified by works, and not be faith only.

26 For as the body without the spirit is dead, so faith without works is dead also.

Romans 4:

4 Now to him who works, the wages are not counted as grace but as debt.
5 But to him who does not work but believes on Him who justifies the ungodly, his faith is accounted for righteousness.

Titus 3:

7 that having been justified by His grace we should become heirs according to the hope of eternal life.
8 This is a faithful saying, and these things I want you to affirm constantly, that those who have believed in God should be careful to maintain good works. These things are good and profitable to men.

Luke 6:

45 "A good man out of the good treasure of his heart brings forth good; and an evil man out of the evil treasure of his heart brings forth evil. For out of the abundance of the heart his mouth speaks.
46 "But why do you call Me 'Lord, Lord,' and do not do the things which I say? **!**

Hebrews 10:

35 Therefore do not cast away your confidence, which has great reward.
36 For you have need of endurance, so that after you have done the will of God, you may receive the promise:
37 "For yet a little while,
And He who is coming will come and will not tarry.
38 Now the just shall live by faith;
But if anyone draws back,
My soul has no pleasure in him."
39 But we are not of those who draw back to perdition, but of those who believe to the saving of the soul. **!**

Romans 8:

5 For those who live according to the flesh set their minds on the things of the flesh, but those who live according to the Spirit, the things of the Spirit.
6 For to be carnally minded is death, but to be spiritually minded is life and peace.
7 Because the carnal mind is enmity against God; for it is not subject to the law of God, nor indeed can be.
8 So then, those who are in the flesh cannot please God.

Human Religion (Denomination/Divisions)

See Pg. 24.B.3 & 25.A.1b. + Pg. 51-52

Romans 10:
1 Brethren, my heart's desire and prayer
to God for Israel is that they may be !
saved.
2 For I bear them witness that they have
a zeal for God, but not according to
knowledge.
3 For they being ignorant of God's
righteousness, and seeking to establish
their own righteousness, have not
submitted to the righteousness of God.
4 For Christ is the end of the law for
righteousness to everyone who believes.

Romans 9:
32 Why? Because they did not seek it by faith,
but as it were, by the works of the law. For
they stumbled at that stumbling stone.
33 As it is written:
"Behold, I lay in Zion a stumbling stone and rock of offense,
And whoever believes on Him will not be put to shame."

Mark 7:
7 'And in vain they worship Me, Teaching
as doctrines the commandments of men.'
8 "For laying aside the commandment of God,
you hold the tradition of men – the washing of
pitchers and cups, and many other such things
you do."

Philippians 3:
3 For we are the circumcision, who worship
God in the spirit, rejoice in Christ Jesus, and
have no confidence in the flesh,

Matthew 23:
8 "But you, do not be called 'Rabbi';
for One is your Teacher, the Christ, !
and you are all brethren.
9 "Do not call anyone on earth your father;
for One is your Father, He who is in heaven.
10 "And do not be called teachers; for One is
your Teacher, the Christ.
11 "But he who is greatest among you shall be
your servant.
12 And whoever exalts himself will be abased,
and he who humbles himself will be exalted.

* <See also Pg.107B3 >

< See also Pg. 5.A.2, Pg. 80.A.6, And Pg. 80.B.2-3 >

I Corinthians 1:
10 Now I plead with you, brethren, by the name
of our Lord Jesus Christ, that you all speak the
same thing, and that there be no divisions among
you, but that you be perfectly joined together in
the same mind and in the same judgment.

I Corinthians 3:
3 for you are still carnal. For where there are envy,
strife, and divisions among you, are you not carnal
and behaving like mere men?
4 For when one says, "I am of Paul," and another,
"I am of Apollos," are you not carnal?

Romans 16:
17 Now I urge you, brethren, note those who
cause divisions and offenses, contrary to the !
doctrine which you learned, and avoid them.
18 For those who are such do not serve our Lord
Jesus Christ, but their own belly, and by smooth
words and flattering speech deceive the
hearts of the simple.

Ezekiel 33:
31 "So they come to you as people do, they sit
before you as My people, and they hear
your words, but they do not do them; for !
with their mouth they show much love,
but their hearts pursue their own gain.
(see also Pg. 98.A.2)

Luke 11:
27 And it happened, as He spoke these things, that
a certain woman from the crowed raised her
voice and said to Him, "Blessed is the womb
that bore You, and the breasts which nursed
You!"
28 But He said, "More than that, blessed are
those who hear the word of God and keep
it!" *

Galatians 5:
9 A little leaven leavens the whole lump.

Colossians 2:
16 So let no one judge you in food or in drink,
or regarding a festival or a new moon or
Sabbaths,
17 which are a shadow of things **to come**, but
the substance is Christ.
18 Let no one cheat you of your reward, taking
delight in false humility and worship of
angels, ...

Conscience/Heart
(Our hot line from God when pure and clear.)

I John 3:
21 Beloved, if our heart does not condemn us, we have confidence toward God.

Matthew 7: !
1 "Judge not, lest you be judged."

Hebrews 10:
15 And the Holy Spirit also witnesses to us; for after He had said before,
16 "This is the covenant that I will make with them after those days, says the Lord: I will put My laws into their hearts, and in their minds I will write them."
17 And then He adds, "Their sins and their lawless deeds I will remember no more."

II Corinthians 13:
5 Examine yourselves as to whether you are in the faith. Prove yourselves. Do you not know yourselves, that Jesus Christ is in you? – unless indeed you are disqualified.

Hebrews 9:
14 how much more shall the blood of Christ, who through the eternal Spirit offered Himself without spot to God, purge your conscience from dead works to serve the living God?

I Timothy 1:
4 nor give heed to fables and endless genealogies, which cause disputes rather than godly edification which is in faith.
5 Now the purpose of the commandment is love from a pure heart, from a good conscience, and from sincere faith,
6 from which some, having strayed, have turned aside to idle talk.

Titus 1:
15 To the pure all things are pure, but to those who are defiled and unbelieving nothing is pure; but even their mind and conscience are defiled.
16 They profess to know God, but in works they deny Him, being abominable, disobedient, and disqualified for every good work.

II Timothy 2:
22 Flee also youthful lusts; but pursue righteousness, faith, love, peace with those who call on the Lord out of a pure heart.

Romans 9:
1 I tell the truth in Christ, I am not lying, my conscience also bearing me witness in the Holy Spirit.

I John 2:
28 And now, little children, abide in Him, that when He appears, we may have confidence and not be ashamed before Him at His coming.

I Timothy 3:
9 holding the mystery of the faith with a pure conscience.

Hebrews 13:
18 Pray for us; for we are confident that we have a good conscience, in all things desiring to live honorably.

I Corinthians 6:
12 All things are lawful for me, but all things are not helpful. All things are lawful for me, but I will not be brought under the power of any.

Hebrews 10:
22 let us draw near with a true heart in full assurance of faith, having our hearts sprinkled from an evil conscience and our bodies washed with pure water.
23 Let us hold fast the confession of our hope without wavering, for He who promised is faithful.

Romans 2:
13 (for not the hearers of the law are just in the sight of God, but the doers of the law will be justified;
14 for when Gentiles, who do not have the law, by nature do the things contained in the law, these, although not having the law, are a law to themselves,
15 who show the work of the law written in their hearts, their conscience also bearing witness, and between themselves their thoughts accusing or else excusing them)

Law of Liberty Under Conscience

I Corinthians 10:

23 All things are lawful for me, but all things are not helpful; all thing are lawful for me, but all things do not edify.
24 Let no one seek his own, but each one the other's well-being.
25 Eat whatever is sold in the meat market, asking no questions for conscience' sake;
26 for "The earth is the Lord's and all its fullness."
27 If any of those who do not believe invites you to dinner, and you desire to go, eat whatever is set before you, asking no question for conscience' sake.
28 But if anyone says to you, "This was offered to idols," do not eat it for the sake of the one who told you, and for conscience sake; for "The earth is the Lord's and all its fullness."
29 Conscience, I say, not your own, but that of the other. For why is my liberty judged by another man's conscience?
30 But if I partake with thanks, why am I evil spoken of for the food over which I give thanks?

I Corinthians 8:

6 yet for us there is only one God, the Father, of whom are all things, and we for Him; and one Lord Jesus Christ, through whom all things, and through whom we live.
7 However, there is not in everyone that knowledge; for some, with consciousness of the idol, until now eat it as a thing offered to an idol; and their conscience, being weak, is defiled.
8 But food does not commend us to God; for neither if we eat are we the better; nor if we do not eat are we the worse.
9 But beware lest somehow this liberty of yours become a stumbling block to those who are weak.
10 For if anyone sees you who have knowledge eating in an idol's temple, will not the conscience of him who is weak be emboldened to eat those things offered to idols?

I Timothy 5:

23 No longer drink only water, but use a little wine for your stomach's sake and your frequent infirmities.

Romans 15:

1 We then who are strong ought to bear with the scruples of the weak, and not to please ourselves.
2 Let each of us please his neighbor for his good leading to edification.

Romans 14:

20 Do not destroy the work of God for the sake of food. All things indeed are pure, but it is evil for the man who eats with offense.
21 It is good neither to eat meat nor drink wine nor do anything by which your brother stumbles or is offended or is made weak.
22 Do you have faith? Have it to yourself before God. Happy is he who does not condemn himself in what he approves.
23 But he who doubts is condemned if he eats, because he does not eat from faith; <u>for whatever is not from faith is sin.</u> <_* ***Sin defined!*** * > **!**

Romans 14:

1 Receive one who is weak in the faith, but not to disputes over doubtful things.
2 For one believes he may eat all things, but he who is weak eats only vegetables.
3 Let not him who eats despise him who does not eat, and let not him who does not eat judge him who eats; for God has received him.
4 Who are you to judge another's servant? To his own master he stands or falls. Indeed, he will be made to stand, for God is able to make him stand.
5 One person esteems one day above another; another esteems every day alike. Let each be fully convinced in his own mind.
6 He who observes the day, observes it to the Lord; and he who does not observe the day, to the Lord he does not observe it. He who eats, eats to the Lord, for he gives God thanks; and he who does not eat, to the Lord he does not eat, and gives God thanks.
7 For none of us lives to himself, and no one dies to himself.
8 For if we live, we live to the Lord; and if we die, we die to the Lord. Therefore, whether we live or die, we are the Lord's.
9 For to this end Christ died and rose and lived again, that He might be Lord of both the dead and the living.

Warnings Against the Snares of the Devil

Within Ourselves ("old sin nature" differs from external deception by Devil) See Pg.51-52

Matthew 26:

41 "Watch and pray, lest you enter into temptation. The spirit indeed is willing, but the flesh is weak."

II Peter 2:

10 Therefore, brethren, be even more diligent to make your calling and election sure, for if you do these things you will never stumble.

Hebrews 12:

12 Therefore strengthen the hands which hang down, and the feeble knees,
13 and make straight paths for your feet, so that what is lame may not be dislocated, but rather be healed.
14 Pursue peace with all men, and holiness, without which no one will see the Lord:
15 looking diligently lest anyone fall short of the grace of God; lest any root of bitterness springing up cause trouble, and by this many become defiled.

Hebrews 10:

26 For if we sin willfully after we have received the knowledge of the truth, there no longer remains a sacrifice for sins.

Hebrews 3:

6 but Christ as a Son over His own house, whose house we are if we hold fast the confidence and the rejoicing of the hope firm to the end.

12 Beware, brethren, lest there be in any of you an evil heart of unbelief in departing from the living God;
13 but exhort one another daily, while it is called "Today," lest any of you be hardened through the deceitfulness of sin.
14 For we have become partakers of Christ if we hold the beginning of our confidence steadfast to the end.

I Corinthians 15:

1 Moreover, brethren, I declare to you the gospel which I preached to you, which also you received and in which you stand,
2 by which also you are saved, if you hold fast that word which I preached to you – unless you believed in vain.

II Peter 2:

20 For if, after they have escaped the pollutions of the world through the knowledge of the Lord and Savior Jesus Christ, they are again entangled in them and overcome, the latter end is worse for them than the beginning.
21 For it would have been better for them not to have known the way of righteousness, than having known it, to turn from the holy commandment delivered to them.
22 But it has happened to them according to the true proverb: "A dog returns to his own vomit," and "a sow, having washed, to her wallowing in the mire."

Acts 20:

29 "For I know this, that after my departure savage wolves will come in among you, not sparing the flock.
30 "Also from among yourselves men will rise up, speaking perverse things, to draw away the disciples after themselves.
31 "Therefore watch, and remember that for three years I did not cease to warn everyone night and day with tears.
32 "And now, brethren, I commend you to God and to the word of His grace, which is able to build you up and give you an inheritance among all those who are sanctified.

Ephesians 6:

12 For we do not wrestle against flesh and blood, but against principalities, against powers, against the rulers of the darkness of this age, against spiritual hosts of wickedness in the heavenly places.
13 Therefore take up the whole armor of God, that you may be able to withstand in the evil day, and having done all, to stand.
14 Stand therefore, having girded your waist with truth, having put on the breastplate of righteousness,
15 and having shod your feet with the preparation of the gospel of peace;
16 above all, taking the shield of faith with which you will be able to quench all the fiery darts of the wicked one.
17 And take the helmet of salvation, and the sword of the Spirit, which is the word of God

A. **Warnings** against Devil & his Deceptions

(see pgs 51-52 for deceit by Devil)

I Peter 5:

8 Be sober, be vigilant; because your adversary the devil walks about like a roaring lion, seeking whom he may devour.
9 Resist him, steadfast in the faith, knowing that the same sufferings are experienced by your brotherhood in the world.
10 But may the God of all grace, who called us to His eternal glory by Christ Jesus, after you have suffered a while, perfect, establish, strengthen, and settle you.

<see also Pg. 89.B.5 >

James 4:

5 Or do you think that the Scripture says in vain, "The Spirit who dwells in us yearns jealously"?
6 But He gives more grace. Therefore He says:
"God resists the proud,
But gives grace to the humble."
7 Therefore submit to God. Resist the devil and he will flee from you.
8 Draw near to God and He will draw near to you. Cleanse your hands, you sinners; and purify your hearts, you double-minded.

Ephesians 2:

1 And you He made alive, who were dead in trespasses and sins,
2 in which you once walked according to the course of this world, according to <u>the prince of the power of the air</u>, the spirit who now works in the sons of disobedience.

Hebrews 12:

16 lest there be any fornicator or profane person like Esau, who for one morsel of food sold his birthright.
17 For you know that afterward, when he wanted to inherit the blessing, he was rejected, for he found no place for repentance, though he sought it diligently with tears.

B. **Watch** for Christ's return and your accounting (Judgment)

II Corinthians 5:

10 For we must all appear before the judgment seat of Christ, that each one may receive the things done in the body, according to what he has done, whether good or bad.
11 Knowing, therefore, the terror of the Lord, we persuade men; but we are well-known to God, and I also trust are well-known in your consciences.

<Paul's motivation for evangelism.>

I Corinthians 3:

13 each one's work will become manifest; for the Day will declare it, because it will be revealed by fire; and the fire will test each one's work, of what sort it is.
14 If anyone's work which he has built on it endures, he will receive a reward.
15 If anyone's work is burned, he will suffer loss; but he himself will be saved, yet so as through fire.

Matthew 12:

36 "But I say to you that for every idle word men speak, they will give account of it in the day of judgment.
37 "For by your words you will be justified, and by your words you will be condemned."

Luke 12:

46 "the master of that servant will come on a day when he is not looking for him, and at an hour when he is not aware; and will but him in two and appoint him his portion with the unbelievers.
47 "And that servant who knew his master's will, and did not prepare himself or do according to his will, shall be beaten with many stripes.
48 "But he who did not know, yet committed things worthy of stripes, shall be beaten with few. For everyone to whom much is given, from him much has been committed, of him they will ask the more.

Romans 11:

22 Therefore consider the goodness and severity of God: on those who fell, severity; but toward you, goodness, if you continue in His goodness. Otherwise you will be cut off.

Spirit vs. Flesh *(See also Pg.13 & Pg.78.B.4)*

Mark 14:
38 "Watch and pray, lest you enter into temptation. The spirit truly is ready, the flesh is weak."

John 6:
63 "It is the Spirit who gives life; the flesh profits nothing. The words that I speak to you are spirit, and they are life."

Galatians 5:
16 I say then: Walk in the Spirit, and you shall not fulfill the lust of the flesh.
17 For the flesh lusts against the Spirit, and the Spirit against the flesh; and these are contrary to one another, so that you do not do the things that you wish.
18 But if you are lead by the Spirit, you are not under the law.
22 But the fruit of the Spirit is love, joy, peace, longsuffering, kindness, goodness, faithfulness,
23 gentleness, self-control. Against such there is no law.

Romans 7:
14 For we know that the law is spiritual, but I am carnal, sold under sin.
15 For what I am doing, I do not understand. For what I will to do, that I do not practice; but what I hate, that I do.
16 If, then, I do what I will not to do, I agree with the law that it is good.
17 But now, it is no longer I who do it, but sin that dwells in me.
18 For I know that in me (that is, in my flesh) nothing good dwells; for to will is present with me, but how to perform what is good I do not find.
19 For the good that I will to do, I do not do; but the evil I will not to do, that I practice.
20 Now if I do what I will not to do, it is no longer I who do it, but sin that dwells in me.
21 I find then a law, that evil is present with me, the one who wills to do good.
22 For I delight in the law of God according to the inward man.
23 But I see another law in my members, warring against the law of my mind, and bringing me into captivity to the law of sin which is in my members.
24 O wretched man that I am! Who will deliver me from this body of death?
25 I thank God – through Jesus Christ our Lord! So then, with the mind I myself serve the law of God, but with the flesh the law of sin.

II Corinthians 5:
17 Therefore, if anyone is in Christ, he is a new creation; old things have passed away; behold, all thing have become new.

Romans 8:
12 Therefore, brethren, we are debtors – not to the flesh, to live according to the flesh.
13 For if you live according to the flesh you will die; but if by the Spirit you put to death the deeds of the body, you will live.
14 For as many as are led by the Spirit of God, these are sons of God.
15 For you did not receive the spirit of bondage again to fear, but you received the Spirit of adoption by whom we cry out, "Abba, Father."
16 The Spirit Himself bears witness with our spirit that we are children of God.

John 15:
4 "Abide in Me, and I in you. As the branch cannot bear fruit of itself, unless it abides in the vine, neither can you, unless you abide in Me.
5 "I am the vine, you are the branches. He who abides in Me, and I in him, bears much fruit; for without Me you can do nothing.

Galatians 2:
20 "I have been crucified with Christ; it is no longer I who live, but Christ lives in me; and the life which I now live in the flesh I live by faith in the Son of God, who loved me and gave Himself for me.

Philippians 1:
21 For to me, to live is Christ, and to die is gain.
22 But if I live on in the flesh, this will mean fruit from my labor; yet what I shall choose I cannot tell.
23 For I hard pressed between the two, having a desire to depart and be with Christ, which is far better.

II Corinthians 5:
6 Therefore we are always confident, knowing that while we are at home in the body we are absent from the Lord.
7 For we walk by faith, not by sight.
8 We are confident, yes, well pleased rather to be absent from the body and to be present with the Lord.

Proverbs 18:
14 The spirit of a man will sustain him in sickness,
But who can bear a broken spirit ?

Sanctification

A.1-3 of the Spirit
A.4-6 by the Truth

I Corinthians 6:
17 But he who is joined to the Lord is one spirit with Him.
19 Or do you now know that your body is the temple of the Holy Spirit who is in you, whom you have from God, and you are not your own?

I Corinthians 3:
16 Do you not know that you are the temple of God and that the Spirit of God dwells in you?
17 If anyone defiles the temple of God, God will destroy him. For the temple of God is holy, which temple you are.
<see Temple Pg.8.B & 22.A.2-3>

Galatians 5:
24 And those who are Christ's have crucified the flesh with its passions and desires.
25 If we live in the Spirit, let us also walk in the Spirit.
26 Let us not become conceited, provoking one another, envying one another.

Ephesians 5:
8 For you were once darkness, but now you are light in the Lord. Walk as children of light
9 (for the fruit of the Spirit is in all goodness, righteousness, and truth),
10 proving what is acceptable to the Lord.
11 And have no fellowship with the unfruitful works of darkness, but rather expose them.

I John 4:
4 You are of God, little children, and have overcome them, because He who is in you is greater than he who is in the world.
5 They are of the world. Therefore they speak as of the world, and the world hears them.

John 17:
16 "They are not of the world,
just as I am not of the world.
17 "Sanctify them by Your truth.
Your word is truth.
18 "As You sent Me into the world,
I also have sent them into the world.
19 "And for their sakes I sanctify Myself, that
they also may be sanctified by the truth.
<see also Pg. 27.B.2c ref by angel to "Scripture of Truth">

From the World
(B. 4-7 the Evil of Riches)

John 15:
19 "If you were of the world, the world would love its own. Yet because you are not of the world, but I chose you out of the world, therefore the world hates you.

I John 2:
15 Do not love the world or the things in the world. If anyone loves the world, the love of the Father is not in him.
16 For all that is in the world – the lust of the flesh, the lust of the eyes, and the pride of life – is not of the Father but is of the world.

James 4:
4 Adulterers and adulteresses! Do you not know that friendship with the world is enmity with God? Whoever therefore wants to be a friend of the world makes himself an enemy of God.

I Timothy 6:
10 For the love of money is the root of all kinds of evil, for which some have strayed from the faith in their greediness, and pierced themselves through with many sorrows.
17 Command those who are rich in this present age not to be haughty, not to trust in uncertain riches but in the living God, who gives us richly all things to enjoy.

Matthew 6:
21 "For where your treasure is, there your heart will be also.
24 "No one can serve two masters; for either he will hate the one and love the other, or else he will be loyal to the one and despise the other. You cannot serve God and mammon."

Matthew 13:
22 "Now he who received seed among the thorns is he who hears the word, and the cares of this world and the deceitfulness of riches choke the word, and he becomes unfruitful."

Job 1:
21 "Naked I came from my mother's womb,
And naked shall I return there.
The LORD gave, and the LORD has taken away;
Blessed be the name of the LORD."

< See also Pg. 103.B >

A. Sanctification from the World of Unbelievers

I John 1:
4 And these things we write to you
that your joy may be full.

Romans 12:
1 I beseech you therefore, brethren, by the mercies of God, that you present your bodies a living sacrifice, holy, acceptable to God, which is your reasonable service.
2 And do not be conformed to this world, but be transformed by the renewing of your mind, that you may prove what is that good and acceptable and perfect will of God.

II Corinthians 6:
14 Do not be unequally yoked together with unbelievers. For what fellowship has righteousness with lawlessness? And what communion has light with darkness? !
15 And what accord has Christ with Belial? Or
what part has a believer with an unbeliever?
16 And what agreement has the temple of god with idols? For you are the temple of the living God. As God has said:

"I will dwell in them
And walk among them.
I will be their God,
And they shall be My people."

17 Therefore

"Come out from among them
And be separate, says the LORD,
Do not touch what is unclean,
And I will receive you."

18 "I will be a Father to you,
And you shall be My sons and daughters,
Says the LORD Almighty."

Matthew 7:
6 "Do not give what is holy to the dogs; nor cast your pearls before swine, lest they trample them under their feet, and turn and tear you in pieces.

B. 1-3 Christian Walk
B. 4-6 Warnings

Ephesians 4:
1 I, therefore, the prisoner of the Lord, beseech you to have a walk worthy of the calling with which you were called,
2 with all lowliness and gentleness, with longsuffering, bearing with one another in love,
3 endeavoring to keep the unity of the Spirit in the bond of peace.

Ephesians 5:
1 Therefore be followers of God as dear children.
2 And walk in love, as Christ also has loved us and given Himself for us, an offering and a sacrifice to God for a sweet-smelling aroma.

Colossians 4:
5 Walk in wisdom toward those who are outside, redeeming the time.
6 Let your speech always be with grace, seasoned with salt, that you may know how you ought to answer each one.

Colossians 2:
8 Beware lest anyone cheat you through philosophy and empty deceit, according to the tradition of men, according to the basic principles of the world, and not according to Christ.

II Timothy 2:
23 But avoid foolish and ignorant disputes, knowing that they generate strife. !
24 And a servant of the Lord must not quarrel but be gentle to all, able to teach, patient,
25 in humility correcting those who are in opposition, if God perhaps will grant them repentance, so that they may know the truth,
26 and that they may come to their senses and escape the snare of the devil, having been taken captive by him to do his will.

II John:
9 Whoever transgresses and does not abide in the doctrine of Christ does not have God. He who abides in the doctrine of Christ has both the Father and the Son.
10 If anyone comes to you and does not bring this doctrine, do not receive him into your house nor greet him; !
11 for he who greets him shares in his evil deeds.

A. Christian Walk (Lifestyle)

<see also Pg. 94 & Pg. 87.A.>

Ephesians 5:
15 See then that you walk circumspectly, not as
fools but as wise,
16 redeeming the time, because the days are evil.
17 Therefore do not be unwise, but understand
what the will of the Lord is.
18 And do not be drunk with wine, in which is
dissipation; but be filled with the Spirit,
19 speaking to one another in psalms and hymns
and spiritual songs, singing and making melody in
your heart to the Lord,
20 giving thanks always for all things to God the
Father in the name of our Lord Jesus Christ,
21 submitting to one another in the fear of God.

Titus 2:
6 Likewise exhort the young men to be soberminded,
7 in all things showing yourself to be a pattern of
good works; in doctrine showing integrity,
reverence, incorruptibility,
8 sound speech that cannot be condemned, that one
who is an opponent may be ashamed, having nothing
evil to say of you.

II Peter 1:
5 But also for this very reason, giving all diligence,
add to your faith virtue, to virtue knowledge,
6 to knowledge self control, to self-control
perseverance, to perseverance godliness,
7 to godliness brotherly kindness, and to brotherly
kindness love.
8 For if these things are yours and abound, you will
be neither barren nor unfruitful in the knowledge
of our Lord Jesus Christ.
9 For he who lacks these things is short-sighted, even
to blindness, and has forgotten that he was purged
from his old sins.

James 1:
27 Pure and undefiled religion before God and the
Father is this: to visit orphans and widows in their
trouble, and to keep oneself unspotted from the
world.

Philippians 2:
13 for it is God who works in you both to will
and to do for *His* good pleasure.
14 Do all things without complaining and disputing.
15 that you may be become blameless and harmless
children of God without fault in the midst of a
crooked and perverse generation, among whom you
shine as lights in the world,
16 holding fast the word of life, so that I may
rejoice in the day of Christ that I have not run in
vain or labored in vain.

B. Love

<see also Pg. 79.B.s & Pg. 107.A.1>

I Corinthians 13:
13 And now abide faith, hope, love, these
three; but the greatest of these is love.

4 Love suffers long and is kind; love does not
envy; love does not parade itself, is not puffed
up;
5 does not behave rudely, does not seek its own,
is not provoked, thinks no evil;
6 does not rejoice in iniquity, but rejoices in the
truth;
7 bears all things, believes all things, hopes all
things, endures all things.

I John 5:
1 Whoever believes that Jesus is the Christ is
born of God, and everyone who loves Him
who begot also loves him who is begotten of
Him.
2 By this we know that we love the children
of God, when we love God and keep His
commandments.
3 For this is the love of God, that we keep His
commandments. And His commandments are
not burdensome.
4 For whatever is born of God overcomes the
world. And this is the victory that has
overcome the world – our faith.
5 Who is he who overcomes the world, but he
who believes that Jesus is the Son of God?

I John 3:
13 Do not marvel, my brethren, if the world
hates you.
14 We know that we have passed from death to
life, because we love the brethren. He who
does not love his brother abides in death.
15 Whoever hates his brother is a murderer,
and you know that no murderer has eternal
life abiding in him.

I Corinthians 13:
1 Though I speak with the tongues of men and
of angels, but have not love, I have become
as sounding brass or a clanging cymbal.
2 And though I have the gift of prophecy, and
understand all mysteries and all knowledge,
and though I have all faith, so that I could
remove mountains, but have not love, I am
nothing.

Matthew 5:
46 "For if you love those who love
you, what reward have you? Do not
even the tax collectors do the same?

Warnings Against Sin

(Sins that Christians commit.) (Yes, Christians do sin.)

<See also Pg. 20.A.5 & Pg. 86.B.>

Proverbs 28:

13 He who covers his sins will not prosper,
But whoever confesses and forsakes them will have mercy.

Ephesians 4:

30 And do not grieve the Holy Spirit of God, by whom you were sealed for the day of redemption. !!
31 Let all bitterness, wrath, anger, clamor, and evil speaking be put away from you, with all malice.
32 And be kind to one another, tender-hearted, forgiving one another, just as God in Christ also forgave you.

Ephesians 4:

29 Let no corrupt communication proceed out of your mouth, but what is good for necessary edification, that it may impart grace to the hearers.

James 1:

19 Therefore, my beloved brethren, let every man be swift to hear, slow to speak, slow to wrath;
20 for the wrath of man does not produce the righteousness of God.

Psalm 37:

8 Cease from anger, and forsake wrath;
Do not fret – it only causes harm.

Ephesians 6:

26 "Be angry, and do not sin": do not let the sun go down on your wrath,
27 nor give place to the devil.

Colossians 3:

8 But now you must also put off all these: anger, wrath, malice, blasphemy, filthy language out of your mouth.
9 Do not lie to one another, since you have put off the old man with his deeds.

I John 1:

5 This is the message which we have heard from Him and declare to you, that God is light and in Him is no darkness at all.
6 If we say that we have fellowship with Him, and walk in darkness, we lie and do not practice the truth.

James 1:

26 If anyone among you thinks he is religious, and does not bridle his tongue but deceives his own heart, this one's religion is useless.

Galatians 5:

19 Now the works of the flesh are evident, which are: adultery, fornication, uncleanness, licentiousness,
20 idolatry, sorcery, hatred, contentions, jealousies, outbursts of wrath, selfish ambitions, dissensions, heresies,
21 envy, murders, drunkenness, revelries, and the like; of which I tell you beforehand, just as I also told you in time past, that those who practice such things will not inherit the kingdom of God.

Ephesians 5:

3 But fornication and all uncleanness or covetousness, let it not even be named among you, as is fitting for saints;
4 neither filthiness, nor foolish talking, nor coarse jesting, which are not fitting, but rather giving of thanks.
5 For this you know, that no fornicator, unclean person, nor covetous man, who is an idolater, has any inheritance in the kingdom of Christ and God.
6 Let no one deceive you with empty words, for because of these things the wrath of God comes upon the sons of disobedience.
7 Therefore do not be partakers with them.

I Corinthians 6:

15 Do you not know that your bodies are members of Christ? Shall I then take the members of Christ and make them members of a harlot? Certainly not!
16 Or do you not know that he who is joined to a harlot is one body with her? For "The two," He says, "shall become one flesh."

Ephesians 5:

12 For it is shameful even to speak of those things which are done by them in secret.
13 But all things that are exposed are made manifest by the light, for whatever makes manifest is light.
14 Therefore He says:
"Awake, you who sleep,
Arise from the dead,
And Christ will give you light."

A. 1-3 Positive Commands

A. 3-4 Confession

(Purging the Conscience)

<see also Pg. 91.A.1;
Pg. 101.A.7; Pg 100.A.1 >!

I Peter 5: *(Do Not Worry!)*
7 casting all your care upon Him, for He cares for you. !

I Thessalonians 5:
16 Rejoice always,
17 Pray without ceasing,
18 in everything give thanks; for this is the will of God in Christ Jesus for you.
19 Do not quench the Spirit.
20 Do not despise prophecies.
21 Test all things; hold fast what is good.
22 Abstain from every form of evil.

I John 1:
7 But if we walk in the light as He is in the light, we have fellowship with one another, and the blood of Jesus Christ His Son cleanses us from all sin.
8 If we say that we have no sin, we deceive ourselves, and the truth is not in us.
9 If we confess our sins, He is faithful and just to forgive us our sins and to cleanse us from all unrighteousness.
10 If we say that we have not sinned, we make Him a liar, and His word in not in us.

I Corinthians 11: (Of "Lord's Supper")
27 Therefore whoever eats this bread or drinks this cup of the Lord in an unworthy manner will be guilty of the body and blood of the Lord.
28 But let a man examine himself, and so let him eat of that bread and drink of that cup.
29 For he who eats and drinks in an unworthy manner eats and drinks judgment to himself, not discerning the Lord's body.
30 For this reason many are weak and sick among you, and many sleep.
31 For if we would judge ourselves, we would not be judged.
32 But when we are judged, we are chastened by the Lord, that we may not be condemned with the world. !

A.4 – B.4

Chastisement

<see also Pg. 123; Pg 78.A.4>

Proverbs 3:
11 My son, do not despise the chastening of the Lord,
Nor detest His correction;
12 For whom the Lord loves He corrects,
Just as a father the son in whom he delights.

Revelation 3:
19 "As many as I love, I rebuke and chasten. Therefore be zealous and repent."

Deuteronomy 8:
5 "So you should know in your heart that as a man chastens his son, so the LORD your God chastens you."

Job 5:
17 "Behold, happy is the man whom God corrects;
Therefore do not despise the chastening of the Almighty."

Hebrews 12:
5 And you have forgotten the exhortation which speaks to you as to sons:
"My son, do not despise the chastening of the LORD,
Nor be discouraged when you are rebuked by Him;
6 For whom the LORD loves He chastens,
And scourges every son whom He receives."
7 If you endure chastening, God deals with you as with sons; for what son is there whom a father does not chasten?
8 But if you are without chastening, of which all have become partakers, then you are illegitimate and not sons. !
9 Furthermore, we have had human fathers who corrected us, and we paid them respect. Shall we not much more readily be in subjection to the Father of spirits and live?
10 For they indeed for a few days chastened us as seemed best to them, but He for our profit, that we may be partakers of His holiness.
11 Now no chastening seems to be joyful for the present, but grievous; nevertheless, afterward it yields the peaceable fruit of righteousness to those who have been trained by it.

Trials and Temptations of Believers

II Timothy 3:
12 Yes, and all who desire to live godly in Christ Jesus will suffer persecution.

Lamentations 3:
23b Great is Your faithfulness.
24 "The LORD is my portion," says my soul,
"Therefore I hop in Him!"
25 The LORD is good to those who wait for Him,
To the soul who seeks Him.
26 It is good that one should hope and wait quietly
For the salvation of the LORD.
27 It is good for a man to bear
The yoke in his youth.
28 Let him sit alone and keep silent,
Because God has laid it on him.

James 1:
2 My brethren, count it all joy when you fall into various trials,
3 knowing that the testing of your faith produces patience.
4 But let patience have its perfect work, that you may be perfect and complete, lacking nothing.

I Peter 1:
6 In this you greatly rejoice, though now for a little while, if need by, you have been grieved by various trials,
7 that the genuineness of your faith, being much more precious than gold that perishes, though it is tested by fire, may be found to praise, honor, and glory at the revelation of Jesus Christ.

I Peter 2:
19 For this is commendable, if because of conscience toward God one endures grief, suffering wrongfully.
20 For what credit is it if, when you are beaten for your faults, you take it patiently? But when you do good and suffer for it, if you take it patiently, this is commendable before God.
21 For to this you were called, because Christ also suffered for us, leaving us an example, that you should follow His steps. !

<see also Pg. 106.B.3-4>

Philippians 4:
13 <u>I can do all things through Christ who strengthens me.</u> !

Ephesians 6:
10 Finally, my brethren, be strong in the Lord and in the power of His might.
11 Put on the whole armor of God, that you may be able to stand against the wiles of the devil.

I Corinthians 10:
13 No temptation has overtaken you except such as is common to man; but God is faithful, who will not allow you to be tempted beyond what you are able, but with the temptation will also make the way of escape, that you may be able to bear it.
14 Therefore, my beloved, flee from idolatry.
15 I speak as to wise men; judge for yourselves what I say.

James 1:
12 Blessed is the man who endures temptation; for when he has been proved, he will receive the crown of life which the Lord has promised to those who love Him.
13 Let no one say when he is tempted, "I am tempted by God"; for God cannot be tempted by evil, nor does He Himself tempt anyone.
14 But each one is tempted when he is drawn away by his own desires and enticed.
15 Then, when desire has conceived, it gives birth to sin; and sin, when it is full-grown, brings forth death.
16 Do not be deceived, my beloved brethren.

Matthew 10:
33 "But whoever denies Me before men, him I will also deny before My Father who is in heaven.
34 "Do not think that I came to bring peace on earth, I did not come to bring peace but a sword.
35 "For I have come to 'set a man against his father, a daughter against her mother, and a daughter-in-law against her mother-in-law.'
36 "And 'a man's foes will be those of his own household.'"

I Peter 4:
13 but rejoice to the extent that you partake of Christ's sufferings, that when His glory is revealed, you may also be glad with exceeding joy.

Spiritual Growth

<See Pg. 89-90
& Pg. 50.B.1 (I Cor. 14:20) >

I Corinthians 2:

6 However, we speak wisdom among those who are mature, yet not the wisdom of this age, nor of the rulers of this age, who are coming to nothing.

7 But we speak the wisdom of God in a mystery, the hidden wisdom which God ordained before the ages for our glory,

8 which none of the rulers of this age knew; for had they known, they would not have crucified the Lord of glory.

Hebrews 5:

11 of whom we have much to say, and hard to explain, since you have become dull of hearing.

12 For though by this time you ought to be teachers, you need someone to teach you again the first principles of the oracles of God; and you have come to need milk and not solid food.

13 For everyone who partakes only of milk is unskilled in the word of righteousness, for he is a babe.

14 But solid food belongs to those who are of full age, that is, those who by reason of use have their senses exercised to discern both good and evil. !

Hebrews 6:

1 Therefore, leaving the discussion of the elementary principles of Christ, let us go on to perfection, not laying again the foundation of repentance from dead works and of faith toward God,

2 of the doctrine of baptisms, of laying on of hands, of resurrection of the dead, and of eternal judgment.

I Corinthians 2:

14 But the natural man does not receive the things of the Spirit of God, for they are foolishness to him; nor can he know them, because they are spiritually discerned. !

15 But he who is spiritual judges all things, yet he himself is rightly judged by no one.

16 For "Who has known the mind of the Lord that he may instruct Him?" But we have the mind of Christ.

James 3:

13 Who is wise and understanding among you? Let him show by good conduct that his works are done in the meekness of wisdom.

17 But the wisdom that is from above is first pure, then peaceable, gentle, willing to yield, full of mercy and good fruits, without partiality and without hypocrisy.

II Timothy 2:

19 Nevertheless the solid foundation of God stands, having this seal: "The Lord knows those who are His," and, "Let everyone who names the name of Christ depart from iniquity."

20 But in a great house there are not only vessels of gold and silver, but also of wood and clay, some for honor and some for dishonor.

21 Therefore if anyone cleanses himself from the latter, he will be a vessel for honor, sanctified and useful for the Master, prepared for every good work.

I Corinthians 9:

27 But I discipline my body and bring it into subjection, lest, when I have preached to others, I myself should become disqualified.

Acts 24:

25 Now as he reasoned about righteousness, self-control, and the judgment to come, Felix was afraid and answered, "Go away for now; when I have a convenient time I will call for you."

I John 2:

12 I write to you, little children,
Because your sins are forgiven you for His name's sake.
13 I write to you, fathers,
Because you have known Him who is from the beginning.
I write to you, young men,
Because you have overcome the wicked one.
I write to you, little children,
Because you have known the Father.
14 I have written to you, fathers,
Because you have known Him who is from the beginning.
I have written to you, young men,
Because you are strong, and the word of God abides in you.

The "Word" (Food for Spiritual Growth)

< Tie to Pg. 94.A.96-4 >

Psalm 138:
2d For You have magnified Your word above all
Your name.

I Corinthians 3:
1 And I, brethren, could not speak to you as to
spiritual people but as to carnal, as to babes in
Christ.
2 I fed you with milk and not with solid food;
for until now you were not able to receive it, and
even now you are still not able.

I Peter 2:
2 as newborn babes, desire the pure milk of the
word, that you may grow thereby,
3 if indeed you have tasted that the Lord is
gracious.

II Timothy 3:
14 But as for you, continue in the things which
you have learned and been assured of, knowing
from whom you have learned them,
15 and that from childhood you have known the
Holy Scriptures, which are able to make you
wise for salvation through faith which is in
Christ Jesus.
16 All Scripture is given by inspiration !
of God, and is profitable for doctrine,
for reproof, for correction, for
instruction in righteousness,
17 that the man of God may be complete,
thoroughly equipped for every good work.

Isaiah 55:
10 "For as the rain comes down and the snow
from heaven,
And do not return there,
But water the earth,
And make it bring forth and bud,
That it may give seed to the sower
And bread to the eater,
11 So shall My word be that goes forth from
My mouth;
It shall not return to Me void,
But it shall accomplish what I please,
And it shall prosper in the thing for which
I sent it.

Matthew 5:
18 For assuredly, I say to you, till heaven and
earth pass away, one jot or one tittle will by no
means pass from the law till all is fulfilled.

II Timothy 2:
15 Be diligent to present yourself approved to God,
a worker who does not need to be ashamed,
rightly dividing the word of truth.
14 Remind them of these things, charging them
before the Lord not to strive about words to no
profit, to the ruin of their hearers.

I Corinthians 4:
20 For the kingdom of God is not in word but in
power.
21 What do you want? Shall I come to you with a
rod, or in love and a spirit of gentleness?

Concerning Inspiration:

II Peter 1:
20 knowing this first, that no prophecy of Scripture
is of any private interpretation,
21 for prophecy never came by the will of man, but
holy men of God spoke as they were moved by the
Holy Spirit.

Romans 15:
4 For whatever things were written before
were written for our learning, that we through
the patience and comfort of the Scriptures
might have hope.

Ephesians 3:
3 ...by revelation He made known to me the
mystery (as I have briefly written already,
4 by which, when you read, you may understand
my knowledge in the mystery of Christ),
5 which in other ages was not made known to the
sons of men, as it has now been revealed by the
Spirit to His holy apostles and prophets.

I Corinthians 10:
11 Now all these things happened to them !
as examples, and they were written for our
admonition, on whom the ends of the
ages have come.

Proverbs 30:
5 Every word of God *is* pure;
He *is* a shield to those who put their trust in Him.
6 Do not add to His words,
Lest He rebuke you, and you be found a liar.

II Samuel 7:
21 "For Your word's sake, and according to Your
own heart, You have done all these great things,
to make Your servant know them."

The "Word" (continued)
("The Sword of the Spirit")

<See Pg. 104.A.1.>

Hebrews 4:

12 For the word of God is living and powerful, and sharper than any two-edged sword, piercing even to the division of soul and spirit, and of joints and marrow, and is a discerner of the thoughts and intents of the heart. !

Psalm 119:

105 Your word is a lamp to my feet
And a light to my path.

Isaiah 8:

20 To the law and to the testimony! If they do not speak according to this word, it is because there is no light in them.

Deuteronomy 8:

3 "So He humbled you, allowed you to hunger, and fed you with manna which you did not know nor did your fathers know, that He might make you know that man shall not live by bread alone; but man lives by every word that proceeds from the mouth of the LORD."

Isaiah 59:

21 "As for Me," says the LORD, "this is My covenant with them: My Spirit who is upon you, and My words which I have put in your mouth, shall not depart from your mouth, nor from the mouth of your descendants, nor from the mouth of your descendants' descendants," says the LORD, "from this time and forevermore."

Revelation 22:

18 For I testify to everyone who hears the words of the prophecy of this book: If anyone adds to these things, God will add to him the plagues that are written in this book;
19 and if anyone takes away from the words of the book of this prophecy, God shall take away his part from the Book of Life, from the holy city, and from the things which are written in this book.

II Timothy 2:

2 And the things that you have heard from me among many witnesses, commit these to faithful men who will be able to teach others also.

7 Consider what I say, and may the Lord give you understanding in all things.

Zechariah 7:

12 "Yes, they made their hearts like flint, refusing to hear the law and the words which the LORD of hosts had sent by His Spirit through the former prophets. Thus great wrath came from the LORD of hosts.

I John 1:

26 But the anointing which you have received from Him abides in you, and you have no need that anyone teach you; but as the same anointing teaches you concerning all things, and is true, and is not a lie, and just as it has taught you, you will abide in Him.

Deuteronomy 6:

6 "And these words which I command you today shall be in your heart:
7 "you shall teach them diligently to your children, and shall talk of them when you sit in your house, when you walk by the way, when you lie down, and when you rise up.
8 "You shall bind them as a sign on your hand, and they shall be as frontlets between your eyes.
9 "You shall write them on the doorposts of your house and on your gates."

II Samuel 23:

1 Now these are the last words of David.
Thus says David the son of Jesse;
Thus says the man raised up on high,
The anointed of the God of Jacob,
And the sweet psalmist of Israel:
2 "The Spirit of the LORD spoke by me,
And his word was on my tongue."

Romans 16:

25 Now to Him who is able to establish you according to my gospel and the preaching of Jesus Christ, according to the revelation of the mystery which was kept secret since the world began
26 but now has been made manifest, and by the prophetic Scriptures has been made known to all nations, according to the commandment of the everlasting God, for obedience to the faith. !

Proverbs 18:

15 The heart of the prudent acquires knowledge,
And the ear of the wise seeks knowledge.

The "Word" (continued) Exhortations

Colossians 3:

16 Let the word of Christ dwell in you richly in all wisdom,
teaching and admonishing one another
in psalms and hymns and spiritual songs,
singing with grace in your hearts to the Lord.

Colossians 2:

2 that their hearts may be encouraged, being knit together in love, and *attaining* to all riches of the full assurance of understanding, to the knowledge of the mystery of God, both of the Father and of Christ, in whom are hidden all the treasures of wisdom and knowledge.

II Corinthians 10:

4 For the weapons of our warfare are not carnal but mighty in God for pulling down strong-holds,
5 casting down arguments and every high thing that exalts itself against the knowledge of God, bringing every thought into captivity to the obedience of Christ.

Titus 1:

9 holding fast the faithful word as he has been taught, that he may be able, by sound doctrine, both to exhort and convict those who contradict.

I Timothy 4:

12 Let no one despise your youth, but be an example to the believers in word, in conduct, in love, in spirit, in faith, in purity.
13 Till I come, give attention to reading, to exhortation, to doctrine.
14 Do not neglect the gift that is in you, which was given to you by prophecy with the laying on of the hands of the presbytery.
15 Meditate on these things; give yourself entirely to them, that your progress may be evident to all.
16 Take heed to yourself and to the doctrine. Continue in them, for in doing this you will save both yourself and those who hear you.

John 8:

31 Then Jesus said to those Jews who believed Him, "If you abide in My word, you are My disciples indeed.
32 And you shall know the truth,
and the truth shall make you free."

II Timothy 4:

2 Preach the word! Be ready in season and out of season. Convince, rebuke, exhort, with all longsuffering and teaching.
3 For the time will come when they will not endure sound doctrine, but according to their own desires, because they have itching ears, they will heap up for themselves teachers;
4 and they will turn their ears away from the truth, and be turned aside to fables.

I Timothy 6:

3 If anyone teaches otherwise and does not consent to wholesome words, even the words of our Lord Jesus Christ, and to the doctrine which is according to godliness,
4 he is proud, knowing nothing, but is obsessed with disputes and arguments over words, from which come envy, strife, reviling, evil suspicions,
5 useless wranglings of men of corrupt minds and destitute of the truth, who suppose that godliness is a means of gain. From such withdraw yourself.

I Timothy 4:

6 If you instruct the brethren in these things, you will be a good minister of Jesus Christ, nourished in the words of faith and of the good doctrine which you have carefully followed.
7 But reject profane and old wives' fables, and exercise yourself rather to godliness.

Prophecy Concerning Divine Revelation

Amos 8:

11 "Behold the days are coming," says the LORD God,
"That I will send famine on the land,
Not a famine of bread,
Nor a thirst for water,
But of hearing the words of the LORD.
12 They shall wander from sea to sea,
And from north to east;
They shall run to and fro,
seeking the word of the LORD,
But shall not find it."

The "Word"
(The Realm of Wisdom)

<See Pg. 94.A.4>

Ecclesiastes 7:

16 Do not be overly righteous,
Nor be overly wise:
Why should you destroy yourself?

Galatians 1:

6 I marvel that you are turning away so soon from Him who called you in the grace of Christ, to a different gospel,
7 which is not another; but there are some who trouble you and want to pervert the gospel of Christ.
8 But even if we, or an angel from heaven, preach any other gospel to you than what we have preached to you, let him be accursed.
9 As we have said before, so now I say again, if anyone preaches any other gospel to you than what you have received, let him be accursed.

II Corinthians 4:

2 But we have renounced the hidden things of shame, not walking craftiness nor handling the word of God deceitfully, but by manifestation of the truth commending ourselves to every man's conscience in the sight of God.

I John 2:

1 But there were also false prophets among the people, even as there will be false teachers among you, who will secretly bring in destructive heresies, even denying the Lord who brought them, and bring on themselves swift destruction.
2 And many will follow their destructive ways, because of whom the way of truth will be blasphemed.

I Corinthians 4:

6 Now these things, brethren, I have figuratively transferred to myself and Apollos for your sakes, that you may learn in us not to think beyond what is written, that none of you may be puffed up on behalf of one against the other.
7 For who makes you differ from another? And what do you have that you did not receive? Now if you did indeed receive it, why do you glory as if you had not received it?

Psalm 131:

1 LORD, my heart is not haughty,
Nor my eyes lofty.
Neither do I concern myself with great matters,
Nor with things too profound for me.

<See also Pg. 105.B.1; Pg. 76B.1; Pg 46.B.1:20 and Pg. 106.A.3>

Psalm 19:

7 The law of the LORD is perfect, converting the soul;
The testimony of the LORD is sure, making wise the simple.

Psalm 111:

10 The fear of the LORD is the beginning of wisdom.

I Corinthians 1:

26 For you see your calling, brethren, that not many wise according to the flesh, not many mighty, not many noble, are called.

Ephesians 3:

17 that Christ may dwell in your hearts through faith; that you, being rooted and grounded in love,
18 may be able to comprehend with all the saints what is the width and length and depth and height -
19 to know the love of Christ which passes knowledge; that you may be filled with all the fullness of God.

I Corinthians 8:

1 Knowledge puffs up, but love edifies.
2 And if anyone thinks that he knows anything, he knows nothing yet as he ought to know.
3 But if anyone loves God, this one is known by Him.

Psalm 1:

1 Blessed is the man
Who walks not in the counsel of the ungodly,
Nor stands in the path of sinners,
Nor sits in the seat of the scornful;
2 But his delight is in the law of the LORD,
And in His law he meditates day and night.

Colossians 1:

26 the mystery which has been hidden from ages and from generations, but now has been revealed to His saints.
27 To them God willed to make known what are the riches of the glory of this mystery among the Gentiles: which is Christ in you, the hope of glory.
28 Him we preach, warning every man and teaching every man in all wisdom, that we may present every man perfect in Christ Jesus.

Basics of Prayer
First Principle: Praise and Thanksgiving

Philippians 4:

4 Rejoice in the LORD always.
Again I will say, rejoice!
5 Let your gentleness be known to all men.
The LORD is at hand.
6 Be anxious for nothing,
but in everything by prayer
and supplication, with thanksgiving,
let your requests be made known to God;
7 and the peace of God,
which surpasses all understanding,
will guard your hearts and minds
through Christ Jesus.
8 Finally, brethren, whatever things are
true, whatever things are noble,
whatever things are just, whatever
things are pure, whatever things are
lovely, whatever things are of good
report, if there is any virtue and if
there is anything praiseworthy –
meditate on these things.

!

Psalm 150:

1 Praise the LORD!
Praise God in His sanctuary;
Praise Him in His mighty firmament!
2 Praise Him for His mighty acts;
Praise Him according to His excellent
greatness!
3 Praise Him with the sound of the trumpet;
Praise Him with the lute and harp!
4 Praise Him with the timbrel and dance;
Praise Him with stringed instruments and
flutes!
5 Praise Him with loud cymbals;
Praise Him with high sounding cymbals!
6 Let everything that has breath praise the LORD.
Praise the LORD!

Ecclesiastes 3:

12 I know that there is nothing better for them
than to rejoice, and to do good in their lives,
13 and also that every man should eat and
drink and enjoy the good of all his labor –
it is the gift of God.

Isaiah 38:

20 "The LORD *was ready* to save me;
Therefore we will sing my songs with
stringed instruments
All the days of our life, in the house of the
LORD."

Hebrews 13:

15 Therefore by Him let us continually offer the
sacrifice of praise to God, that is, the fruit of our
lips, giving thanks to His name.
16 But do not forget to do good and to share, for
with such sacrifices God is well pleased.

Hosea 11:

7 My people are bent on backsliding from Me.
Though they call to the Most High,
None at all exalt Him.

!

Psalm 8:

1 O LORD, our Lord,
How excellent is Your name in all the earth,
You who set Your glory above the heavens!
2 Out of the mouth of babes and infants
You have ordained strength,
Because of Your enemies,
That You may silence the enemy and the
avenger.
3 When I consider Your heavens,
the work of Your fingers,
The moon and the stars,
which You have ordained,
4 What is man that You are mindful of him,
And the son of man that You visit him?
5 For You have made him a little lower than the
angels,
And You have crowned him with glory and
honor.
6 You made him to have dominion over the
works of Your hands;
You have put all things under his feet,
7 All sheep and oxen –
Even the beasts of the field,
8 The birds of the air,
And the fish of the sea
That pass through the paths of the seas.
9 O LORD, our Lord,
How excellent is Your name in all the earth!

Psalm 63:

1 O God, You are my God;
Early I will seek you;
My soul thirsts for You;
My flesh longs for you
In a dry and thirsty land
Where there is no water.

Basics of Prayer (continued)

Psalm 51

A Prayer of Repentance

To the Chief Musician. A Psalm of David when Nathan the prophet went to him, after he had gone in to Bathsheba.

1 Have mercy upon me, O God,
According to Your loving-kindness;
According to the multitude of Your tender mercies,
Blot out my transgressions.
2 Wash me thoroughly from my iniquity,
And cleanse me from my sin.
3 For I acknowledge my transgressions,
And my sin is ever before me.
4 Against You, You only, have I sinned,
And done this evil in Your sight –
That You may be found just when You speak,
And blameless when You judge.
5 Behold, I was brought forth in iniquity,
And in sin my mother conceived me.

16 For You do not desire sacrifice, or else I would give it;
You do not delight in burnt offering.
17 The sacrifices of God are a broken spirit,
A broken and contrite heart –
These, O God, You will not despise.

Psalm 23:

1 The LORD is my shepherd; I shall not want.
2 He makes me to lie down in green pastures;
He leads me beside the still waters.
3 He restores my soul;
He leads me in the paths of righteousness
For His name's sake.
4 Yea, though I walk through the valley of the shadow of death,
I will fear no evil;
For You are with me;
Your rod and Your staff, they comfort me.
5 You prepare a table before me in the presence of my enemies;
You anoint my head with oil;
My cup runs over.
6 Surely goodness and mercy shall follow me
All the days of my life;
And I will dwell in the house of the LORD
Forever.

Isaiah 29:

6 With my soul I have desired You in the night,
Yes, by my spirit within me I will seek You early;

Psalm 103:

A Psalm of David

1 Bless the LORD, O my soul;
And all that is within me,
bless His holy name!
2 Bless the LORD, O my soul,
And forget not His benefits:
3 Who forgives all your iniquities,
Who heals all your diseases,
4 Who redeems your life from destruction,
Who crowns you with loving-kindness and tender mercies.

Psalm 33:

1 Rejoice in the LORD O you righteous!
For praise from the upright is beautiful.
2 Praise the LORD with the harp;
Make melody to Him with an instrument of ten strings.
3 Sing to Him a new song;
Play skillfully with a shout of joy.

Psalm 34:

A Psalm of David when he pretended madness before Abimelech, who drove him away, and he departed.

1 I will bless the LORD at all times;
His praise shall continually be in my mouth.
2 My soul shall make its boast in the LORD;
The humble shall hear of it and be glad.
3 O magnify the LORD with me,
And let us exalt His name together.

Psalm 136:

1 Oh, give thanks to the LORD, for He is good!
For His mercy endures forever.
2 Oh, give thanks to the God of gods!
For His mercy endures forever.
3 Oh, give thanks to the LORD of Lords!
For His mercy endures forever;
4 To Him who alone does great wonders,
For His mercy endures forever;
5 To Him who by wisdom made the heavens,
For His mercy endures forever;
6 To Him who laid out the earth above the waters,
For His mercy endures forever;
7 To Him who made great lights,
For His mercy endures forever -
8 The sun to rule by day,
For His mercy endures forever;
9 The moon and stars to rule by night,
For His mercy endures forever.

Instructions for Prayer

<See Pg. 92.A first and Pg. 99.A.1 and Correlate Pg. 22.A.3b & Pg. 88.A.1-2 & see Pg. 24.B.1>

Colossians 3:

17 And <u>whatever</u> you do in word or deed, <u>do all in the name of the Lord Jesus</u>, giving thanks to God the Father through Him.

Hebrews 4:

16 Let us therefore come boldly to the throne of grace, that we may obtain mercy and find grace to help in time of need.

I Timothy 2:

1 Therefore I exhort first of all that supplications, prayers, intercessions, and giving of thanks be made for all men,
2 for kings and all who are in authority, that we may lead a quiet and peaceable life in all godliness and reverence.

Ephesians 6:

18 praying always with all prayer and supplication in the Spirit, being watchful to this end with all perseverance and supplication for all the saints.

I Timothy 4:

4 For every creature of God is good, and nothing is to be refused if it is received with thanksgiving;
5 for it is sanctified by the word of God and prayer.

Psalm 63:

6 When I remember You on my bed,
I meditate on You in the night watches.

Psalm 32:

3 When I kept silent, my bones grew old
Through my groanings all the day long.
4 For day and night Your hand was heavy upon me.
5 I acknowledge my sin to You,
And my iniquity I have not hidden.
I said, "I will confess my transgressions to the LORD."
And You forgave the iniquity of my sin.
Selah
6 For this cause everyone who is godly shall pray to You
In a time when You may be found.

Matthew 6:

5 "And when you pray, you shall not be like the hypocrites. For they love to pray standing in the synagogues and on the corners of the streets, that they may be seen by men. Assuredly, I say to you, they have their reward. !
6 "But you, when you pray, go into your room, and when you have shut your door, pray to your Father who is in the secret place; and your Father who sees in secret will reward you openly.
7 "But when you pray, do not use vain repetitions as the heathen do. For they think that they will be heard for their many words.
8 "Therefore do not be like them. For your Father knows the things you have need of before you ask Him.

Psalm 22:

22 I will declare Your name to My brethren;
In the midst of the congregation I will praise You.

Psalm 77:

3 I remembered God, and was troubled;
I complained, and my spirit was overwhelmed.
Selah
4 You hold my eyelids open;
I am so troubled I cannot speak.
5 I have considered the days of old,
The years of ancient times.
6 I call to remembrance my song in the night;
I meditate within my heart,
And my spirit makes diligent search.

Matthew 6:

9 "In this manner, therefore, pray:
Our Father in heaven,
Hallowed by Your name.
10 Your kingdom come.
Your will be done
On earth as it is in heaven.
11 Give us this day our daily bread.
12 And forgive us our debts
As we forgive our debtors.
13 And do not lead us into temptation,
But deliver us from the evil one.
For Yours is the kingdom and the power and the glory forever. Amen.
14 "For if you forgive men their trespasses, your heavenly Father will also forgive you.

Prayer Principles

A.1-B.3 Fasting (defined)

Matthew 6:

16 "Moreover, when you fast, do not be like the hypocrites, with a sad countenance. For they disfigure their faces that they may appear to men to be fasting. Assuredly, I say to you, they have their reward.
17 "But you, when you fast, anoint your head and wash your face, 18 "so that you do not appear to men to be fasting, but to your Father who is in the secret place; and your Father who sees in secret will reward you openly."

Psalm 69:

When I wept and chastened my soul with fasting,
That became my reproach.

Ezra 8:

21 Then I proclaimed a fast there at the river of Ahava, that we might humble ourselves before our God, to seek from Him the right way for us and our little ones and all our possessions.

Psalm 35:

13 But as for me, when they were sick,
My clothing was sackcloth;
I humbled myself with fasting;
And my prayer would return to my own heart.

Isaiah 58:

3 'Why have we fasted,' they say,
'and You have not seen?
Why have we afflicted our souls,
and You take no notice?'
"In fact, in the day of your fast you find pleasure,
And exploit all your laborers.
Indeed you fast for strife and debate,
And to strike with the fist of wickedness.
You will not fast as you do this day,
To make your voice heard on high.
Is it a fast that I have chosen,
A day for a man to afflict his soul?
Is it to bow down his head like a bulrush,
And to spread out sackcloth and ashes?
Would you call this a fast,
And an acceptable day to the LORD?

B.4, 5 Misc. Public Prayer

Isaiah 58: cont.

6 "Is this not the fast that I have chosen:
To loose the bonds of wickedness,
To undo the heavy burdens,
To let the oppressed go free.
And that you break every yoke?
7 Is it not to share your bread with the hungry,
And that you bring to your house the poor who are cast out;
When you see the naked, that you cover him,
And not hide yourself from your own flesh?
8 Then your light shall break forth like the morning,
Your healing shall spring forth speedily,
And your righteousness shall go before you.

Acts 14:

22 strengthening the souls of the disciples, exhorting them to continue in the faith, and saying, "We must through many tribulations enter the kingdom of God."
23 So when they had anointed elders in every church, and prayed with fasting, they commended them to the Lord in whom they had believed.

II Samuel 12:

22 So he said, "While the child was still alive, I fasted and wept; for I said, 'Who can tell whether the LORD will be gracious to me, that the child may live?'
23 "But now he is dead; why should I fast? Can I bring him back again? I shall go to him, but he shall not return to me."

Ezra 10:

1 Now while Ezra was praying, and while he was confessing, weeping, and bowing down before the house of God, a very large congregation of men, women, and children assembled to him from Israel; for the people wept very bitterly.

I Corinthians 14:

16 Otherwise, if you bless with the spirit, how will he who occupies the place of the uninformed say "Amen" at your giving of thanks, since he does not understand what you say?

<see also Pg. 43.B.3>

Prayer Principles Cont. - Principles of Asking for Worldly Things

< Think: What Requests are truly "in His name"?>

James 4:

2 You lust and do not have.
You murder and covet and cannot obtain.
You fight and war.
Yet you do not have because you do not ask.
3 You ask and do not receive, because you ask amiss, that you may spend it on your pleasures.

Romans 8:

26 Likewise the Spirit also helps in our weaknesses. For we do not know what we should pray for as we ought, but the Spirit Himself makes intercession for us with groanings which cannot be uttered.
27 Now He who searches the hearts knows what the mind of the Spirit is, because He makes intercession for the saints according to the will of God.

Luke 11:

9 "And I say to you, ask, and it will be given to you; seek, and you will find; knock, and it will be opened to you.
10 "For everyone who asks receives, and he who seeks finds, and to him who knocks it will be opened.
11 "If a son asks for bread from any father among you, will he give him a stone? Or if he asks for a fish, will he give him a serpent instead of a fish?
12 "Or if he asks for an egg, will he offer him a scorpion?
13 "If you then, being evil, know how to give good gifts to your children, how much more will your heavenly Father give the Holy Spirit to those who ask Him!"

Matthew 7:

7 "Ask, and it will be given to you; seek, and you will find; knock, and it will be opened to you."

I Timothy 2:

8 Therefore I desire that the men pray everywhere, lifting up holy hands, without wrath and doubting;
9 in like manner also, that the women adorn themselves in modest apparel, with propriety and moderation, not with braided hair or gold or pearls or costly clothing,
10 but, which is proper for women professing godliness, with good works.

Hebrews 13:

5 Let your conduct be without covetousness, and be content with such things as you have. For He Himself has said, "I will never leave you nor forsake you."

Matthew 6:

31 "Therefore do not worry, saying, 'What shall we eat?' or 'What shall we drink?' or 'What shall we wear?'
32 "For after all these things the Gentiles seek. For your heavenly Father knows that you need all these things.
33 "But seek first the kingdom of God and His righteousness, and all these things shall be added to you.
34 "Therefore do not worry about tomorrow, for tomorrow will worry about its own things. Sufficient for the day is its own trouble.

Luke 18:

1 Then He spoke a parable to them that men
always ought to pray and not lose heart, 2 saying,
"There was in a certain city a judge who did not fear God nor regard man.
3 "Now there was a widow in that city; and she came to him, saying, 'Avenge me of my adversary.'
4 "And he would not for a while; but afterward he said within himself, 'Though I do not fear God nor regard man,
5 'yet because this widow troubles me I will avenge her, lest by her continual coming she weary me.' "
6 Then the Lord said, "Hear what the unjust judge said.
7 "And shall God not avenge His own elect who cry out day and night to Him, though He bears long with them?
8 "I tell you that He will avenge them speedily. Nevertheless, when the Son of Man comes, will He really find faith on earth?"

I Timothy 6:

6 But godliness with contentment is great gain.
7 For we brought nothing into this world, and it is certain we can carry nothing out.
8 And having food and clothing, with these we shall be content.
9 But those who desire to be rich fall into temptation and a snare, and into many foolish and harmful lusts which drown men in destruction and perdition.

Philippians 4:

11 Not that I speak in regard to need, for I have learned in whatever state I am, to be content:
12 I know how to be abased, and I know how to abound.

Prayer Principles Continued
(Faith and In Name) *<See Pg. 26.A.1. *Note>*

< See Pg. 77A.1. & Pg. 84.B.1>

Romans 10:

17 So then faith comes by hearing,
and hearing by the word of God.

Hebrews 11:

1 Now faith is the substance of things hoped for,
the evidence of things not seen.

2 For by it the elders obtained a good testimony.

6 But without faith it is impossible to please Him, for he who comes to God must believe that He is, and that He is a rewarder of those who diligently seek Him.

John 15:

7 "If you abide in Me, and My words abide in you, you will ask what you desire, and it shall be done for you.

8 "By this My Father is glorified, that you bear much fruit; so you will be My disciples.

John 14:

12 "Most assuredly, I say to you, he who believes in Me, the works that I do he will do also; and greater works than these he will do, because I go to My Father.

13 "And whatever you ask in My name, that I will do, that the Father may be glorified in the Son.

14 "If you ask anything in My name, I will do it."

Matthew 18:

17 "And if he refuses to hear them, tell it to the church. But if he refuses even to hear the church, let him be to you like a heathen and a tax collector.

18 "Assuredly, I say to you, whatever you bind on earth will be bound in heaven, and whatever you loose on earth will be loosed in heaven.

19 "Again I say to you that if two of you agree on earth concerning anything that they ask, it will be done for them by My Father in heaven.

20 "For where two or three are gathered together in My name, I am there in the midst of them."

Ephesians 3:

20 Now to Him who is able to do exceedingly abundantly above all that we ask or think, according to the power that works in us,

Mark 5:

30 And Jesus, immediately knowing in Himself that power had gone out of Him, turned around in the crowd and said, "Who touched My clothes?"

34 And He said to her, "Daughter, your faith has made you well. Go in peace, and be healed of your affliction."

Matthew 17:

16 "So I brought him to Your disciples, but they could not cure him."

17 Then Jesus answered and said, "O faithless and perverse generation, how long shall I be with you? How long shall I bear with you? Bring him here to Me."

18 And Jesus rebuked the demon, and he came out of him; and the child was cured from that very hour.

19 Then the disciples came to Jesus privately and said, "Why could we not cast him out?"

20 So Jesus said to them, "Because of your unbelief; for assuredly, I say to you, if you have faith as a mustard seed, you will say to this mountain, 'Move from here to there,' and it will move; and nothing will be impossible for you.

21 "However, this kind does not go out except by prayer and fasting."

Matthew 21:

21 So Jesus answered and said to them, "Assuredly, I say to you, if you have faith and do not doubt, you will not only do what was done to the fig tree, but also if you say to this mountain, 'Be removed and be cast into the sea,' it will be done.

22 "And all things, whatever you ask in prayer, believing, you will receive."

Mark 6:

4 But Jesus said to them, "A prophet is not without honor except in his own country, among his own relatives, and in his own house."

5 Now He could do no mighty work there, except that He laid His hands on a few sick people and healed them.

6 And He marveled because of their unbelief. Then He went about the villages in a circuit, teaching.

7 And He called the twelve to Him, and began to send them out two by two, and gave them power over unclean spirits.

Prayer Principles Continued - Behind the Scenes: Requirements for Answers to Prayer

Mark 9:

23 Jesus said to him, "If you can believe, all things are possible to him who believes."
24 Immediately the father of the child cried out and said with tears, "Lord, I believe; help my unbelief!"

I John 3:

22 And whatever we ask we receive from Him, because we keep His commandments and do those things that are pleasing in His sight.
23 And this is His commandment; that we should believe on the name of His Son Jesus Christ and love one another, as He gave us commandment.

I John 2:

3 Now by this we know that we know Him, if we keep His commandments.
4 He who says, "I know Him," and does not keep His commandments, is a liar, and the truth is not in him.
5 But whoever keeps His word, truly the love of God is perfected in him. By this we know that we are in Him.
6 He who says he abides in Him ought himself also to walk just as He walked.

I John 3:

16 By this we know love, because He laid down His life for us. And we also ought to lay down our lives for the brethren.
17 But whoever has this world's goods, and sees his brother in need, and shuts up his heart from him, how does the love of God abide in him?

John 15:

12 "This is My commandment,
that you love one another
as I have loved you.
13 Greater love has no one than this,
than to lay down one's life for his friends.

!

Exodus 15:

26 and said, "If you diligently heed the voice of the LORD your God and do what is right in His sight, give ear to His commandments and keep all His statutes, I will put none of these diseases on you which I have brought on the Egyptians. For I am the LORD who heals you."

Romans 12:

3 For I say, through the grace given to me, to everyone who is among you, not to think of himself more highly than he ought to think, but to think soberly, as God has dealt to each one a measure of faith.

Mark 11:

22 So Jesus answered and said to them, "Have faith in God.
23 "For assuredly, I say to you, whoever says to this mountain, 'Be removed and be cast into the sea,' and does not doubt in his heart, but believes that those things he says will come to pass, he will have whatever he says.
24 "Therefore I say to you, whatever things you ask when you pray, believe that you receive them, and you will have them.
25 "And whenever you stand praying, if you have anything against anyone, forgive him, that your Father in heaven may also forgive you your trespasses."

John 16:

22 "Therefore you now have sorrow; but I will see you again and your heart will rejoice, and your joy no one will take from you.
23 "And in that day you will ask Me nothing. Most assuredly, I say to you, whatever you ask the Father in My name He will give you.
24 "Until now you have asked nothing in My name. Ask, and you will receive, that your joy may be full.
25 "These things I have spoken to you in figurative language; but the time is coming when I will no longer speak to you in figurative language, but I will tell you plainly about the Father.
26 "In that day you will ask in My name, and I do not say to you that I shall pray the Father for you;
27 "for the Father Himself loves you, because you have loved Me, and have believed that I came forth from God.
28 "I came forth from the Father and have come into the world. Again, I leave the world and go to the Father."
29 His disciples said to Him, "See, now You are speaking plainly, and using no figure of speech!"

Prayer Principles Continued

A, B.2:

Pray for Spiritual Health and Wisdom

Revelation 3:
20 "Behold, I stand at the door and knock. If anyone hears My voice and opens the door, I will come in to him and dine with him, and he with Me.
21 "To him who overcomes I will grant to sit with Me on My throne, as I also overcame and sat down with My Father on His throne."

I John 5:
14 Now this is the confidence that we have in Him, that if we ask anything according to His will, He hears us.
15 And if we know that He hears us, whatever we ask, we know that we have the petitions that we have asked of Him.
16 If anyone sees his brother sinning a sin which does not lead to death, he will ask, and He will give him life for those who commit sin not leading to death. There is sin leading to death. I do not say that he should pray about that.
17 All unrighteousness is sin, and there is sin not leading to death.

James 1:
5 If any of you lacks wisdom, let him ask of God, who gives to all liberally and without reproach, and it will be given to him.
6 But let him ask in faith, with no doubting, for he who doubts is like a wave of the sea driven and tossed by the wind.
7 For let not that man suppose that he will receive anything from the Lord;
8 he is a double-minded man, unstable in all his ways.

II Peter 1:
3 as His divine power has given to us all things that pertain to life and godliness, through the knowledge of Him who called us by glory and virtue,
4 by which have been given to us exceedingly great and precious promises, that through these you may be partakers of the divine nature, having escaped the corruption that is in the world through lust. !

B.1, 3-5: Physical Suffering in the Will of God

<See also Pg. 48A2-4, B1 + Pg 118A4,5>

John 16:
33 "These things I have spoken to you, that in Me you may have peace. In the world you will have tribulation; but be of good cheer, I have overcome the world."

James 5:
13 Is anyone among you suffering? Let him pray. Is anyone cheerful? Let him sing psalms.
14 Is anyone among you sick? Let him call for the elders of the church, and let them pray over him, anointing him with oil in the name of the Lord.
15 And the prayer of faith will save the sick, and the Lord will raise him up. And if he has committed sins, he will be forgiven.
16 Confess your trespasses to one another, and pray for one another, that you may be healed. The effective, fervent prayer of a righteous man avails much.

I Peter 4:
19 Therefore let those who suffer according to the will of God commit their souls to Him in doing good, as to a faithful Creator. !

Hebrews 5:
7 who, in the days of His flesh, when He had offered up prayers and supplications, with vehement cries and tears to Him who was able to save Him from death, and was heard because of His godly fear,
8 though He was a Son, yet He learned obedience by the things which He suffered.
9 And having been perfected, He became the author of eternal salvation to all who obey Him,
10 called by God as High Priest "according to the order of Melchizedek."

Philippians 2:
25 Yet I considered it necessary to send to you Epaphroditus, my brother, fellow worker, and fellow soldier, but your messenger and the one who ministered to my need;
26 since he was longing for you all, and was distressed because you had heard that he was sick.
27 For indeed he was sick almost unto death; but God had mercy on him, and not only on him but on me also, lest I should have sorrow upon sorrow.

The Church Family/Body

<See Pg. 49.A.2. See also Pg. 102.B.2 and Pg. 104.A.5>

I Peter 4:

8 And above all things have fervent love for one another, for "love will cover a multitude of sins."

9 Be hospitable to one another without grumbling.

10 As each one has received a gift, minister it to one another, as good stewards of the manifold grace of God.

Hebrews 10:

24 And let us consider one another in order to stir up love and good works,

25 not forsaking the assembling of ourselves together, as is the manner of some, but exhorting one another, and so much the more as you see the Day approaching.

I Corinthians 11: ("Lord's Supper")

24 and when He had given thanks, He broke it and said, "Take, eat; this is My body which is broken for you; do this in remembrance of Me."

25 In the same manner He also took the cup after supper, saying, "This cup is the new covenant in My blood. This do, as often as you drink it, in remembrance of Me."

26 For as often as you eat this bread and drink this cup, you proclaim the Lord's death till He comes.

Ephesians 4:

11 And He Himself gave some to be apostles, some prophets, some evangelists, and some pastors and teachers,

12 for the equipping of the saints for the work of ministry, for the edifying of the body of Christ,

13 till we all come to the unity of the faith and the knowledge of the Son of God, to a perfect man, to the measure of the stature of the fullness of Christ;

14 that we should no longer be children, tossed to and fro and carried about with every wind of doctrine, by the trickery of men, in the cunning craftiness by which they lie in wait to deceive,

15 but, speaking the truth in love, may grow up in all things into Him who is the head – Christ –

16 from whom the whole body, joined and knit together by what every joint supplies, according to the effective working by which every part does its share, causes growth of the body for the edifying of itself in love.

Romans 12:

5 so we, being many, are one body in Christ, and individually members of one another.

6 Having then gifts differing according to the grace that is given to us, let us use them; if prophecy, let us prophesy in proportion to our faith;

7 or ministry, let us use it in our ministering; he who teaches, in teaching;

8 he who exhorts, in exhortation; he who gives, with liberality; he who leads, with diligence; he who shows mercy, with cheerfulness.

9 Let love be without hypocrisy. Abhor what is evil. Cling to what is good.

10 Be kindly affectionate to one another with brotherly love, in honor giving preference to one another;

11 not lagging in diligence, fervent in spirit, serving the Lord;

12 rejoicing in hope, patient in tribulation, continuing steadfastly in prayer;

13 distributing to the needs of the saints, given to hospitality.

14 Bless those who persecute you; bless and do not curse.

15 Rejoice with those who rejoice, and weep with those who weep.

16 Be of the same mind toward one another. Do not set your mind on high things, but associate with the humble. Do not be wise in your own opinion. !

Ecclesiastes 5:

1 Walk prudently when you go to the house of God; and draw near to hear rather than to give the sacrifice of fools, for they do not know that they do evil.

2 Do not be rash with your mouth,
And let not your heart utter anything hastily before God.
For God is in heaven, and you on earth;
Therefore let your words be few.

Mark 3:

32 And a multitude was sitting around Him; and they said to Him, "Look, Your mother and Your brothers are outside seeking You."

33 But He answered them, saying, "Who is My mother, or My brothers?"

34 And He looked around in a circle at those who sat about Him, and said, "Here are My mother and My brothers!

35 "For whoever does the will of God is My brother and My sister and mother."

The Church Family/Body - Continued

I Corinthians 12:
21 And the eye cannot say to the hand, "I have
no need of you"; nor again the head to the feet,
"I have no need of you."
22 No, much rather, those members of the body
which seem to be weaker are necessary.
23 And those members of the body which we think
to be less honorable, on these we bestow greater
honor; and our unpresentable parts have greater
modesty,
24 but our presentable parts have no need. But
God composed the body, having given greater
honor to that part which lacks it,
25 that there should be no schism in the body,
but that the members should have the same care
for one another.
26 And if one member suffers, all the members
suffer with it; or if one member is honored, all
the members rejoice with it.
27 No you are the body of Christ, and members
individually.

Colossians 3:
12 Therefore, as the elect of God, holy and
beloved, put on tender mercies, kindness,
humbleness of mind, meekness, longsuffering;
13 bearing with one another, and forgiving one
another, if anyone has a complaint against
another; even as Christ forgave you, so you also
must do.
14 But above all these things put on love,
which is the bond of perfection.
15 And let the peace of God rule in your !
hearts, to which also you were called in
one body; and be thankful.

I John 5: <see Pg. 90.B.3>
20 If someone says, "I love God," and hates his
brother, he is a liar; for he who does not love
his brother whom he has seen, how can he love
God whom he has not seen?
21 And this commandment we have from Him:
that he who loves God must love his brother
also.

Galatians 6:
9 And let us not grow weary while doing good,
for in due season we shall reap if we do not lose
heart.
10 Therefore, as we have opportunity, let us do
good to all, especially to those who are of the
household of faith.

Galatians 3:
26 For you are all sons of God through faith in
Christ Jesus.
27 For as many of you as were baptized into Christ
have put on Christ.
28 There is neither Jew nor Greek, there is neither
slave nor free, there is neither male nor female; for
you are all one in Christ Jesus.
29 And if you are Christ's, then you are Abraham's
seed, and heirs according to the promise.

Philippians 2:
3 Let nothing be done through selfish ambition or
conceit, but in lowliness of mind let each esteem
others better than himself.

I Timothy 5:
20 Those who are sinning rebuke in the !
presence of all, that the rest also may fear.

Galatians 6:
1 Brethren, if a man is overtaken in any trespass,
you who are spiritual restore such a one in a spirit
of gentleness, considering yourself lest you also be
tempted.
2 Bear one another's burdens, and so fulfill the law
of Christ.

II Thessalonians 3:
13 But as for you, brethren, do not grow weary in
doing good.
14 And if anyone does not obey our word in this
epistle, note that person and do not keep company
with him, that he may be ashamed.
15 Yet do not count him as an enemy, but
admonish him as a brother.

I Corinthians 6:
1 Dare any of you, having a matter against another,
go to law before the unrighteous, and not before
the saints?
2 Do you not know that the saints will judge the
world? And if the world will be judged by you, are
you unworthy to judge the smallest matters?
3 Do you not know that we shall judge angels?
How much more, things that pertain to this life?
4 If then you have judgments concerning things
pertaining to this life, do you appoint those who
are least esteemed by the church to judge?

<See also I Peter 5:1-5>

The Church Family/Body Continued

A. Financial Support of the Church

Matthew 6:

3 "But when you do a charitable deed, do not let your left hand know what your right hand is doing,
4 "that your charitable deed may be in secret; and your Father who sees in secret will Himself reward you openly."

I Corinthians 16:

1 Now concerning the collection for the saints, as I have given orders to the churches of Galatia, so you must do also:
2 On the first day of the week let each one of you lay something aside, storing up as he may prosper, that there be no collections when I come.

II Corinthians 9:

6 But this *I say*: He who sows sparingly will also reap sparingly, and he who sows bountifully will also reap bountifully.
7 *So let* each one *give* as he purposes in his heart, not grudgingly or of necessity; for God loves a cheerful giver.
8 And God *is* able to make all grace abound toward you, that you, always having all sufficiency in all *things*, may have an abundance for every good work.

I Timothy 5:

16 If any believing man or woman has widows, let them relieve them, and do not let the church be burdened, that it may relieve those who are really widows.

Galatians 6:

6 Let him who is taught the word share in all good things with him who teaches.

I Timothy 5:

17 Let the elders who rule well be counted worthy of double honor, especially those who labor in the word and doctrine.
18 For the Scripture says, "You shall not muzzle an ox while it treads out the grain," and "The laborer is worthy of his wages."

I Corinthians 9:

14 Even so the Lord has commanded that those who preach the gospel should live from the gospel.

B. Regarding Male/Female

I Corinthians 11:

3 But I want you to know that the head of every man is Christ, the head of woman in man, and the head of Christ is God.

Ephesians 5:

31 "For this reason a man shall leave his father and mother and be joined to his wife, and the two shall become one flesh."
32 This is a great mystery, but I speak concerning Christ and the church.
33 Nevertheless let each one of you in particular so love his own wife as himself, and let the wife see that she respects her husband.

Ephesians 5:

22 Wives, submit to your own husbands, as to the Lord.
23 For the husband is the head of the wife, as also Christ is head of the church; and He is the Savior of the body.
24 Therefore, just as the church is subject to Christ, so let wives be to their own husbands in everything.
25 Husbands, love your wives, just as Christ also loved the church and gave Himself for it,
26 that He might sanctify and cleanse it with the washing of water by the word,
27 that He might present it to Himself a glorious church, not having spot or wrinkle or any such thing, but that it should be holy and without blemish.
28 So husband ought to love their own wives as their own bodies; he who loves his wife loves himself.
29 For no one has ever hated his own flesh, but nourishes and cherishes it, just as the Lord does the church.
30 For we are members of His body, of His flesh and of His bones.

I Timothy 2:

11 Let a woman learn in silence with all submission.
12 And I do not permit a woman to teach or to have authority over a man, but to be in silence.
13 For Adam was formed first, then Eve.
14 And Adam was not deceived, but the woman being deceived, fell into transgression.
15 Nevertheless she will be saved in childbearing if they continue in faith, love, and holiness, with self-control.

Male/Female Principles

I Corinthians 14:

33 For God is not the author of confusion but
of peace, as in all the churches of the saints.
34 Let your women keep silent in the churches,
for they are not permitted to speak; but they are
to be submissive, as the law also says.
35 And if they want to learn something, let them
ask their own husbands at home; for it is
shameful for women to speak in church.
36 Or did the word of God come originally
from you? Or was it you only that it reached?
37 If anyone thinks himself to be a prophet or
spiritual, let him acknowledge that the things
which I write to you are the commandments of
the Lord.
38 But if anyone is ignorant, let him be ignorant.

I Corinthians 11:

5 But every woman who prays or prophesies
with her head uncovered dishonors her head,
for that is one and the same as if her head were
shaved.
6 For if a woman is not covered, let her also be
shorn. But if it is shameful for a woman to be
shorn or shaved, let her be covered.
7 For a man indeed ought not to cover his head,
since he is the image and glory of God; but
woman is the glory of man.
8 For man is not from woman, but woman from
man.
9 Nor was man created for the woman, but
woman for the man.
10 For this reason the woman ought to have a
symbol of authority on her head, because of the
angels.*

13 Judge among yourselves. Is it proper for a
woman to pray to God with her head
uncovered?
14 Does not even nature itself teach you that if a
man has long hair, it is a dishonor to him?
15 But if a woman has long hair, it is a glory to
her; for her hair is give to her for a covering.
16 But if anyone seems to be contentious, we
have no such custom, nor do the churches of
God.

***Note the principle, not the contemporary example.**

I Corinthians 11:

11 Nevertheless, neither is man independent of
woman, nor woman independent of man, in the
Lord.
12 For as the woman was from the man, even so the
man also is through the woman; but all things are
from God.

Genesis 2:

16 And the LORD God commanded the man,
saying, "Of every tree of the garden you may freely
eat;
17 "but of the tree of the knowledge of good and
evil you shall not eat, for in the day that you eat of
it you shall surely die."
18 And the LORD God said, "It is not good that
man should be alone; I will make him a helper
comparable to him."
19 Out of the ground the LORD God formed every
beast of the field and every bird of the air, and
brought them to Adam to see what he would call
the. And whatever Adam called each living
creature, that was its name.
20 So Adam gave names to all cattle, to the birds of
the air, and to every beast of the field. But for
Adam there was not found a helper comparable to
him.
21 And the LORD God caused a deep sleep to fall
on Adam, and he slept; and He took one of his
ribs, and closed up the flesh in its place.
22 Then the rib which the LORD God had taken
from man He made into a woman, and He
brought her to the man.
23 And Adam said:

> "This is now bone of my bones
> And flesh of my flesh;
> She shall be called Woman,
> Because she was taken out of Man."

24 Therefore a man shall leave his father and
mother and be joined to his wife, and they shall
become one flesh.

Genesis 3:

16 To the woman He said:

> "I will greatly multiply your sorrow and your conception;
> In pain you shall bring forth children;
> Your desire shall be for your husband,
> And he shall rule over you."

Family

A. Family Relations

I Peter 3:

1 Likewise you wives, be submissive to your own husbands, that even if some do not obey the word, they, without a word, may be won by the conduct of their wives,
2 when they observe your chaste conduct accompanied by fear.
3 Do not let your beauty be that outward adorning of arranging the hair, of wearing god, or of putting on fine apparel;
4 But let it be the hidden person of the heart, with the incorruptible ornament of a gentle and quiet spirit, which is very precious in the sight of God.
5 For in this manner, in former times, the holy women who trusted in God also adorned themselves, being submissive to their own husbands,
6 as Sarah obeyed Abraham, calling him lord, whose daughters you are if you do good and are not afraid with any terror.

A Word to Husbands

7 Likewise you husbands, dwell with them with understanding, giving honor to the wife, as to the weaker vessel, and as being heirs together of the grace of life, that your prayers may not be hindered.

Colossians 3:

18 Wives, submit to your own husbands, as is fitting in the Lord.
19 Husbands, love your wives and do not be bitter toward them.
20 Children, obey your parents in all things, for this is well pleasing to the Lord.
21 Fathers, do not provoke your children, lest they become discouraged.

Ephesians 6:

1 Children, obey your parents in the Lord, for this is right.
2 "Honor your father and mother," which is the first commandment with promise:
3 "that it may be well with you and you may live long on the earth."
4 And you, fathers, do not provoke your children to wrath, but bring them up in the training and admonition of the Lord.

B.1.: Sex

B. 2-3: Female Pattern Desired

I Corinthians 7:

3 Let the husband render to his wife the affection due her, and likewise also the wife to her husband.
4 The wife does not have authority over her own body, but the husband does. And likewise the husband does not have authority over his own body, but the wife does.
5 Do not deprive one another except with consent for a time, that you may give yourselves to fasting and prayer; and come together again so that Satan does not tempt you because of your lack of self-control.
6 But I say this as a concession, not as a commandment.

I Timothy 5:

9 Do not let a widow under sixty years old be taken into the number, and not unless she has been the wife of one man,
10 well reported for good works: if she has brought up children, if she has lodged strangers, if she has washed the saints' feet, if she has relieved the afflicted, if she has diligently followed every good work.
11 But refuse the younger widows; for when they have begun to grow wanton against Christ, they desire to marry,
12 having condemnation because they have cast off their first faith.
13 And besides they learn to be idle, wandering about from house to house, and not only idle but also gossips and busybodies, saying things which they ought not.
14 Therefore I desire that the younger widows marry, bear children, manage the house, give no opportunity to the adversary to speak reproachfully.
15 For some have already turned aside after Satan.

Titus 2:

3 the older women likewise, that they be reverent in behavior, not slanderers, not give to much wine, teachers of good things –
4 that they admonish the young women to love their husbands, to love their children,
5 to be discreet, chaste, homemakers, good obedient to their own husbands, that the word of God may not be blasphemed.

Family - Continued

A. Virtuous Wife

10 Who can find a virtuous wife?
For her worth is far above rubies.
11 The heart of her husband safely trusts her;
So he will have no lack of gain.
12 She does him good and not evil
All the days of her life.
13 She seeks wool and flax,
And willingly works with her hands.
14 She is like the merchant ships,
She brings her food from afar.
15 She also rises while it is yet night,
And provides food for her household,
And a portion for her maidservants.
16 She considers a field and buys it;
From her profits she plants a vineyard.
17 She girds herself with strength,
And strengthens her arms.
18 She perceives that her merchandise is good,
And her lamp does not go out by night.
19 She stretches out her hands to the distaff,
And her hand holds the spindle.
20 She extends her hand to the poor,
Yes, she reaches out her hands to the needy.
21 She is not afraid of snow for her household,
For all her household is clothed with scarlet.
22 She makes tapestry for herself;
Her clothing is fine linen and purple.
23 Her husband is known in the gates,
When he sits among the elders of the land.
24 She makes linen garments and sells them,
And supplies sashes for the merchants.
25 Strength and honor are her clothing;
She shall rejoice in time to come.
26 She opens her mouth with wisdom,
And on her tongue is the law of kindness.
27 She watches over the ways of her household,
And does not eat the bread of idleness.
28 Her children rise up and call her blessed;
Her husband also, and he praises her:
29 " Many daughters have done well,
But you excel them all."
30 Charm is deceitful and beauty is passing,
But a woman who fears the LORD, she shall
be praised.
31 Give her of the fruit of her hands,
And let her own works praise her in the gates

B. Family Relations Continued:

Marriage, Widows.

See Page 123 for Child Raising.

I Timothy 5:

8 But if anyone does not provide for his own, and especially for those of his household, he has denied the faith and is worse than an unbeliever.

II Corinthians 12:

14 Now for the third time I am ready to come to you. And I will not be burdensome to you; for I do not seek yours, but you. For the children ought not to lay up for the parents, but the parents for the children.

I Corinthians 7:

32 But I want you to be without care. He who is unmarried cares for the things that belong to the Lord – how he may please the Lord.
33 But he who is married cares about the things of the world – how he may please his wife.
34 There is a difference between a wife and a virgin. The unmarried woman cares about the things of the Lord, that she may be holy both in body and in spirit. But she who is married cares about the things of the world – how she may please her husband.
35 And this I say for your own profit, not that I may put a leash on you, but for what is proper, and that you may serve the Lord without distraction.

I Corinthians 7:

8 But I say to the unmarried and to the widows: It is good for them if they remain even as I am;
9 but if they cannot exercise self-control, let them marry. For it is better to marry than to burn with passion.

I Timothy 5:

5 Now she who is really a widow, and left alone, trusts in God and continues in supplications and prayers night and day.
6 But she who lives in pleasure is dead while she lives.

Family - Continued

A. Marriage

Mark 10:

7 'For this reason a man shall leave his father and mother and be joined to his wife,
8 and the two shall become one flesh', so then they are no longer two, but one flesh.
9 "Therefore what God has joined together, let not man separate."

I Corinthians 7:

27 Are you bound to a wife? Do not seek to be loosed. Are you loosed from a wife? Do not seek a wife.
28 But even if you do marry, you have not sinned; and if a virgin marries, she has not sinned. Nevertheless such will have trouble in the flesh, but I would spare you.

!

I Corinthians 7:

14 For the unbelieving husband is sanctified by the wife, and the unbelieving wife is sanctified by the husband; otherwise your children would be unclean, but now they are holy.
15 But if the unbeliever departs, let him depart; a brother or a sister is not under bondage in such cases. But God has called us to peace.

Matthew 5:

32 "But I say to you that whoever divorces his wife for any reason except sexual immorality causes her to commit adultery; and whoever marries a woman who is divorced commits adultery.

<See Pg. 72 B.6: adultery>

Submission, Not Revenge

Romans 12:

17 Repay no one evil for evil. Have regard for good things in the sight of all men.
18 If it is possible, as much as depends on you, live peaceably with all men.
19 Beloved, do not avenge yourselves, but rather give place to wrath; for it is written, "Vengeance is Mine, I will repay," says the LORD.

B. Submissive Life

Matthew 5:

16 "Let your light so shine before men, that they may see your good works and glorify your Father in heaven.

I Peter 5:

5 Likewise you younger people, submit yourselves to your elders. Yes, all of you be submissive to one another, and be clothed with humility, for

"God resists the proud,
But gives grace to the humble."

6 Therefore humble yourselves under the mighty hand of God, that He may exalt you in due time.

Ephesians 6:*

5 Servants, be obedient to those who are your masters according to the flesh, with fear and trembling, in sincerity of heart, as to Christ;
6 not with eyeservice, as men-pleasers, but as servants of Christ, doing the will of God from the heart,
7 with good will doing service, as to the Lord, and not to men,
8 knowing that whatever good anyone does, he will receive the same from the Lord, whether he is slave or free.
9 And you, masters, do the same things to them, giving up threatening, knowing that your own Master also is in heaven, and there is no partiality with Him.

Colossians 3:

22 Servants, obey in all things your masters according to the flesh, not with eyeservice, as men-pleasers, but in sincerity of heart, fearing God.
23 And whatever you do, do it heartily, as to the Lord and not to men.

I Peter 2:

18 Servants, be submissive to your masters with all fear, not only to the good and gentle, but also to the harsh.

Colossians 4:

1 Masters, give your servants what is just and fair, knowing that you also have a Master in heaven.

**Apply to employer/employee today.*

A. Submission to Governments

I Peter 2:

13 Therefore submit yourselves to every ordinance of man for the Lord's sake, whether to the king as supreme,
14 or to governors, as to those who are sent by him for the punishment of evildoers and for the praise of those who do good.
15 For this is the will of God, that by doing good you may put to silence the ignorance of foolish men.

Romans 13:

3 For rulers are not a terror to good works, but to evil. Do you want to be unafraid of the authority? Do what is good, and you will have praise from the same.
4 For he is God's minister to you for good. But if you do evil, be afraid; for he does not bear the sword in vain; for his is God's minister, an avenger to execute wrath on him who practices evil.
5 Therefore you must be subject, not only because of wrath but also for conscience' sake.
6 For because of this you also pay taxes, for they are God's ministers attending continually to this very thing.
7 Render therefore to all their due: taxes to whom taxes are due, customs to whom customs, fear to whom fear, honor to whom honor.

Romans 13:

1 Let every soul be subject to the governing authorities. For there is no authority except from God, and the authorities that exist are appointed by God.
2 Therefore whoever resists the authority resists the ordinance of God, and those who resist will bring judgment on themselves.

Hebrews 13:

3 Remember the prisoners* as if chained with them, and those who are mistreated, since you yourselves are in the body also.

*(* Political/religious prisoners)*

Genesis 9:

6 "Whoever sheds man's blood,
By man his blood will be shed;
For in the image of God
He made man."

B. Missionary/Evangelism

Romans 10:

14 How then shall they call on Him in whom they have not believed? And how shall they believe in Him of whom they have not heard? And how shall they hear without a preacher?
15 And how shall they preach unless they are sent? As it is written:
"How beautiful are the feet of those who preach the gospel of peace,
Who bring glad tidings of good things!"

Mark 14:

13 And He said to them, "Do you not understand this parable? How then will you understand all the parables?
14 "The sower sows the word.
15 "And these are the ones by the wayside where the word is sown. And when they hear, Satan comes immediately and takes away the word that was sown in their hearts.
16 "These likewise are the ones sown on stony ground who, when they hear the word, immediately receive it with gladness;
17 "and they have no root in themselves, and so endure only for a time. Afterward, when tribulation or persecution arises for the word's sake, immediately they stumble.
18 "Now these are the ones sown among thorns; they are the ones who hear the word,
19 "and the cares of this world, the deceitfulness of riches, and the desires for other things entering in choke the word, and it becomes unfruitful.

Luke 18:

29 So He said to them, "Assuredly, I say to you, there is no one who has left house or parents or brothers or wife or children, for the sake of the kingdom of God,
30 "who shall not receive many times more in this present time, and in the age to come everlasting life."

I Timothy 3:

5 (for if a man does not know how to rule his own house, how will he take care of the church of God?);

Section 2B - Miscellaneous non-Sequential Topics

A. Pride vs. Humility

<See also Pg. 98.B.7. and Pg. 21.A.3>

Proverbs 16:

18 Pride goes before destruction,
And a haughty spirit before a fall.
19 Better to be of a humble spirit with the lowly,
Than to divide the spoil with the proud.

Habakkuk 2:

4 "Behold the proud,
His soul is not upright in him;
But the just shall live by his faith."

Proverbs 8:

13 The fear of the LORD is to have evil;
Pride and arrogance and the evil way
And the perverse mouth I hate.

I Timothy 3:

6 not a novice, lest being puffed up with pride he fall into the same condemnation as the devil.
7 Moreover he must have a good testimony among those who are outside, lest he fall into reproach and the snare of the devil.

Beatitudes

Matthew 5:

3 "Blessed are the poor in spirit,
For theirs is the kingdom of heaven.
4 Blessed are those who mourn,
For they shall be comforted.
5 Blessed are the meek,
For they shall inherit the earth.
6 Blessed are those who hunger and thirst for righteousness,
For they shall be filled.
7 Blessed are the merciful,
For they shall obtain mercy.
8 Blessed are the pure in heart,
For they shall see God.
9 Blessed are the peacemakers,
For they shall be called the sons of God.
10 Blessed are those who are persecuted for righteousness' sake,
For theirs is the kingdom of heaven.

40 Days after Birth of Jesus (returned from Egypt)

Luke 2:

22 Now when the days of her purification
according to the law of Moses were completed,
they brought Him to Jerusalem to present Him
to the Lord 23 (as it is written in the law of the
Lord, "Every male who opens the womb shall
be called holy to the LORD"),

B. Kingdom of God

Mark 8:

37 "Or what will a man give in exchange for his soul?
38 "For whoever is ashamed of Me and My words in this adulterous and sinful generation, of him the Son of Man also will be ashamed when He comes in the glory of His Father with the holy angels."

Mark 9:

1 And He said to them, "Assuredly, I say to you that there are some standing here who will not taste death till they see the kingdom of God present with power."

Luke 17:

20 Now when He was asked by the Pharisees when the kingdom of God would come, He answered them and said, "The kingdom of God does not come with observation;
21 "nor will they say, 'See here!' or 'See there!' For indeed, the kingdom of God is within you."

Matthew 7:

13 "Enter by the narrow gate; for wide is the gate and broad is the way that leads to destruction, and there are many who go in by it.
14 "Because narrow is the gate and difficult is the way which leads to life, and there are few who find it."

Mark 4:

10 But when He was alone, those around Him with the twelve asked Him about the parable.
11 And He said to them, "To you it has been given to know the mystery of the kingdom of God; but to those who are outside, all things come in parables,
12 "so that
'Seeing they may see and not perceive,
And hearing they may hear and not understand;
Lest they should turn,
And their sins be forgiven them.' "

Mark 4:

33 And with many such parables He spoke the word to them as they were able to hear it.
34 But without a parable He did not speak to them. And when they were alone, He explained all things to His disciples.

Christology

Philippians 2:
5 Let this mind be in you which was also in Christ Jesus,
6 who, being in the form of God, did not consider it robbery to be equal with God,
7 but made Himself of no reputation, taking the form of a servant, and coming in the likeness of men.
8 And being found in appearance as a man, He humbled Himself and became obedient to the point of death, even the death of the cross.

Mark 14:
61 But He kept silent and answered nothing. Again the high priest asked Him, saying to Him, "Are You the Christ, the Son of the Blessed?"
62 And Jesus said, "I am. And you will see the Son of Man sitting at the right hand of the Power, and coming with the clouds of heaven."

Mark 12:
35 Then Jesus answered and said, while He taught in the temple, "How is it that the scribes say that the Christ is the Son of David?"
36 "For David himself said by the Holy Spirit:
'The LORD said to my Lord,
"Sit at My right hand,
Till I make Your enemies Your footstool." '
37 "Therefore David himself calls Him 'Lord'; how is He then his Son?" And the common people heard Him gladly.

II Corinthians 1:
2 Grace to you and peace from God our Father and the Lord Jesus Christ.
3 Blessed be the God and Father of our Lord Jesus Christ, the Father of mercies and God of all comfort,
4 who comforts us in all our tribulation, that we may be able to comfort those who are in any trouble, with the comforted by God
5 For as the <u>sufferings of Christ abounds in us</u>, so our consolation also abounds through Christ.

Colossians 1:
24 I now rejoice in my sufferings for you, and fill up in my flesh what is lacking in the afflictions of Christ, for the sake of His body, which is the church,

II Timothy 1:
8 … Share with me in the sufferings for the Gospel according to the power of God,

Hebrews 4:
15 For we do not have a high priest who cannot sympathize with out weaknesses, but was in all *points* tempted as *we are, yet* without sin.

Ephesians 2:
14 For He Himself is our peace, who has made both one, and has broken down the middle wall of division between us.

Physical Resurrection

< See also Lazarus Pg. 39B >

Luke 24:
39 "Behold My hands and My feet, that it is I Myself. Handle Me and see, for a spirit does not have flesh and bones as you see I have."
40 When He had said this, He showed them His hands and His feet.
41 But while they still did not believe for joy, and marveled, He said to them, "Have you any food here?"
42 So they gave Him a piece of broiled fish and some honeycomb.
43 And He took it and ate it in their presence.

Compassion Felt by the Lord

Matthew 25:
37 "Then the righteous will answer Him, saying, 'Lord, when did we see You hungry and feed You, or thirsty and give You drink?
38 'When did we see You a stranger and take You in, or naked and clothe You?
39 'Or when did we see You sick, or in prison, and come to You?'
40 "And the King will answer and say to them, 'Assuredly, I say to you, inasmuch as you did it to one of the least of these My brethren, you did it to Me.' "

Christ's Commandments

Matthew 22:
37 Jesus said to him, " ' You shall love the LORD your God with all your heart, with all your soul, and with all your mind.'
38 "This is the first and great commandment.
39 "And the second is like it: 'You shall love your neighbor as yourself.' "

"Hail Mary" *< cont. from Pg37B1>*

Luke 1:
41 And it happened, when Elizabeth heard the greeting of Mary, that the babe leaped in her womb; and Elizabeth was filled with the Holy
Spirit. 42 Then she spoke out with a loud voice and said, "Blessed *are* you among women, and blessed *is* the fruit of your womb!
46 And Mary said: " My soul magnifies the Lord,
48 For He has regarded the lowly state of His maidservant; For behold, henceforth all generations will call me blessed.

Angels

Matthew 18: **(Guardian Angels)**

10 "Take heed that you do not despise one of these little ones, for I say to you that in heaven their angels always see the face of My Father who is in heaven.

11 "For the Son of Man has come to save that which was lost.

12 "What do you think? If a man has a hundred sheep, and one of them goes astray, does he not leave the ninety-nine and go to the mountains to seek the one that is straying?

13 "And if he should find it, assuredly, I say to you, he rejoices more over that sheep than over the ninety-nine that did not go astray.

14 "Even so it is not the will of your Father who is in heaven that one of these little ones should perish."

Hebrews 13:

1 Let brotherly love continue.

2 Do not forget to entertain strangers, for by so doing some have unwittingly entertained angels.

Psalm 68:

17 The chariots of God are twenty thousand,
Even thousands of thousands;
The LORD is among them as in Sinai, in the Holy Place.

I Corinthians 15:

39 All flesh is not the same flesh, but there is one kind of flesh of men, another flesh of beasts, another of fish, and another of birds.

40 There are also celestial bodies and terrestrial bodies; but the glory of the celestial is one, and the glory of the terrestrial is another.

41 There is one glory of the sun, another glory of the moon, and another glory of the stars; for one star differs from another star in glory.

42 So also is the resurrection of the dead. The body is sown in corruption, it is raised in incorruption.

44 It is sown a natural body, it is raised a spiritual body. There is a natural body, and there is a spiritual body.

Jude

6 And the angels who did not keep their proper domain, but left their own habitation, He has reserved in everlasting chains under darkness for the judgment of the great day;

Luke 15:

10 "Likewise, I say to you, there is joy in the presence of the angels of God over one sinner who repents."

Colossians 2:

10 and you are complete in Him, who is the head of all principality and power.

15 Having disarmed principalities and powers, He made a public spectacle of them, triumphing over then in it.

Hebrews 1:

13 But to which of the angels has He ever said:
"Sit at My right hand,
Till I make Your enemies Your footstool"?

14 Are they not all ministering spirits sent forth to minister for those who will inherit salvation?

Luke 16:

22 "So it was that the beggar died, and was carried by the angels to Abraham's bosom. The rich man also died and was buried.

23 "And being in torments in Hades, he lifted up his eyes and saw Abraham afar off, and Lazarus in his bosom.

24 "Then he cried out and said, 'Father Abraham, have mercy on me, and send Lazarus that he may dip the tip of his finger in water and cool my tongue; for I am tormented in this flame.'

I Kings 22:

19 Then Micaiah said, "Therefore hear the word of the LORD: I saw the LORD sitting on His throne, and all the host of heaven standing by, on His right hand and on His left.

20 "And the LORD said, 'Who will persuade Ahab to go up, that he may fall at Ramoth Gilead?' So one spoke in this manner, and another spoke in that manner.

21 "Then a spirit came forward and stood before the LORD, and said, 'I will persuade him.'

22 "The LORD said to him, 'In what way?' So he said, 'I will go out and be a lying spirit in the mouth of all his prophets.' And He said, 'You shall persuade him, and also prevail. Go out and do so.'

23 "Now therefore, look! The LORD has put a lying spirit in the mouth of all these prophets of yours, and the LORD has declared disaster against you."

Angels + the Dead

Hebrews 2:

16 For indeed He does not give aid to angels, but He does give aid to the seed of Abraham.

Matthew 22:

30 "For in the resurrection they neither marry nor are given in marriage, but are like angels of God in heaven.
31 "But concerning the resurrection of the dead, have you not read what was spoken to you by God, saying,
32 'I am the God of Abraham, the God of Isaac, and the God of Jacob'? God is not the God of the dead, but of the living."

Heaven

John 14:

2 "In My Father's house are many mansions; if it were not so, I would not have told you. I go to prepare a place for you.
3 "And if I go and prepare a place for you, I will come again and receive you to Myself; that where I am, there you may be also."

Hebrews 12:

22 But you have come to Mount Zion and to the city of the living God, the heavenly Jerusalem, to an innumerable company of angels,

Genealogy of Christ

Mary (Mother)

Luke 3:

23 Now Jesus Himself began His ministry at about thirty years of age, being (as was supposed) the son of Joseph, the son of Heli,
24 the son of Matthat, the son of Levi, the son of Melchi, the son of Janna, the son of Joseph,
25 the son of Mattathiah, the son of Amos, the son of Nahum, the son of Esli, the son of Naggai,
26 the son of Maath, the son of Mattathiah, the son of Semei, the son of Joseph, the son of Judah,
27 the son of Joannas, the son of Rhesa, the son of Zerubbabel, the son of Shealtiel, the son of Neri,
28 the son of Melchi, the son of Addi, the son of Cosam, the son of Elmodam, the son of Er,
29 the son of Jose, the son of Eliezer, the son of Jorim, the son of Matthat, the son of Levi,
30 the son of Simeon, the son of Judah, the son of Joseph, the son of Jonan, the son of Eliakim,
31 the son of Melea, the son of Menan, the son of Mattathah, the son of Nathan, the son of David,
32 the son of Jesse, the son of Obed, the son of Boaz, the son of Salmon, the son of Nahshon,
33 the son of Amminadab, the son of Ram, the son of Hezron, the son of Perez, the son of Judah,
34 the son of Jacob, the son of Isaac, the son of Abraham, the son of Terah, the son of Nahor,
35 the son of Serug, the son of Reu, the son of Peleg, the son of Eber, the son of Shelah,
36 the son of Cainan, the son of Arphaxad, the son of Shem, the son of Noah, the son of Lamech,
37 the son of Methuselah, the son of Enoch, the son of Jared, the son of Mahalalel, the son of Cainan,
38 the son of Enosh, the son of Seth, the son of Adam, the son of God.

Joseph (Stepfather)

Matthew 1:

2 Abraham begot Isaac, Isaac begot Jacob, and Jacob begot Judah and his brothers.
3 Judah begot Perez and Zerah by Tamar, Perez begot Hezron, and Hezron begot Ram.
4 Ram begot Amminadab, Amminadab begot Nahshon, and Nahshon begot Salmon.
5 Salmon begot Boaz by Rahab, Boaz begot Obed by Ruth, Obed begot Jesse,
6 and Jesse begot David the king. David the king begot Solomon by her who had been the wife of Uriah.
7 Solomon begot Rehoboam, Rehoboam begot Abijah, and Abijah begot Asa.
8 Asa begot Jehoshaphat, Jehoshaphat begot Joram, and Joram begot Uzziah.
9 Uzziah begot Jotham, Jotham begot Ahaz, and Ahaz begot Hezekiah.
10 Hezekiah begot Manasseh, Manasseh begot Amon, and Amon begot Josiah.
11 Josiah begot Jeconiah and his brothers about the time they were carried away to Babylon.
12 And after they were brought to Babylon, Jeconiah begot Shealtiel, and Shealtiel begot Zerubbabel.
13 Zerubbabel begot Abiud, Abiud begot Eliakim, and Eliakim begot Azor.
14 Azor begot Zadok, Zadok begot Achim, and Achim begot Eliud.
15 Eliud begot Eleazar, Eleazar begot Matthan, and Matthan begot Jacob.
16 And Jacob begot Joseph the husband of Mary, of whom was born Jesus who is called Christ.
17 So all the generations from Abraham to David are fourteen generations, from David until the captivity in Babylon are fourteen generations, and from the captivity in Babylon until the Christ are fourteen generations.

Dinosaurs Seen in Old Testament Days

Job 40:

15 "Look now at the behemoth, which I mad
along with you;
He eats grass like an ox.
16 See now, his strength is in his hips,
And his power is in his stomach muscles.
17 He moves his tail like a cedar;
The sinews of his thighs are tightly knit.
18 His bones are like beams of bronze,
His ribs are like bars of iron.
19 He is the first of the ways of God;
Only He who made him can bring near His
sword.
20 Surely the mountains yield food for him,
And all the beasts of the field play there.
21 He lies under the lotus trees,
In a covert of reeds and marsh.
22 The lotus trees cover him with their shade;
The willows by the brook surround him.
23 Indeed the river may rage,
Yet he is not disturbed;
He is confident, though the Jordan gushes
into his mouth,
24 Though he takes it in his eyes.
Or one pierces his nose with a snare.

Job 41:

1 "Can you draw out Leviathan with a hook,
Or snare his tongue with a line which you
lower?
2 Can you put a reed through his nose,
Or pierce his jaw with a hook?
3 Will he make many supplications to you?
Will he speak softly to you?
4 Will he make a covenant with you?
Will you take him as a servant forever?
5 Will you play with him as with a bird,
Or will you leash him for your maidens?
6 Will your companions make a banquet of him?
Will they apportion him among the merchants?
7 Can you fill his skin with harpoons,
Or his head with fishing spears?
8 Lay your hand on him;
Remember the battle – Never do it again!
9 Indeed, any hope of overcoming him is vain;
Shall one not be overwhelmed at the sight of
him?
10 No one is so fierce that he would dare stir
him up.
Who then is able to stand against Me?
11 Who has precede Me, that I should pay him?
Everything under heaven in Mine.
12 "I will not conceal his limbs,
His mighty power, or his graceful proportions.

Psalm 104:

25 This great and wide sea,
In which are innumerable teeming things,
Living things both small and great.
26 There the ships sail about;
And there is that Leviathan
Which You have made to play there.

Psalm 74:

13 You divided the sea by Your strength;
You broke the heads of the sea serpents in the
waters.
14 You broke the heads of Leviathan in pieces.
14b And gave him as food to the people
inhabiting the wilderness.

Job 41: continued

13 Who can remove his outer coat?
Who can approach him with a double bridle?
14 Who can open the doors of his face,
With his terrible teeth all around.
15 His rows of scales are his pride,
Shut up tightly as with a seal;

21 His breath kindles coals,
And a flame goes out of his mouth.
22 Strength dwells in his neck,
And sorrow dances before him.
23 The folds of his flesh are joined together;
They are firm on him and cannot be moved.
24 His heart is as hard as stone,
Even as hard as the lower millstone.
25 When he raises himself up, the mighty are
afraid;
Because of his crashings they are beside
themselves.
26 Though the sword reaches him, it cannot avail;
Nor does spear, dart, or javelin.

29 Darts are regarded as straw;
He laughs at the threat of javelins.
30 His undersides are like sharp potsherds;
He spreads pointed marks in the mire.
31 He makes the deep boil like a pot;
He makes the sea like a pot of ointment.
32 He leaves a shining wake behind him;
One would think the deep had white hair.
33 On earth there is nothing like him,
Which is made without fear.
34 He beholds every high thing;
He is king over all the children of pride."

Creation misc.

<see also Pg.31A1v6, and Pg.13A7 >

Psalm 104:

1 Bless the Lord, O my soul !
You are very great;
2 Who cover *Yourself* with light
as *with* a garment,
Who stretch out the heavens like a curtain.
3 Who lays the beams of His upper chambers
in the waters,
Who makes the clouds His chariot,
Who walks on the wings of the wind.
4 Who makes His angels spirits
His ministers a flame of fire

Job 41: continued

16 One is so near another
That no air can come between them;
17 They are joined one to another,
They stick together and cannot be parted.
18 His sneezings flash forth light,
And his eyes are like the eyelids of the morning.
19 Out of his mouth go burning lights;
Sparks of fire shoot out.
20 Smoke goes out of his nostrils,
As from a boiling pot and burning rushes.
27 He regards iron as straw,
And bronze as rotten wood.
28 The arrow cannot make him flee;
Slingstones become like stubble to him.

Jeremiah 27:

5 'I have made the earth, the man and the beast
that *are* on the ground, by My great power
and by My outstretched arm, and have
given it to whom it seemed proper to Me.

Mark 10:

6 'But from the beginning of the creation,
God *'made them male and female.'*

I Corinthians 15:

45 And so it is written, *"The first man Adam
became a living being."*[1] The last Adam
became a life-giving spirit.
46 However, the spiritual is not first, but the
natural, and afterward the spiritual.
47 The first man *was* of the earth, *made* of dust;
the second Man *is* the Lord from heaven.
48 As *was* the *man* of dust, so also *are* those
who are made of dust; and as *is* the heavenly
Man, so also *are* those *who are* heavenly.
49 And as we have borne the image of the
man of dust, we shall also bear the image of
the heavenly *Man.* *<see also Pg.109B4 >*

The Great Flood

Psalm 148:

4 Praise Him, you heavens of heavens,
And you waters above the heavens!

Psalm 74:

14b And gave him as food to the people
inhabiting the wilderness.
15 You broke open the fountain and the
flood;
You dried up mighty rivers.
16 The day is Yours, the night is also Yours;
You have prepared the light and the sun.
17 You have set all the borders of the earth;
You have made summer and winter.

Psalm 104: (Creation, or flood?)

5 You who laid the foundations of the earth,
So that it should not be moved forever,
6 You covered it with the deep as with a
garment;
The waters stood above the mountains.
7 At Your rebuke they fled;
At the voice of Your thunder they hastened
away.
8 They went up over the mountains;
They went down into the valleys,
To the place which You founded for
them.
9 You have set a boundary that they may
not pass over,
That they may not return to cover the
earth.

II Peter 3:

5 For this they willfully forget: that by the
word of God the heavens were of old, and the
earth standing out of water and in the water.
6 by which the world that then existed
perished, being flooded with water.

Matthew 24:

38 For as in the days before the flood, they were
eating and drinking, marrying and giving in
marriage, until the day that Noah entered the ark,
. . . 39 and did not know until the flood came
and took them all away, . . .

< note creation of "strata">

Amos 9:

6 He who builds his layers in the sky,
And has founded His strata in the earth;
Who calls for the waters of the sea,
And pours them out on the face of the
earth–
The LORD is His name.

Miscellaneous

(Demon Possession)

Luke 11:

24 "When an unclean spirit goes out of a man, he goes through dry places, seeking rest; and finding none, he says, 'I will return to my house from which I came.'

25 "And when he comes, he finds it swept and put in order.

26 "Then he goes and takes with him seven other spirits more wicked than himself, and they enter and dwell there; and the last state of that man is worse than the first."

(Power of His "name")

Mark 9:

39 But Jesus said, "Do not forbid him, for no one who works a miracle in My name can soon afterward speak evil of Me.

40 "For he who is not against us in on our side."

Leviticus 20:

13 If a man lies with a male as he lies with a woman, both of them have committed an abomination. They shall surely be put to death. Their blood shall be upon them.

Deuteronomy 22:

5 A woman shall not wear anything that pertains to a man, nor shall a man put on a woman's garment, for all who do so are an abomination to the LORD your God.

II Samuel 24:

1 Again the anger of the LORD was aroused against Israel, and he moved David against them to say, "Go, number Israel and Judah."

10 And David's heart condemned him after he had numbered the people. So David said to the LORD, "I have sinned greatly in what I have done; but now, I pray, O LORD, take away the iniquity of Your servant, for I have done very foolishly."

15 So the LORD sent a plague upon Israel from the morning till the appointed time. From Dan to Beersheba seventy thousand men of the people died.

16 And when the Angel stretched out His hand over Jerusalem to destroy it, the LORD relented from the destruction, and said to the angel who was destroying the people, "It is enough; now restrain your hand." And the angel of the LORD was by the threshing floor of Araunah the Jebusite.

(Relevant to the length of stay of Israelites in Egypt.) *(See Pg. 4.B.1,2)*

I Chronicles 6:

1 The sons of Levi were Gershon, Kohath, and Merari.

2 The sons of Kohath were Amram, Izhar, Hebron, and Uzziel.

3 The children of Amram were Aaron, Moses, and Miriam. And the sons of Aaron were Nadab, Abihu, Eleazar, and Ithamar.

Numbers 26:

58 These are the families of the Levites: the family of the Libnites, the family of the Hebronites, the family of the Mahlites, the family of the Mushites, and the family of the Korathites. And Kohath begot Amram.

59 The name of Amram's wife was Jochebed the daughter of Levi, who was born to Levi in Egypt; and to Amram she bore Aaron and Moses and their sister Miriam.

(Apparent cheapness of human life)

Judges 21:

10 So the congregation sent out there twelve thousand of their most valiant men, and commanded them, saying, "Go and strike the inhabitants of Jabesh Gilead with the edge of the sword, including the women and children.

11 "And this is the thing that you shall do: You shall utterly destroy every male, and every woman who has known a man intimately."

14 So Benjamin came back at that time, and they gave them the women whom they had saved alive of the women of Jabesh Gilead; and yet they had not found enough for them.

<*See also Pg. 17.A.2; Pg. 18.A.2-B.1* + Pg. 123.A.7>

(Exercise)

I Timothy 4:

8 For bodily exercise profits a little, but godliness is profitable for all things, having promise of the life that now is and of that which is to come.

9 *This is a faithful saying and worthy of all acceptance.*

Miscellaneous

A. Trivia

(Forests in Egypt cut down)

Jeremiah 46:

23 "They shall cut down her forest," says the
LORD,
"Though it cannot be searched,
Because they are innumerable,
And more numerous than grasshoppers.
24 The daughter of Egypt shall be ashamed."

(Slavery)

Leviticus 25:

44 'And as for your male and female slaves
whom you have – from the nations that are
around you, from them you may buy male and
female slaves.
45 'Moreover you may buy the children of the
strangers who sojourn among you, and their
families who are with you, which they beget in
your land; and they shall become your property.
46 'And you may take them as an inheritance for
your children after you, to inherit them as
possession; they shall be your permanent slaves.
But regarding your brethren, the children of
Israel, you shall not rule over one another with
rigor.'

(Athletic skills of Lefties)

Judges 20:

16 Among all this people there were seven
hundred select men who were left-handed; every
one could sling a stone at a hair's breadth and
not miss.

(Well Witnessed Miracle)

Exodus 14:

22 So the children of Israel went into the midst
of the sea on the dry ground, and the waters
were a wall to them on their right hand and on
their left.
23 And the Egyptians pursued and went after
them into the midst of the sea, all Pharaoh's
horses, his chariots, and his horsemen.

B.1-3: Blaspheme

I Peter 4:

14 If you are reproached for the name of Christ,
blessed are you, for the Spirit of glory and of God
rests upon you. On their part He is blasphemed,
but on your part He is glorified.

II Samuel 12:

13 Then David said to Nathan, "I have sinned
against the LORD." And Nathan said to David,
"The LORD also has put away your sin; you shall
not die.
14 "However, because by this deed you have given
great occasion to the enemies of the LORD to
blaspheme, the child also who is born to you shall
surely die."

Mark 3:

29 "but he who blasphemes against the Holy Spirit
never has forgiveness, but is subject to eternal
condemnation" –
30 because they said, "He has an unclean spirit."

(Significance of Dispensations)

Mark 7:

25 For a woman whose young daughter had an
unclean spirit heard about Him, and she came and
fell at His feet.
26 The woman was a Greek, a Syro-Phoenician by
birth, and she kept asking Him to cast the demon
out of her daughter.
27 But Jesus said to her, "Let the children be filled
first, for it is not good to take the children's bread
and throw it to the little dogs."
28 And she answered and said to Him, "Yes, Lord,
yet even the little dogs under the table east from
the children's crumbs."

(Settling Relationships Problems)

Matthew 18:

15 "Moreover if your brother sins against you, go
and tell him his fault between you and him alone.
If he hears you, you have gained your brother.

God and His Children

A. 1-6: The Real Generation Gap

A: 7 – B.1-5 Raising Children

Matthew 12:

39 But He answered and said to them, "An evil
and adulterous generation seeks after a
sign, and no sign will be given to it except
the sign of the prophet Jonah."

Matthew 8:

12 But He sighed deeply in His spirit, and
said, "Why does this generation seek a
sign? Assuredly, I say to you, no sign
shall be given to this generation."

Mark 9:

19 He answered him and said, "O faithless
generation, how long shall I be with you?
How long shall I bear with you? Bring him to
Me."

Mark 13:

30 "Assuredly, I say to you, this generation
will by no means pass away till all these
things take place."

Luke 9:

40 "So I implored Your disciples to cast it out,
but they could not."
41 Then Jesus answered and said, "O faithless
and perverse generation, how long shall
I be with you and bear with you? …"

Luke 18:

25 "But first He must suffer many things and be
rejected by this generation."

Deuteronomy 21:

18 If a man has a stubborn and rebellious son
who will not obey the voice of his father or
the voice of his mother, and who, when they
have chastened him, will not heed them,
21 Then all the men of his city shall stone
him to death with stones; so you shall put
away the evil person from among you, and
all Israel shall hear and fear.

Proverbs 13:

24 He who spares his rod hates his son,
But he who loves him disciplines him promptly.

Deuteronomy 1:

39 '… your children, … , who today have
no knowledge of good and evil, …

Proverbs 22:

6 Train up a child in the way he should go,
And when he is old he will not depart from it.

Proverbs 19:

18 Chasten your son while there is hope,
And do not set your heart on his destruction.

Proverbs 23:

13 Do not withhold correction from a child,
For if you beat him with a rod, he will not die.
14 You shall beat him with a rod,
And deliver his soul from hell.

Ecclesiastes 11:

9 Rejoice, O young man, in your youth,
And let your heart cheer you in the days of your
youth;
Walk in the ways of your heart,
And in the sight of your eyes;
But know that for all these
God will bring you into judgment.
Therefore remove sorrow from your heart,
And put away evil from your flesh,
For childhood and youth are all vanity.

Ecclesiastes 12:

Remember now your Creator in the days of your
youth,
Before the difficult days come,
And the years draw near when you say,
"I have no pleasure in them."

Mark 7:

9 And He said to them, "All too well you reject the
commandment of God, that you may keep your
tradition.
10 "For Moses said, 'Honor your father and your
mother'; and 'He who curses father or mother, let
him be put to death.'
11 "But if you say, 'If a man says to his father or
mother, "Whatever profit you might have received
from me is Corban (that is, dedicated to temple)";
12 "and you no longer let him do anything for his
father or his mother,
13 "making the word of God of no effect through
your tradition which you have handed down. And
many such things you do."

Proverbs 29:

15 The rod and rebuke give wisdom,
But a child left *to himself* brings shame to
his mother.

*<See also Pg. 92.B; Pg. 111.A.3;
Pg. 112.B.2; Pg. 93.A.2:27
and Pg. 83.B.1>*

Notes

< YOU FILL THIS SPACE !

Excerpts from the Original Busy Man's Bible

George W. Cable was one of the great southern American authors, famous in his time for his vivid realism in his historical fiction stories set in meticulously accurate depictions of old Louisiana. He was virtually driven out of the south because his realistic and sympathetic descriptions of the plight of African Americans before and after the Civil War, were so well juxtaposed to the accurate and thus scandalous depictions of the gentry creoles of the day. A brief biography of Mr. Cable is located just behind this section of excerpts, if you want to know more about him.

After he moved to Massachusetts, he wrote a mostly forgotten book to challenge the busy people of the world to learn to study the Bible independently, as a businessman would study a proposal for business, or an employee would study his or her employer's instructions for a job.

In the following pages I have tried to select and present some highlights of George Washington Cable's 1891 book, because it is not in copyright and not easily available, yet needs to be read. I hope this will kindle your interest enough to search for and find and read his whole book, and get your own reaction to his message.

I am setting up a website (BusyMansBible.com) in the hopes that you and others will do more research and share your findings and opinions with me and others. I want to know things like how many copies sold, where, to whom, and with what impact. When you read his original BMB, try to imagine yourself as living in the 1890', attending a church like most people.

Note that all emphasis, underlining and bolding, was added by me. I couldn't help myself in those moments. It does not make those parts more important, because maybe my mind mood fluctuated as I read the book in several sittings. I hope that by now you know me well enough to realize that we will often have to agree to disagree, at least for the fn of it. ☺

Enjoy!

THE BUSY MAN'S BIBLE. AND How to Study and Teach It

George Washington Cable, 1891

I.
WHY STUDY IT?

THE very essence of Christ's teaching is that religion is not a mere province of life, but the whole empire of life both in the individual and throughout human society. Everything that is right at all is, in so far, "good religion," and nothing is entirely right until it is "good religion." Religion is not to be grouped with, but comprises and appropriates, science, art, literature, commerce, handicraft, unskilled labor, sleep, recreative pleasures, and the furnishing of recreative pleasures. All these, be they essentials or only aids to life's fullest development, are but parts and phases of religion. ...

II.
HOW TO BEGIN

Said a talented young man to a musician,

"Tell me how to play the sonatas of Beethoven in their true spirit."

Said the musician, " You ask too much of me; yet I will do what I can. What do you play these days?"

"Nothing."

"My friend!

How shall I tell you how to play Beethoven when it is not your habit to play anything at all? To know how to play Beethoven you must first of all know how to play."

So with the Bible. To know how to study it,

we must first of all know how to study.

... [Pg.13] ...

... But for the Bible thousands of teachers and scholars claim an immunity from fundamental methods of correct study, without which we cannot get a firmly founded, genuine conviction of the meaning and merits of anything.

... [Pg.14] ...

Oh for the rare gift to come to the study of the Word of God as if strangers to men's claims for it, until its truth, sinking into mind and heart, establish its authority and convince us of its inspiration ! The true way to begin the study of all books is the true way for the Bible.

Not in a spirit of carping unbelief, or of contempt or suspicion of our teachers; yet, in faithfulness to God, truth, and humanity, bearing in mind that things are not true because they are in the Bible, and cannot truly be Bible to us.

[Pg.15,16]
until they would be just as true to us if they were not in the Bible.

What? Shall we hold the Scriptures in diminished reverence! No; there need be no decrease in the quantity of our reverence that may not be immeasurably offset by increase in its quality. An ounce of reverence founded on one's own personal conviction and experience of Scripture truth is worth in God's sight a hundredweight of mere traditional reverence. Scripture truth; is the term a good one ? Truth suffers every time we put upon her the manacles of a limiting adjective. Scripture truth, scientific truth, gospel truth, practical truth! There is but one kind of truth; and to it, wherever and however found, we owe the solemn reverence we are prone to give to the Bible as its greatest vehicle, instead of to itself.

But even this is not saying enough. Truth itself, God's pure eternal truth, simply discovered, observed, and emotionally reverenced, is but treasure still buried. "The kingdom of God cometh not by [mere admiring] observation " of it. Only as truth melts and runs into our hearts, our lives, our daily conduct, and is there molded and coined into justice, righteousness, holiness, and universal love, do its latent powers become actual values. There cannot be even a correct approach to the study of truth, that regards truth or beauty as an ultimate and adequate end. All such studyings are, as to their spiritual value, but unfinished bridges ending in air, to be swept away by the first high wind of our intellectual pride, or the first high water of our physical appetites. Any real spiritual profit nay, any permanent, potential conviction of truth so got, is got without genuine credit to ourselves or our method, and, as it were, by lucky accident. Only the student who hungers and thirsts after righteousness shall be profitably filled.

If this be so, then how much less correct is an approach to the study of the Bible when prompted by the advance purpose to justify some theory of our own, orthodox or heterodox, or some belief of our church or of our social circle, or of our public community, concerning God's nature or man's duty. ...

... [Pg.17] ...

It was a pious monk who said, "Whoever seeketh an interpretation in this book shall get an answer from God; whoever bringeth an interpretation to this book shall get an answer from the Devil."

(Cont, - Excerpts from the Original Busy Man's Bible)

III.
HOW TO STUDY

... [Pg.21-23] ...

have we only the habit of studying books, or have we that vastly better gift, a studious habit of mind? For brains are so much better than books! And for our busy people there follows this welcome word: that it is only the habit of book study, and not the mere studious habit of mind, that taxes our time and leisure. Also, and better yet, that thousands who are too busy for book study are, in the few directions their minds take, more constant, diligent, genuine students, than thousands who, poring over books, have won the high degree of gold spectacles. The term "hard study" has got most lamentably entangled with the notion of printed pages, book-covers, and feats of memory; but when we substitute for it the nobler word, "hard thinking," we see how much of it there is, and how much more there might still be, in this great, busy world. We see how much of it there is good chance for, largely free from the time-devouring captivity of the student's desk and the late-glimmering lamp. True study is older than printing, or papyrus, or Moses' tables of stone.

We emphasize, then, these two points: First, the true spirit for the undertaking; the spirit whose incessant search is for truth, to turn it into holy being and lovely doing, and that proves, not truth from authority, but authority only from truth, and truth only from discernment and conviction in the mind and conscience of the inquirer himself; and, second, the true spirit for the method; the spirit that bids the mind be always diligent rather than docile; the spirit that weds a diligent mind to a docile heart; the spirit that values the studious mind above the study of books; the spirit of faithful, humble, hard thinking. Until we have in some degree possessed ourselves of these two essentials, this spirit for the undertaking and this spirit for the method, let as not say we know how to study the Bible.

(Cont, - Excerpts from the Original Busy Man's Bible)

IV.
BRAINS ARE BETTER THAN BOOKS.

… [Pg.28-29]

Let them simply give a seventh or tenth of that hard daily and hourly thinking which they give to their business, to the plainest utterances of the Bible upon God's nature and man's duty, and they will gain more knowledge and spiritual refreshment than by poring with eager receptiveness and docile assent over whole commentaries. They will get less learning, it may be, but more wisdom.

And so I make bold to say, when you do sit down to study Scripture, dispense, or at least try to dispense, from the beginning, with commentaries and the various other forms of lessonhelps. What! At the very start? Yes; rather then than later. Book-helps oftener narcotize than stimulate our own thought. They make us think we are thinking, when we are only locking step with the thought of some one else. Even when they help us to think, they are apt to make thinking too easy. Easy thinking yields but flimsy thought

V.
COGITATION FIRST COMMENTATORS LAST.

… [Pg.32,33] …

Get an answer from your own soul. Be it right or wrong, a shout or a whisper, get it from yourself. Then to press the school-room figure bring your slate to the class; look into the commentators and lesson-helps of past and present with diligence, with caution, with humility, and with hunger and thirst after righteousness "prove all things, hold fast that which is good."

VI.
COMPARE WATCHES.

… [Pg.40]

The mind the spirit that has accustomed itself to see that the fundamental truth and essential part of any sincere utterance remains potentially the same whether its literary form be mythus, legend, allegory, poetry, song, drama, romance, philosophy, or history, has learned the most important single thing that can be learned of how to study the Bible.

(Cont, - Excerpts from the Original Busy Man's Bible)

VII.

THE RIGHT SPIRIT IS NINE-TENTHS OF THE RIGHT METHOD.

[Pg.41] ...

What we come to the Bible for when we come rightly is not rules of life. What, not even them? No; we come for principles of life, not rules. Alas ! it is still our lower man that is speaking when we ask to be driven in harness by rules, instead of following, unharnessed, the beckoning guidance of principles. The essence of Christian conduct is to rise beyond the schoolmastership of rules and commandments into the fulfillment of principles and precepts, where duty is swallowed up in an understanding choice and an all-embracing love.

... [Pg.42-46]

To call a thing right without feeling it right, is wrong. To try to feel it right merely because it has been called right, is to yield that homage to authority which God has nowhere given us any right to yield to anything but that which we see to be true and right. And here we are put in mind that some truths in the Bible are worth vastly more than others, both for their essential importance and for the degree of our ability truly to possess them. The truth is worth nothing to us merely for being in the Bible. Its value begins with and is bounded by our spiritual discernment of it; not a consciousness of some supernatural operation, but a discernment that enlists the consent of our whole spirit, and no more depends any longer on whether the rest of mankind believe or deny it than if God had spoken it to us audibly out of the sky. Spiritual experience is authority. "Blessed art thou, Simon Bar-jona" and "The truth shall make you free."

Still, Bible students will say, "Give us rules. To give us only principles takes us by surprise. "We yearn for rules; a few, at least. Give us a method." Very well.

Bring to the study of the Bible such habits of study as belong to your particular daily life. Are you an employee? You give studious consideration to all your employer's orders and instructions. You observe minutely their letter; but you do so, not to evade, but the more surely to understand and execute, their spirit; and you decide the spirit of any particular order by the spirit of his whole business. You view his commands very practically. Your study of them is not speculative or controversial; it is always to know what to do, how to behave ! Bring that habit of study to God's and God's prophets' orders and instructions. Are you an employer? Have you a large and important business

Correspondence? Then you are a laborous student whenever you open your mail. You have to discern the exact intent, as far as you can, of each and every epistle. Now and then one puzzles you. Then you try to put yourself as far as you may into its writer's place. You call in all the knowledge you can get from others to help you to a conclusion, yet just as diligently you see to it that you catch no false bias from them, or accept their conclusions without truly making them your own. You beware, too, of all inelastic rules of interpretation. You also keep down your own self-assertion. You put away all ingenious constructions. And so you read and weigh, and read and weigh. Do so with the Bible.

Study, we say again, is a kind of eating. If your mind has not eaten much for a long time, feed lightly, but often. Line upon line. Three lines a day are far better than twenty-one lines once a week. Yet remember the Bible is no mere wood-pile, from which to draw a fagot or an armful at random. It is a structure. Enter in by its door. Never take up a book of the Bible to study it, or any part of it, without studying first the great main subject and motive of the book. To consider to whom, and specifically for what, it was written, is of more worth than to know by whom it is written. Never lose sight of these as you press on into the study of its parts. Never be content with an understanding of less than the eternal moral principle underlying the narrative or discourse, and its practical bearings on your own life. Push for these as a storming party pushes for the citadel, not stopping on the right hand or on the left to gather intellectual booty. **Never conclusively call an interpretation of God's Word your own because your church or mine declares or denies it, but only when you could not help but call it your own if all the churches on earth forbade it.** Yet remember the church is your teacher and your mother. Jesus Christ is her husband. ...

(Cont, - Excerpts from the Original Busy Man's Bible)

VIII.
LAPPING AS A LAP DOG LAPPETH.

... [Pg.46] ...

Don't cry "help" till your strength fails. Go straight to the Scripture text itself. Helps will be good by and by, not to give us first conceptions, but to supplement and confirm our right conceptions and correct our wrong ones. Read the Scripture text of the lesson carefully, with as much context as may be needed to make the meaning of the passage as plain as context can. Then read the text again, slowly and with great scrutiny. Read it aloud, distributing the emphasis with your best accuracy; this often sheds a sudden flood of light upon the page, and meanings that have been hiding away persistently start from cover at sound of a voice. Read again, noting marginal readings. Read again in the Revised Version. Read again. Sooner or later, this rubbing will bring out a new lustre. Note the lesson's time, place, circumstances, personages, their relations to each other, etc. ; but do not let these or any other by-paths carry you far from the main road. You are a busy man, seeking food and refreshment. Seek the vital, practical truth of the lesson. Try to find some central idea for which the passage seems to have been written. So found, it will be worth ten times as much as if found, without search, in a lesson-help. But do not be fanciful; do not be ingenious. Seek out the great simplicities of the science, art, and practice of living: "the way, the truth, the life." Try to simplify truth. You can never be sure that truth is truth until it is simple. The doctrines of first importance are all simple; what cannot be simplified is not of first importance; put it to one side. Christ never made the essentials of his religion hard to understand. . . . you meet your class-leader in the class hour, not "with the lesson prepared," every hour in the week would not be enough for that; it is a bottomless deep, but with yourself somewhat prepared for the lesson, and the leader enabled to teach you twice, thrice, four times as much as he could if you came to get your first impressions from him. If he cannot, you may suspect him of having "glanced over the lesson" for the first time a half-hour before the time for meeting his class: If so, quit him ! Find one who can teach you something, or else become a teacher yourself. Men fully as busy as you manage to do it, and grow in grace by it. So can you or I.

... [Pg.54] ...

It is a sad perversion of the true art of teaching, and saddest when the things taught are those of the Bible, for a teacher, either directly or by implication, to ask his pupils to pay assents and consents in advance of convictions imparted.

Too many "of us unconsciously satisfy ourselves with trying to teach the Bible, instead of simply using the Bible to teach Christianity."

X.

TEACH THE CHRIST-LIFE.

Studying or teaching, it is one; the pursuit of truth or beauty for mere truth or beauty's sake is a vain mistake of means for ends. The end of Bible teaching is not only not the Bible, it is not even truth or beauty; not even the beauty of holiness. It is the impartation to nay, better, it is the development of, truth all kinds of truth in the pupil's daily conduct, and of all kinds of beauty in his character. The end of all true Bible teaching we all know it; the only trouble is to remember it and not the ultimate end alone, but the immediate end every time we sit down to it is the developtment of a better likeness of Christ in the pupil's conduct and character.

... [Pg.62] ...

No follower of Christ may hope to profit any soul to whom he teaches the Bible except when he so teaches it as to widen and intensify the Christ-life in the affections and daily actions of his learners. This is the whole final purpose of the Bible. Whenever we do not in some degree accomplish this we do not succeed in really teaching the Bible at all. And since every counterfeit sort of Bible-teaching is easier than this sort, we should make this sort our paramount purpose . . .

... [Pg.63] ...

the noblest and most indispensable part of real study is not hard study, but hard thinking,

... [Pg.67] ...

it is a hundred times easier to get the essentials of Christianity into "the pupil's" head by way of his heart than into his heart by way of his head.

... [Pg.72] ...

Rules are risky things, soon worn out, easily spoiled, and, however good, bad as soon as they obscure our view of principles.

(Cont, - Excerpts from the Original Busy Man's Bible)

... [Pg.73] ...

teach always visibly and absorbingly in the pupil's personal interest, ... If we cannot begin our teaching with such love, if for a time only "the love of Christ constraineth us," yet let that move us dilligently to make ourselves love our pupils, few or many, in general and in particular, all and singular. If we can begin no better we can at least act out the love we only wish we felt; acting it out not in mere manners, but in acts and works lovingly and lovably performed, which by impulse we would do only for those we love.

... [Pg.76] ...

Religion is not a knowledge of certain things; it is a state of the heart in which all knowledge should be received and used. . . . It is coextensive with the universe.

But unselfishness is not self annihilation nor any effort after it. It is but the subordination of Self to its place in the universal harmony.

... [Pg.77] ...

True teaching, then, whether in the Bible or not, can be only that sort which moves the student to ask of every offered acquisition, not, How can this serve Self? but, What self-equipment will this add for that blessed service of the Universal Harmony which by its nature tends to make the whole universe myself and saves me from the folly and ruin of trying to make Self my universe.

... [Pg.79-81] ...

But you are a busy man or woman! So much the better ; you are in practice ; you have so many daily practical experiences of life by which to test the moral recipes of the Bible. But your calling, you insist, is not of a religious character. Then there is something wrong with it; or, more likely, only with you. Can it be that you are but an amateur Christian?

. . .

Going into Christianity professionally does not necessarily change our visible calling, but only its fundamental purposes, the Master for whom it is performed, and the ends to which its product is really and unreservedly dedicated. A man may be a Right Reverend missionary and not be a professional Christian. Another may be a professional Christian yet only saw logs or sell toys if that is the best he can do to help the world toward the likeness of God.

Take your Bible, busy Christian and, with it, teach that.

About the Original Author - George Washington Cable

I am just so fascinated with Mr. Cable, and wish I could find a recording of him reading, or better yet, singing. I have chosen to include a biographical excerpt from Little Pilgrimages, by E.F.Harkins published in 1903, (and thus in the public domain, so feel free to copy this section if you like). I hope this will stir you to find more about him, and like me, want to emulate him.

There is also a somewhat harsh literary criticism, with good biographical background on George Cable in the book *Social Historians*, By Harry Aubrey Toulmin, Jr., published in 1911 (and also in the public domain). Based on that criticism, I would probably not read some of his early short stories, because George Cable was trying too hard to prove his position on the wrongness of the Creoles of his time and the attitudes that allowed slavery to continue before the war. However, other of his writings sound like must reads to me, since I lived in New Orleans for over three years, and would certainly enjoy his intimate historical pictures.

Despite his failures to write fiction without overbearing liberal axe-grinding (something still done too much today), I think you will agree that he was a brilliant, logical, and extremely complicated man, with an amazing life story. Here is a short excerpt from *Social Historians* (Pgs. 36-37):

> George Washington Cable was born October twelfth, 1844, thus attaining the age of fourteen before the death of his father, which left the family in cramped circumstances. It, therefore, became necessary for the future author to start to work in the commission firm of Violet & Black. This was the beginning of his commercial career.
>
> In 1863 young Cable enlisted in the Fourth Mississippi Cavalry of the Confederate Army, in General Wirt Adam's Brigade. So very youthful was the boy's appearance at the age of nineteen that frequently he provoked the enlivening question from the Federal soldiers, " Are you sending babies to fight us? " The youngster made an excellent soldier, serving with daring, courage, and promptness, proving himself a strict disciplinarian; he spent his spare hours around the camp fire in the study of the Bible, Latin, and Mathematics. He was finally dangerously wounded in the armpit and forced to retire from the service.
>
> Upon the scattering of the forces after the surrender, young Cable procured a position as errand boy, while he studied civil engineering. When he finally became sufficiently competent, he joined a surveying party that was to go along the Achafalaya River in the Teche country. Here he contracted the breakbone fever " or malaria, which prevented him from doing active work for two years, but he was not entirely idle during this time, as he applied himself to the natural history and the human history of that section since the time of the first settlers.

Excerpt from ***Little Pilgrimages***, by E.F.Harkins

George Washington Cable was born in New Orleans on October 12, 1844. His father was of Virginian descent; his mother of New England. They were married in Indiana ten years before George was born, and they moved to New Orleans after the hard times of 1837. The father died in 1859, and then George, at the age of fifteen, went to work to help support the family. He was a very small boy for his age; and indeed it is related that in 1863, when the family was sent outside the Union lines for refusing to take the oath of allegiance, his sisters had no difficulty in obtaining permission to have their "little brother " accompany them. The "little brother," however, was not so harmless as he looked. He volunteered to fight for the Confederacy, and was mustered into the Fourth Mississippi Cavalry, then in Gen. Wirt Adams's brigade.

For a time after the war he rolled cotton on the New Orleans levees and carried a surveyor's chain along the banks of the Atchafalaya; and by and by he found a place on the New Orleans Picayune. He is therefore to be counted among the authors whose literary career started in the reporter's room. His strong taste for culture and his zeal for the public welfare soon made an outlet for themselves in short articles touching on current topics; and, though the articles were much enjoyed by the readers of the Picayune, the young writer before long felt the distaste for newspaper work which, early or late, comes to almost every journalist with high literary aims. Journalism is the best school of experience in the world, but it can be attended too long.

Cable resisted the fascinations of journalism firmly and wisely. At the height of his success he left the Picayune and went into the counting-room of a cotton house. He had a good eye for the picturesque features of daily life, the features met commonly in the daily papers, and at his leisure he wrote a few short stories based on New Orleans characters. One day these stories, which he had made no attempt to sell, came into the hands of an agent of the old Scribner's Monthly, who happened to visit Louisiana in connection with the well-remembered Great South papers. This agent, by name Edward King, praised the stories, and, at the author's request, sent one of them to New

(Cont. - excerpt from Little Pilgrimages, by E.F.Harkins)

York. The story, for some reason, came back; but the next one sent, "Sieur George," brought a note of acceptance and encouragement from Richard Watson Gilder, Doctor Holland's associate. A few years later a volume of these Louisiana sketches was published under the title of "Old Creole Days." It was immediately recognized as a notable addition to our short story literature. Nevertheless, the author stuck to his desk in the counting-room. Many another ambitious young writer, in the circumstances, would have given up his position and leaned entirely upon his pen. Young Cable had a cool head. He knew that he was moving forward handsomely, and that if he yielded to the excitement of the situation for a moment he might fall back. So his pen rusted for two years, when he accepted an order for a serial story. This turned out to be "The Grandissimes," a clear and entertaining exposition of the author's views of the old-fashioned Southern life, a happy mingling of fact and fiction, of fun and sobriety, of calm appreciation of the Louisiana aristocracy and a warm toleration of the struggles of the poor negro slaves. Of course, this attitude added nothing to the author's popularity among Southerners.

In 1879, when Mr. Cable was thirty-five years old, the business house in which he had worked to keep his feet on earth dissolved, and the clerk had to choose between returning to journalism and devoting him self entirely to literature. By this time he seems to have been more self-reliant and more confident. At any rate, he chose literature. The first thing he did was to decline to write for more than one publisher. It must be said again that a steadier head never produced a story.

A strong sense of duty, in fact, early established control of his work. His interests were not permitted to grow narrow. He realized that he possessed exceptionally abundant resources for the production of miscellaneous literature touching on the development of the middle South, and he determined to make the most of his possessions. In 1880, for example, we find him engaged in a special article on New Orleans for the Census Bureau, and his native city was also the theme of an article which he wrote for the "Encyclopedia Britannica." One of his critics has said: "Since Hawthorne's Custom House reports, few pages of the Government documents have been enriched by so discriminating a pen as in the exhaustive census monograph upon the past and present of the Southern metropolis." This paper led to a series of articles entitled "The Creoles of Louisiana," written for The Century, in which the reader will note an artistic combination of dry history and vivid imagination.

(Cont. - excerpt from Little Pilgrimages, by E.F.Harkins)

The business life which fortunately imposed so valuable a system upon him incidentally inspired his second novel, "Dr. Sevier," many of the scenes in which are faithful pictures of his own experiences as a youth. As in the historical sketches, so in this second novel the poetic imagination of the author fairly rivals his grasp of the prosaic relations existing between man and man. But such relations were supremely vital from his viewpoint, and his third novel, "Bonaventure," was written in moments stolen from the discussion of the questions of elections, prison systems, and the future of the negro. The reader will note in the hero of this story the personification of the practical strengthening and yet spiritualizing gospel which the author has enunciated in his private and public religious work. For it is important to chronicle that Mr. Cable has done as much to Christianize several communities as the most energetic minister would be expected to do ; and from his scrupulous performance of not merely the ordinary Christian duties but also of duties self-imposed, he has never allowed literature or society to beguile him.

Naturally his social and political studies drew many invitations to address public meetings. It was at Johns Hopkins University, while lecturing on literary art, that, upon the suggestion of President Gilman, he ventured for the first time to read selections from his own stories. The delight of the audience was no less a surprise to him than the realization of his own elocutionary skill. This he set about to cultivate, and with such success that for years afterward he was enthusiastically welcomed to the great cities. It was once estimated that in his busiest years on the platform he traveled more than ten thousand miles every twelve months.

Busy Man's Bible Challenges - Leisure Learning Time Entertaining Thought Exercises -

(Stretching the Truth Accurately Into Controversial Issues)

No, I don't want to encourage you to get into the endless debates on the common controversial doctrinal and philosophical issues that keep dividing "Christians" from others and themselves. But, I'd rather that, instead of watching TV or other unfulfilling forms of entertainment, you spend your leisure time fearlessly "going where no man has gone before" (ala Star Trek) exploring and searching for answers to, or at least a better understanding of, questions and issues usually deemed too mysterious or as simply to be "taken on faith, since we cannot really understand some things" in the Bible. As in Koan Zen practice, you should learn about yourself and God, even if you do not answer the "unanswerable" questions.

My hope is that, after you have made it through the BMB's core Bible passages sections, you will have proven for yourself the thesis that a busy person with business thinking skills can make sense of the Bible, and have developed in yourself a heart felt belief in and hunger for the truths of God, from the surface truths of historical and daily life details to the deeper spiritual "mysteries" of the "mind of Christ" as described in Pg.94B and 97A2,3 passages. (I don't see how you can read those passages and still put off trying to understand "deep" spiritual truths, quoting "His thoughts are so much higher than our[s]" as your excuse.)

Keep in mind that the goal George Cable and I have in mind for you is that your heart will be changed – NOT that you will become knowledgeable. That means you may not feel competent to eloquently express what you have figured out and learned, but now you know what you know and the light of it illuminates all your other perceptions and attitudes and shines out from within you.

The real problem I want to address is that too many people cannot even make up their own mind on some important issues, and appear to be content with rationalizing that they can never really "know" the answer to such issues. The result is a numbing of their sense of the importance of spiritual matters, which then leaves only a life that is materialistically guided. After all, you at least subconsciously think, how can it be important to you if it is too hard to understand, even for the supposed theological experts!

I think what George Cable was saying is that too many people get either lazy or intimidated when it comes to "religious" matters, and simply adopt the beliefs of some "authority" on each issue, especially the issue about whether "Laity" can, and /or should, attempt to study and figure out spiritual matters themselves. This ends up with the masses of layman only knowing what some authority believes, when actually, that so-called "authority" most often merely believes that he or she knows the correct stance to believe, and actually does not possess any true spiritual wisdom on a specific topic that manifests spiritually in their own life.

And, if a topic does not have real potential for being manifest spiritually in your life, then why waste time with it !?!

So, to get you thinking independently of other humans in seeking to understand God's Truth and "spiritual" things, I suggest attempting to think about answers to some difficult, and often controversial, questions often asked about Christianity by skeptics. I have included examples of challenges on some of my favorite topics to study and discuss, just to illustrate and hopefully give you a taste for doing the same. When it comes to these specific topics, I believe we should not be afraid to think in directions that are unpopular or politically incorrect within the church or society.

Yes, these are highly debatable theories and highly controversial topics. That is exactly the point! I think that intelligent, busy people are now seeking mental as well as physical fitness, and the well deserved image of sluggardly avoidance of hard thinking by Christians when it comes to these difficult topics is one big reason that Zen meditation, especially Koan practice, has become so popular with busy people in our western culture. I know I said this before, in my Prologue of this book, but I think it is a real shame that the Christian educators are still clinging to what money making power positions they have, instead of breaking away from their old organized religious megopoly business model altogether, as it slowly loses market share to the New Age message hawkers. It is sad to see the organized church vainly trying to adopt the competition's successful entertainment marketing style, rather than repenting from competition, and trying instead to just imitate Jesus and the apostles.

It is also sad to see the intellectual laziness of the religious establishment as each subdivision declares its own dogma as necessary, and unwilling to attempt the hard thinking to demystify the Bible to debunk all the dogma, whether from other denominations or from secular Humanists, etc. If people who believe in Truth cannot forsake dogma, despite the grip it appears to provide on "the faithful" remnant, and fearlessly seize the high ground of reason, then they will continue to fight in the pits of pretense, and inevitably lose to the only weapon the opposition has – Political Correctness, enforced by entertainment idols and mass media. Oops! I got up on a soapbox there. Sorry.

So, the **Instructions for the BMB Challenges:**

1. Use the same approach as the Koan Zen masters, who, after being fully educated in the philosophy of their religion, then meditated on specific applications (anecdotal stories) and tried to use that effort to cause the "truths" to become clear and take hold in their heart and mind. The analog to the Zen philosophies would be the Truths revealed in rightly dividing the Bible scriptures, and, the analog to meditating on the Zen's "one hand clapping" challenges, at least here, is "hard thinking" on my BMB Challenges. Note that the Koan Zen practice seems an exact shadow of the thought life of the blessed man of Psalm 1:2 who, "in His Law he meditates day and night".

2. You must keep your brain in the right mode of seeking heart growth, rather than simple head knowledge, remembering Psalm 131, verse 1:

> LORD, my heart is not haughty, Nor my eyes lofty.
> Neither do I concern myself with great matters,
> Nor with things too profound for me.

Busy Man's Bible Challenges

Overview

Challenge #1

Dimensions of Truth – Classifying Facts By Levels of Reality

This is a reprint of the first handout diagram for a class I taught at church in 2001. The purpose of the class was to introduce Bible students to an important aspect of interpreting ("rightly dividing") Bible "data" – the skill of categorizing each particular piece of information in the Bible as applying to one aspect (level or layer) of reality to which it was meant to apply. There are **two main points** to this concept. The **first** is that all scripture was written to convey meaningful "data" to the reader, not confuse them. The **second** is that by figuring out what was the intended understanding of each passage we can identify each piece of information (data) and categorize it according to what I call "levels of truth" or "dimensions of reality" before applying it to the larger context of all we know from the Bible.

This first BMB Challenge is meant to be simply an introductory exercise in learning to begin thinking in these terms, and to try doing some categorization. It is only intended to provoke some thought and maybe generate some new thinking along this line, and hopefully some feedback (to BusyMansBible.com) I plan on doing a full chapter in a future book, and would love to have some "community" debate and input.

Challenge #2

Challenging Others to Think – Against PC Propaganda

("in humility correcting those who are in opposition, if God perhaps will grant them…" IITim.2:25)

People today, especially the younger generation, are proud to be blissfully ignorant and **zealously apathetic** towards any idea that is not popular with their peers, no matter if it is an important truth. Most are having such a hard time keeping their lifestyle comfortable and fun, that they just DO NOT want to hear about anything controversial that might potentially bother them enough to actually want to do something about it, especially if it may make them less popular. HORRORS! ☺

So how do you get someone like that to give even a few moments of thought to the war of spiritual truth versus Political Correctness propaganda, and get them to even consider that maybe this is important?

This BMB Challenge asks you to stretch you mind around some thought exercises that will challenge the core values I hope have grown strong in your heart since you have studied hard using the BMB core passages and George Cable's methods. The four pages (again, a hand out for a Sunday School class years ago) presented for this BMB Challenge are actually meant to be an example of this category of teaching, that I want you to consider and debate in your own mind, its merits and weaknesses, hopefully for you to vastly improve, or even rewrite as your own. Do it honestly for yourself, fearlessly willing to give up your previously professed beliefs, no matter how embarrassing it might feel.

Challenge #3

What's Wrong With the Church? – ~~and How to Fix It~~.

This is a reprint of a message I gave at church in the 90's, but is still relevant today. I included it here as an example of a topic which needs the thoughtful time and energies of the BMB type of busy men and women, in the hope of stimulating prayer, study, thought, and dialog about it, in hopes of us truly finding a "Fix" for the much worse situation of the Church today (2009). In this instance I have removed the half of the message that proposed "How to Fix It," because this book is all about You doing your own thinking, and not learning my solutions, just my methods.

I feel we need a new approach for a world in which Christians are increasingly more persecuted, even in America. What should be the strategy of the church in support of Christians in the last days before Christ's return, if you believe (per II Peter 3:9, and II Thess. 2:10) that this will happen only after it become impossible for a human to be "converted" because of the hostile culture. (But that is a different topic; so, I'll stop my intro now.)

Challenge #4

Fractally Thinking – (Is There a Plan for My Life?)

This is a totally new angle on applying the growing understanding of the natural world stemming from the modern mathematics field of Fractal Geometry. This new math has shown that a mathematical model can be built for what so far appears to be any apparently random collections of objects in nature. Scientists are discovering amazing design principles for things like forests and river valleys. So I want to ask the question "why doesn't anyone notice the 'hand of the Creator' in what are essentially elegantly designed systems, and then extrapolate from that discovery and begin to wonder about how far reaching this new math theory might be.

My goal is to spark imagination, discussion and creative research into the logical implications of this. The real payoff to you of participating in this challenge should be a stretching of your mind into handling difficult passages on concepts like "spiritual growth" (pg.87-88A) and "free will" and "predestination" (pg.75-76) from a new, higher vantage point that at least feels more real and scientific, and less mysterious. The "Fractally Thinking" exercise and the resulting new thinking strength can then be used to go back over the Bible passages on those subjects and more and see what you discover from that higher view point. Sure, your thinking won't rise to the level the scripture ascribes to God in Isaiah 55:8-9, but they might reach that promised in John 16:13, I Cor.13:2, I Cor. 2,16, Eph.3:3-4, and I John 1:26, etc.

As with the levels of truth in BMB Challenge #1, there are goals at every level. The innermost goal of this challenge is the same as for all, for that matter, this entire book – that new logic structures will be built and strengthened in your innermost paradigm, so that your view of the world around you and your responses to it will be changed to be more like that of Jesus. May "Christ live in you" be a reality.

Busy Man's Bible Challenge #1

Dimensions of Truth – Classifying Facts By Levels of Reality

Both well meaning and malevolent people have often given "biblical truth" a bad image in the public eye, when they promote a particular passage as having a meaning that is inappropriate at best, and often absurd, although apparently literal. How do you make sense of Bible scriptures that sometimes appear contradictory to logic or even to the Bible itself, without giving in to those who want to say that everything in the Bible is symbolic myth and allegorical stories? The answer, of course, is context.

The graphic below attempts to represent a top level view of the large scale context, or framework, for beliefs and facts of a person who has recognized and accepted the spiritually revealed foundational truth of the Bible, and who desires their personal world view to help them to be in sync with the source, or author, of that harmonious truth. The concentric circles of the framework illustrate the levels, or layers, of reality to which "factual information" found in the Bible applies.

Dimensions of Truth

Within A Paradigm Built on Spiritual Revelation

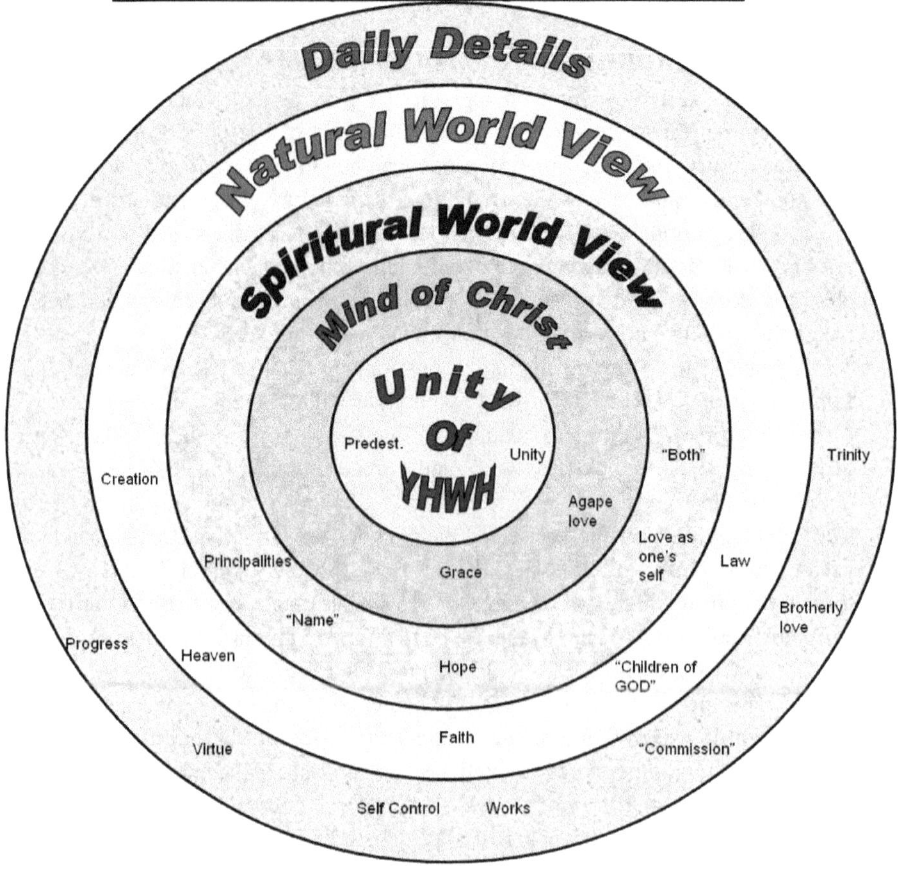

One phrase in a Bible passage may contain such data (facts, reproofs and instructions – see Pg.95A4.c) belonging to more than one dimension of truth.

Please bear with me as I try a metaphor – I challenge you to then try to think up your own. Try to view the diagram as though you are looking down on a mythical fruit tree that represents a person's "world view" framework for life.

In the outer layer, you can study and understand the interaction of the leaves, and hopefully fruit, with the surrounding world. Consider that you could be a successful fruit tree farmer, at least during good years, with only an understanding of the workings of the tree that you can observe without dissecting the tree.

To study and understand the information in the next "Dimension of Truth" layer you would have to dissect it and observe the oozing sap and count the rings and dig out the roots, so that you now understand why the tree thrives in one location more than another (depending on whether it has a tap root or surface spreading roots, etc.).

To study and understand the information in the next layer you would need a modern electron microscope, so that you could discover the DNA of the tree, and observe the cellular specializations of the RNA controlled protein synthesis and nuclear membrane functionalities, etc. To describe these invisible attributes you would need a new language, that is pretty meaningless outside of this field of study.

To study and understand the information in the next layer, you would have to use a computer to compare all the genetic information from all trees, and even all living organisms, to see the amazing commonality, and recognize the common designs found in all, and the nuances of variations that result in different expressions of "Life" forms. You would probably need to employ "fractal theory" math modeling (see http://en.wikipedia.org/wiki/Fractal_analysis and BMB Challenge #3) in this effort.

Before going to the next layer, let me point out that with the four outer layers of data, you can now, for example, work on environmental studies, and try to understand and improve the interacting effects of one form of life with another. You can discover how the toxic wastes from one may start a domino effect that might endanger all if the checks and balances in nature were disrupted. You have in these four layers the equivalent of all that today's Politically Correct notion of science is seen to include.

To study and understand the information in the innermost layer, you would have to first imagine that maybe there is another level of truth as yet unseen, much as it was before we had modern technology and discovered the hidden world and language of DNA, etc. You would have to believe that the adage "where there is smoke, there is fire" applies to all the claims and reports of religious spiritual experiences and other paranormal phenomena. Personally, I am amazed at the phobia that the religiously atheistic scientists show in avoiding what logically appear certain to be the scientific realm wherein we might discover the mechanics of teleportation and time travel! However, for now, all I am trying to point out is that for you to understand the Bible, you must realize that many truths in it were meant to pertain to this realm as a real layer of science. Whether you believe that this realm is real science or not, the scribes and keepers of the Bible did, and you will misunderstand them and be confused when their language is attempting to convey truths at this level, per Isaiah 55:8-9 (Pg.9A3).

The best, if not only way to learn and understand this is by considering examples. I'll try to explain one at each level.

1. A factual truth about "self Control" can be applied to the surface layer of reality – the "Daily Details" of our life, without supporting any extrapolations on aspects of faith or law or any deeper spiritual truths.

2. A passage or even just a phrase may tell us something about the physical aspects of earth, or heaven, or the power of faith, or the strength of God's physical protection for His "children" without giving specific instructions applicable to a daily decision, and without supporting extrapolations concerning our "body as a living sacrifice" or God's Love for us. For example a passage might say "your faith has made you whole" without meaning that it is God's will that all are healed, or that faith is always the key ingredient or essence of healing; any more than if I saw you moving a stack of red paint buckets from the front of a building to the rear and said "Don't run with paint, or you'll end up covered in red!" means that all paint is red or that you certainly will be covered up every time you run with red paint. A statement must be understood to sometimes be about one particular event, and one particular aspect of an event, useful for instruction only as an example of possibilities, and realities at the level of truth intended.

3. This is a hard one. The word "Both" shown in this layer in the diagram refers to "Both the Father and the Son" (e.g. Pg.97A2), that literally seems to say that they are two separate persons. The results of misundertanding this as spiritual term has been both the proliferation of the idea that the "Trinity" includes separate "persons" as well as fodder for phony arguments by cults about Jesus being separate from God. Another example is that John 6:63 (Pg.87A2) only applies to our "Spiritual World View" and does not change the facts that we are "Children of God" and our physical flesh is quite important in defining who we are both in its influences on our soul and our proper or improper use of it.

4. Despite what some churches preach, I John 4:6-8 (Pg.14B4) does not mean you are going to Hell if you listen to the Beatles more than John or Paul's epistles, or if you show less that perfect "agape love" at all times. John especially, often describes the workings of "the mind of Christ" so that we know Him and hope to be more like Him, since we "have the Mind of Christ" in us (and our old brain baggage, too).

5. Truth at the deepest level has no boundaries of space-time or even direct application to it, other than the fact that spiritual and physical manifestations of such truth exist, and indeed were necessary to "prove" and thereby complete the truths. For example, the truths of predestination are not meant to give us guidance in decisions about our daily life, and the infinite grace and love of Christ does not lessen the importance of our doing good works and avoiding sin.

I now hereby challenge you to first ponder and try to improve the above 5 examples; and then, to consider the sample scattering of terms in the diagram, and decide if they are placed in the correct layers, and why or why not, as well as example scriptures for each term placement. [Yes, I was very short in my examples and instructions, because I limited it to just 3 pages. Without boundaries I ramble 4ever!]

BUSY MAN'S BIBLE CHALLENGE #2

Evangelistic Apologetics

("in humility correcting those who are in opposition, if God perhaps will grant them…" IITim.2:25)

People today, especially the younger generation, are proud to be blissfully ignorant, and **zealously apathetic** towards any idea that is not popular with their peers, no matter if it is important truth. Most are having such a hard time keeping their lifestyle comfortable and fun, that they just DO NOT want to hear about anything controversial, that might potentially bother them enough to actually want to do something about it. So how do you get someone like that to give even a few moments of thought to the subject and get them to even consider that maybe this is important?

Try moving a conversation (e.g. about a news story or Ben Stein's movie ***Expelled***) to where you can discuss that a definition of Science which leaves out the supernatural is unnecessarily restricting itself from discovering any truths and scientific discoveries and the power that might be untapped by old fashioned, post-modern notions of science. Make the point that it is undeniable that there are at least two very strong and opposing viewpoints being pushed at the educated population, one by the main-stream entertainment and secular culture, and the other by Christian churches and businesses selling their self and family improvement ideas.

If you can get someone to acknowledge that the issue is important and polarized and somewhat daunting (understatement of the year) for any individual to research and make a truly logical decision, then try to propose the following as possibly the way to get some feel for what direction you should lean, perhaps prior to digging deeper.

Imagine how a good psychologist might help a woman try to choose between two men fighting for her hand in marriage. Suppose this scenario:

> they both look good and seem to have a lot to offer, until each calls the other evil;
> the first one says he has proof that the other is a liar and wants a full debate on it,
> and the second calls the first guy a certified lunatic, and refuses any debate.
> Both warn that it would be a huge and dangerous mistake if she chose the other.

If the poor girl had met and fallen for just of one of them first, either one, she would easily say yes to him and ignore the other, but since she likes them both, she has to admit that at least one of them must be either a liar or a loony. How can she choose?

A trained objective psychologist would have her do the following:

1. Look into each one's history, to learn where he is coming from, and thus better understand him. Answer the questions, "Could he really be a loony? Would he really lie to me? What are his motivations for lying to me?"
2. Look into their accomplishments and reputation, and judge who they are by their "fruit" and other relationships. Try to recall any character inconsistencies.
3. Try to nail down a few specific issues that you can test for truth.
4. Analyze their behavior for body language clues to which one is telling the truth.

Exercise 1 for You: Think about how you would apply the 4 steps above to the culture war between Christians and Secular Humanists. Write down specific results for each case and each contender. Is there more than one suitor for your philosophical affections? After you have figured out how you would argue the above, try it with another person whose beliefs are like yours, and then a friend who is solidly secular.

BMB Challenge # 2 Exercise 2 for You:

Here is a step by step approach to then move into discussions of the scientific view of the Bible. Note this will probably only work with a friend who knows you really care.

1. Bring a conversation to the point where you can ask them "What do you believe, anyway?" If you think it appropriate you could say something like, "There's this guy at church who's arguing about the history and problems of Darwinism and daring us to try and come up with any real reasons to believe in "Macro Evolution" (point out that Gregor Mendel's genetics is "Micro Evolution only). It would be fun to come up with something really strong, but so far I really can't find something he can't soundly put down."
2. Ask them "Well, " (or "So,") "WHY do you believe that? I would really like to understand how people believe that, but so far I can't find ANYONE who actually understands and can give me any good reason to believe that the story of Macro Evolution (not genetics) is any more than just an old pagan religion that has enjoyed very good publicity and financial backing from Hollywood and the news media, and other very rich, greedy, self-centered, people who desperately want to avoid any kind of Guilt trip being put on them."
3. Then say, "As far as I can find out Evolution just became popular by intense publicity and peer pressure to agree with it, and a bunch of heralded "Discoveries" and "Theories" that were ALL later proven to be either out-right hoaxes or plain bad science. Can you tell me even ONE of the major publicized proofs or tenets of Evolution that was used to promote it before, say, 1950, that has not been discredited by the majority of the scientific community? And can you tell me of any one of these that the schools actually took out of their Evolution pushing text books after being scientifically shot down? It seems to me that there is a very solid track record here that anyone can see that those pushing Darwinism have never been bothered by Ethics or the idea that Truth is not something you fabricate!"
4. After they respond by saying "Hey, man! I really don't have time to worry about that kind of stuff! Why should I? You can't tell me that all the schools and all the TV people have been lying to everybody! What does it matter anyway?! What difference does it make if I believe in Darwin?" (And This part is only if they want you to think they believe in God.) "Anyway, I think that God probably used Evolution and helped things along here and there to create stuff."
5. Then ask, "Haven't you heard? 'The Truth will set you Free' and Lies will enslave you. Seems to me it might be worth, maybe, 30 minutes to try to figure out what you actually know about what you believe. After all a guiding principal of marketing is that if people can be made to believe something without understanding it, then you can take advantage of their blissful ignorance. Hey, I'm not asking much. Help me out here, as a favor to me. Enlighten me. Help me understand. Just come up the with the 3 most solid reasons for believing that God did NOT create everything in 6 days 6000 years ago. Please!"
6. If needed you can say, "Hey! Come on! If you won't do it just to help me, I wish you would listen to this. I think it's pretty important. As I see it there are only 4 possibilities in life:

- "1. Evolution is true, there is no afterlife or God and you know it, and you live your whole life trying to pretend life has meaning, but knowing it doesn't, you must work and play hard to keep yourself or at least others from seeing that you are deeply miserable, hating Christians for causing fear of death; then you die into nothingness and are forgotten.
- "2. Evolution is true but you mistakenly think God created everything, and you live your whole life with the strength and hope that your life is important, and that glorious rewards for your sufferings and an eternity with God awaits you; then you die into nothingness and are forgotten.
- "3. Evolution is False and you Know God created everything, and you live your whole life with the real power of the Spirit of God, not to mention the strength and hope that comes from knowing your life is important and that eternity with God awaits you; then you die and enter a wonderful Eternal life with God and all those you have loved.
- "4. Evolution is a Lie, but you believe it, and live your whole life trying to pretend it has meaning, and knowing it doesn't, are at best secretly miserable, until you die and have to spend a conscious eternity with all of the demonic spirits that have had free play with you and enslaved you with lies all your life, and with only tormenting memories of the Good you experienced in life but failed to recognize as gifts from God.

7. "Wow! It seems like a bad bet to me! You have nothing to gain if your view of Truth is right, and everything to loose if your view of Truth is wrong. It seems to me that if you are right, my beliefs will probably provide me with a happier, if no more meaningful life than yours. It seems obvious that this is an important concept to have right!."
8. Then, if you can, bring up some of the things presented below, to challenge them to get answers to those fatal flaws in the popular theory of Evolution.

There are only 2 possible logical views (and one New-Age view) :

1. There is a God

2. There is not

(3.) A new anti-logical view is that We are god (& one with the creation/ Mother-Earth) and Truth and Logic are mere illusions. (This is not a theory but merely the feeling that one does not have to submit to any external idea or illusion, because we create our universe, and since logic does not exist, it cannot be argued. This is not really new, but a mutation of Hinduism confronted by modern science.

What are the features of each of the 2 rational views:

1. Recognition of a Creator in the Creation

Belief that God is Awesome, SuperNatural, SuperPowerful, and puts the 6 or 7000 year history of the "space-time" universe within a larger perspective where it is essentially a "Petrie dish" part of the Eternal Spiritual realm.

Belief that God is good and created us (as His offspring) for a purpose, that we can, and thus should (& thus can) discover and accomplish.

That Evil was created for a purpose and will perform as planned by God. (Evil will deceive man so that man will deny the creator.)

That History (astronomic, geologic, and social) is controlled by God (and was "Catastrophic") to support and accomplish His specific plans in 7000 years.

2. Denial of the Creator must be as active as His own declarations

A high esteem is given to our own personalities, potentials, proclivities, lusts and desires (wants, appetites and freedoms)
Pride in our ability to choose and accomplish our own purpose and destiny
A redefinition of all Truth that points to a Creator, so as to facilitate the above.
A zeal to avoid the pain that a conscience would inflict upon us if anything we choose to do were felt to be wrong.
A constant effort to find "meaning" in life, or, to reinforce the values in life to which one has chosen to ascribe meaningfulness.
That History must be ruled by random chance and "Uniformitarianism" of natural laws such that Nihilistic logic can provide freedom from moral conscience.

The resulting lifestyles ("Fruit") of these views are:

1. Creationist View
    1. Focus on the Eternal
    2. Obedience to God
    3. Success is acquiring eternal life with God, our Father. For others too.
2. Evolutionist (nihilist/hedonist)View
    1. Focus on the Now
    2. Obedience to one's own appetites and desires
    3. Success is acquiring wealth, pleasure, power

Questions to Ponder:

Which one of the above lifestyles will produce more profits for Industrial "Kings"?

Which kind of population would be more attractive to Madison Ave. style Marketing? – a population of :

1. clear headed Free thinking individuals who can spot an untruth easily, and want nothing to do with it - or -
2. confused non-thinking "sheep" who have been enslaved to lies by the strength of their own pride.

That's easy! Slaves to lusts make up the biggest "Market" (Consumers).

Exercise 3 for You: If organizations have been deceptively promoting Evolution, and were put on trial for enslaving humanity, what would be their:

Motives
Opportunity (ability)
Evidence (Errors, Omissions, Lies and Deceptions)

Final Question for You: Do you think discussions and debates, like described above, help you build a heart that is strong and confident in pursuit of truth? The truth that makes you care more about others? Keep in mind Paul's warning to Timothy:

II Timothy 4:
2 Preach the word! Be ready in season and out of season. Convince, rebuke, exhort, with all longsuffering and teaching.
3 For the time will come when they will not endure sound doctrine, but according to their own desires, because they have itching ears, they will heap up for themselves teachers;
4 and they will turn their ears away from the truth, and be turned aside to fables.

Busy Man's Biblical Challenge #3

What's Wrong With The Church Today… ~~AND How to Fix It~~

1st. The Obvious Symptoms

- There is no forward momentum in conquering the world
- There is a real lack of Unity & real Love. Even the world sees us mostly as Spiritually wounded, maimed, dead, or scared, from fighting within ourselves.

The Obvious Problems (that we acknowledge and wish we could fight) **:**

- lack of power – the power of God is not evident in our lives
- proud, fragmented groups – at best, protecting and taking care of themselves

The Not So Obvious Causes (progressive - one leads to the other)

- Lawlessness – Non-Biblical religion, (due to no real, Biblical authority structure)
- Carnal Distraction – addicted to Entertainment, the most glorified god of our culture (results from Lawlessness).
- Fear of Persecution and Discomfort (much less sharing in the sufferings of Christ)

The True Root Cause:

THE SPIRIT OF ANTICHRIST, WHO IS A TRINITY OF LIES:

1. There is no Creator God (Denying the Father)
2. Jesus is not God (Denying the Son)
3. Jesus the man is not alive and involved (Denying the Holy Spirit – the only unforgivable sin)

The Bottom Line Cause: OUR CHOICE

Even though we know that the Word tells us how to fight, WE CHOOSE to not fight against the Spirit of AntiChrist, because we prefer to blend in and avoid persecution, and enjoy entertainment when we know we should be in the fight.

The Result: Unbelief & all the Problems listed above.

Here is a Metaphor that illustrates where we are.

Picture the lawless frontier as seen in the American western movies. Everyone wearing a gun, and ready to settle any argument by blowing away the other side; banding together in gangs to help win feuds and feel strength in numbers, when you inevitably met up at the bar rooms with those who disagree with you, to indulge in your lusts of the flesh, because the only thing that everyone agrees on is that entertainment is important. Politeness and respect are given according to a man's rank in terms of his demonstrated fighting skills, and those of his gang. Authority exists in gangs based on each person's value to the gang, which simply means effectiveness in fighting and strategic planning for winning fights and gaining wealth, to maintain the best lifestyle possible.

Not essentially different from our world today, except that the weapons are different and the gangs are called businesses, families, and churches, etc.

The Problem Restated:

We have chosen to set up church in the lawless frontier, and out of fear, chosen to organize and defend ourselves the same way the non-Christians do; including adopting their rules of social and political conduct, under the guise of making "the lost" feel more comfortable in our midst. This all began when we stopped believing in the power of the Holy Spirit and the value of His "Law".

Here is The "Law":

- let each one esteem the other more highly than himself.
- love your enemies, … do good to those who hate you, pray for those who spitefully use you & persecute you.
- walk as Jesus walked, giving up all for "The Cause", which is to **seek and save the lost**
- make disciples, each one using their **gift**(s) as given by the Holy Spirit, for the edification of the Body
- and thus, Honor the Lord your God. (Love the Lord with **all** your heart, **all** your soul, & **all** your mind.)
- Pray always, and in all things give thanks. (Humble ourselves and pray.) Abide in His Truth.
- < *you complete this!* >
-
-

Therefore, The Fix for the Body of Christ: *(I left just enough to tease you for my own entertainment. It's up to you to fill in the blanks. ☺ Better yet, write a lot.)*

- Refocus _____
- Re-establish _____
- Disarm & practice ____, allowing ____

OK you say, but specifically how?

1st. Review _____

- Let ____
- ____
- Review ____, and begin ____.
- Wait ______ it.

Then Let's _____ and:

BUSY MAN'S BIBLICAL CHALLENGE #4

Fractally Thinking

If you are not aware of the advances in mathematical thinking coming since Fractal Theory has been widely accepted, then I recommend that you go find a PBS documentary or other easy learning reference to learn about it. I was a math major (geek) in college, but was "too smart" to go back to finish my degree, even though I only need a few more hours. I am a bit sad that I missed out on this mathematical excitement, because I was caught up in the strong current of a successful career in the petrochemical engineering world by the time Benoit Mandelbrot's branch of math came to light.

Briefly, Fractal theory introduced the use of a new dimension, called "roughness" or "coarseness" that, when used to vary parameters to special recursive math formula functions, enabled useful computer simulation models of biological systems, and other, previously thought-to-be-too-complex-to-be-modeled, systems like weather, forests, river flood plains, coastal ecosystems, etc. This new math brought about some amazing discoveries such as how, when reduced to their Fractal formulae, things like a "healthy heartbeat" and a mountain range seem to share a common design. How cool is that! Fractal geometry has shown the math and science community that it was definitely wrong to think that a mathematical description is not possible for anything.

What amazes me is how the majority of "scientists" have such a strong mental blindness, due to their powerful religion of atheistic hedonism, which prevents them from realizing that this Fractal theory is not something humans created, but simply are just now discovering. They have this new knowledge but cannot let it enter into the core of their mind, because they subconsciously know and fear it would then confront them with the axiom, that the truth and design of mathematics, or any non contingent idea, are absolute and eternal; and thus, exist outside the dimension of time and space; and thus, can not be assumed to have come into existence suddenly as a result of a hiccup in chaos that began a first "Big Bang". Since the core of their mind is built to support their nihilistic-hedonistic religion, there is no room for such an opposing idea.

Before Fractal theory their delusion required slightly less faith, because of the apparent, chaotic and "non-mathematical" nature of life and so many things and systems in nature. Now, however, "they are without excuse" because God's "eternal power" and "invisible attributes are clearly seen, being understood by" them, and they must truly have hard, corrupt hearts to choose their flimsy self-faith, and reject the Spirit of Truth, which could set them free of their subconscious dread of death.

But enough of the background of Fractal theory. If you want to spend more time pondering the philosophy of Truth, per the above, I suggest, as a start, you read and ponder my web page titled "God or Nothing?" on BusyMansBible.com. But now, on to a new thought exercise extrapolating on this. (This exercise is specifically meant for those I think of as "spiritually handicapped" like myself.)

Could There Be A Plan for My Life?

Do I have "free will" or "Free Will" or am I "pre-destined" and "elected" and "foreknown" or "fore-ordained" to make a fixed set of good and bad "choices" in my life, and (or is it "or"?), do passages like Ephesians 1:4-11 that say "**He chose us in Him before the foundation of the world, ... predestined according to the purpose of Him who works all things according to the counsel of His will**" really mean what they appear to say, and if so, "How fair is that!" ?

Here we have a subject that is right in the center of all those endlessly debatable philosophical subjects that old fashioned religion practitioners (lazy thinkers) like to elevate to the level of "mysteries" that we must simply take on faith, just prior to telling us exactly what we must believe if we don't want to be a heretic.

Before diving into this, because of the risk of this being read outside of the context of the BMB book, I want to remind you (now would be a good time to read skipped pages (iv - xiii) of the "Prologue" of this book if you skipped it as directed, and) to keep in mind that I want you to have fun and not take me too seriously when discussing this serious stuff, so that you can likewise not be taking yourself too seriously, and thus be more likely, in my opinion, to engage the right parts of your whole self, soul, heart, mind and spirit, (more technically: your right spirit within your renewed mind of your humble heart growing your eternal soul – per the exercise of "BMB Challenge #1"), and be able to glean and absorb the essence of the truths that I, like you, need and hope to integrate into "our" (another reference back to "BMB Challenge #1", about "unity") thinking and feelings when this subject, or those like it, comes up in academic discussions and/or real life decision/action moments.

As George W. Cable pointed out, if I am to be successful at teaching you something, you must know me well enough that you actually enjoy my anecdotes of my ponderings on the subject being taught, and feel invited and excited to take up the thought challenges, ready to dissect and challenge every fact and idea tidbit I present, and to dig in and fearlessly come up with your own assessments and ideas that help you feel like some valuable truth is entering your soul in such a way as to make a difference in your life, and thus satisfying a "hunger and thirst" within you.

Integral to this desire of mine, for you, is the silliness of my paragraph long, run-on sentences with truly too many nerdy side-barbs, and flourishes; because, I think this style best resembles the metaphor I think best describes the kind of debate I wish we could have. Picture me as a juggler, who understands that, like any sport, to reach the highest potential, in this case number of objects juggled in the air at the same time, you must be having fun, and at a certain point, to have more fun you must get another juggler involved, and if that juggler is not having fun with you, you will not reach your personal and combined potentials in the sport.

OK! Enough said on all that. Let me tell you a fraction of my ponderings on how Fractal theory relates to "a plan for my life."

I want to propose a new line of study building on the discovery that Fractal geometry can probably describe a mathematical design for what might appear to be a random collection. It seems to me that by making only a little logic leap, we can now say that there is most probably a mathematical, formulaic description for "my life" or anyone else's life, for that matter. And in the next leap after that, extrapolating from how the field of Operations Research uses mathematical models (for more on "OR" go to http://en.wikipedia.org/wiki/Operations_research), we can sanely imagine how there could well be mathematical definitions for every variation that our life might have or may yet take, factoring in all the Physics, Metaphysics, and all the effects of free will in and around us, as well as the occasional Divine interventions enforcing God's purposed will (itself something like the ultimate sentient fractal function).

It is not that huge a step of logic then to postulate the ultimate Fractal processing "machine" as God's omniscient mind, which calculated the result of all the interacting equations, (7 to 10 billion humans?), and then, as in Operations Research, use a master Fractal based equation simulation to choose the optimal set of individual equations, each of which included many chosen points of His own Divine involvement, so as to maximize the final total of priceless, eternal, joyous, souls living together with God, while minimizing the pain and suffering and evil in the sum total as well as each individual human equation that was necessary for the reality of "free will" of spiritually significant individuals.

WOW! What a fun idea!

But, what do you do with that?

Well, at least now I don't feel like the concepts of the innermost, deepest layer of Truth as described in "BMB Challenge #1" is quite so mysterious and, thus, I feel less religious when I accept as true the points from the Bible that I have assigned to that, like pre-destination and election, etc.

"How's that?" you say. (I wish I could define or not use the word "eternally".)

Well, if scientists now say they can no longer see limits to the potential of mathematically modeling seemingly random collections, while at the same time, not in any way lessening the reality of the vast complexity and the existence and importance of random events and "free choices" within the equation; then, I think I feel downright scientific when I accept both my complete responsibility for all my choices as well as give God credit and thanks for all His creative genius and infinite intellectual and mathematical processing abilities in designing the ultimate physical manifestation of the ultimate (I would use the word "fractal" but I suspect that there is at least one more quantum leap in kind to get to the ultimate math) model of the eternal Truths of Life, Love, Hope and Faith, that inherently had the power to require a physical universe in which I could be created to receive those from the perfect physical manifestation of God, in a dirty, space-time continuum Petri dish of life on earth, in order that I and a maximum number of individuals like me would then be united with God, in a new universe that "eternally" models all Truth – or something.

I don't know about you, but that made me want to delve in more deeply trying to dissect the science of the "spirit" and "mind" and "heart" and "soul" concepts, and find the practical applications of those truths. I believe that a scientific approach to the "unseen" world of the "spirit realm" has a huge potential for changing true science, much like the discovery of the unseen world with the microscope led to an end to the old world Political Correctness that vilified as heretics any who practiced the witchcraft of modern medicine. I think it is just so sad that our government is now fallen into the hands of a well organized group of believers in Naturalism and relativism who have usurped the title of "scientific community" and instituted their own new form of thought repression using Political Correctness empowered by emotional rhetoric, using the same tactics as Hitler, Lenin and Stalin, and are now sweeping away freedom of thought and real debate on issues like "Climate Change" and "Choice" and other illogical agenda. Ben's Stein's movie "Expelled – No Intelligence Allowed!" really made me sad. I better stop! This is not constructive. ☺

So, for this BMB Challenge I want to get you started on some hard thinking, drawing from an integrated understanding of all the Bible data on "spirit" and "mind" and "heart" and "soul" concepts, as well as "Love" and "angel" and "faith" and "hope", etc., to try to formulate, only intuitively at first, but eventually a testable theoretical model, that has a "Level Zero DFD" that looks something like this:

1. Eternal Entities (that includes God and us and all truth)
2. Processed as input into a "Spiritual Fractal" (call it a "Spractal Pregression") ultimate mathematical model generation dimensional tool,
3. Producing a spiritual dimension laboratory in which the
4. Primary sentient concepts play by a perfect set of rules in generating
5. "proof of concept manifestations" in a
6. space-time continuum Petri dish of life on earth.

I think you can take it from there, I don't want to taint your imagination with my own fantasies, because I hope to get some unrestrained creative feedback on this at BusyMansBible.com/Spractal ☺. Here are some BMB passage references for you to start with. Of course you can probably figure out to use the table of Contents and Topical Index, too. Happy hard thinking!

Start by rereading the "intro to God" section on pages 7 to 14. Ponder that the Hebrew idea of "name" involved more than simple taxonomy, and might reflect some of the eternal nature of the concept of "Identity" that brings together many different types, entities, attribute and events into a unity under a name. OK, no more of my ideas. Next, read about predestination and spirit and love (use the topical index), and then investigate Satan and angels, trying to understand the science and rules of their "warfare". Oh, and don't forget miracles, heaven, hell, and the idea of Jesus being the "outstretched arm" of God, and the perfect and only physical manifestation of God!

INDEX OF TOPICS

Abrahamic Covenant....3
Adultery....72B6, 113A4
Amen....12A1, 102B5
Angels (see also "Michael")....24B3, 26b2, 27b3, 72A3, 82B7,117-118,121A5
Angels, Fallen....53, 58B, 72A3, 73A4, 111B4
Anger....91A2-A6
Anti-Christ....55A2v15,B4, 58A, 59, 60A3,B1, 62A2, 64A3
Apostolic Signs....41-45,48A1
Apostle recap by Paul....48B1-2, 49B4, 95B5
Arm of God....11, 12, 26B2, 40A1
Assurance of Salvation....77, 78
Atonement by Christ....73
Baptism....43A, 44B1, 45, 46
Barnabas....43, 44
Beatitudes....115
Birth of Messiah....37
Blaspheme....16, 122
Captivity of Judah....25B3
Chastisement of Believers....78A4, 92
Church Family....107, 108
Christology....116
Christ's Ancestry....19B4, 118
Christ's Compassion....116
Christ's Crucifixion and Resurrection....40
Christ's "Name"....44B4, 45, 103
Christ's Second Coming....55
Commands for Believers....92
Communion....92A4, 107A3
Condemnation Under Law....72
Conscience/Heart....46B2, 83, 98A3
Creation....1, 13A1,4,7, 120B2,5
Daniel....25B4, 27, 28
David....21, 22, 96B3, 121A5
Dead, the....20B, 56A, 73B2, 118A1
Death....73
Demonic Activities....52
Dinosaurs....119
Dispensational tidbits....43A, 97B4, 122B4
Divine Nature of God....9, 10
Division of Israel....23
Divorce....113A
Early Church....42
End Times:....See Prophecy-Last Days
Election....75, 76
Elijah and Elisha....23, 24
Enoch....56B2
Esau....3

Eternity 66-68
Evangelism 96B4, 114
Exercise 121B4
Eyes of the LORD 21A2, 121A2
Ezra 29
Faith 77, 84B1, 104
Fall of Mankind 2
False Doctrines 51
Family 111, 112
Fasting 102
Feasts of Tabernacles (Sukkot) 35B6-8, 39A4, 66B4
Firstborn 11A1, 24A2, 37B3, 75B6
Flood, the 2, 55A2v39, 72A3, 120B
Fruit of the Spirit 87A3, 88A4
Giants 2A2, 18A2
Gifts of Spirit 49, 50, 107
Giving to the Church 109
Governments in the World 114
Grace 24B3, 80
"Great Commission" .... , 96B5
Hate 90B3
Heaven 118B1,2
Hell 65B1, 72A3, 73A2-4
Hezekiah 25
High Places 21B3, 25B1
Holy Spirit of God 13, 14
Homosexuality 71B1, 121A5
Hope of Salvation 79, 83B7, 85A5, 95B4, 98B7, 104A2
Human Religion and Sects 82
Humility 21A3, 115
Imposters 44B4, 51-53
Innocent children 71A9
Interpretation of Scripture 95B1-2
Jacob 3
Jesus' Ministry of Signs of His Deity 38, 39
Job 25B4, 54
John the Baptizer 38,116B5
Joseph and Israel Sold Into Egypt 4
Joshua 16-18
Judgment 72A3, 73, 86B
Judges Period 19
"Keys" 43
Killing 16, 121
King David and King Solomon 21, 22
King Saul 20
Last Days .... See Prophecy-Last Days
Law, the 16, 72B, 121A3,4
Laying on of Hands 18, 40B2, 42B2, 43A1, 43B3, 44A1, 44B1
Lazarus (2 different men) 39B,117B4

Liberty and Conscience........84
"Lord's Prayer"........101
Love........14B3, 90, 98B2-3
Male/Female........109, 110
Magic........52
Man as God's Offspring........13
Manna........17B2, 96A4
Marriage........113
Mary (mother of Jesus)........37, 41A3, 116B5,118
Maturity........20, 50B1, 90
Michael........27B2, 54B2, 60B3
Missionary........96B4, 114
Moses the Deliverer........4, 25B4
Murder Penalty........114A5
Mystery (see Prophesies)........
........75A3,76B2,83B4,94A1,95B5,96B5,97A2,98B7,109B2, 115B5
"Name" of Christ........44B4, 45, 103
"Name" of the **Lord** Proclaimed........6, 7, 15, 31, 32
"Name" Making........5, 21A2
Nebuchadnezzar........26
Noah........2B, 25B4
Obedience........20A5, 123A7
Parables........114B2, 115B5
Paul........45-48
Pentecost, the Day of........41
Peter and His "Keys"........43
Physical Presence of God and His Name........8, 11, 22A3, 27B2
Prayer: Examples of Basics........24B1, 99, 100
Prayer: Instructions on Prayer........101
Prayer: Requirements for Prayer........103
Prayer: Principles of Prayer........103-106
Predestination/Election........75, 76, 77A2v3b
Pride........115
Prophesies
  False........51B
  of Last Days, Signs of........55
    Rapture(s?) of the Church........56 (,63A1?)
    Mystery of Lawlessness........51A4B3, 55A2v12, 89A3
    Daniel's 70 Weeks Outline........57
    Babylon........61B3, 62B3, 63A2,B2
    Time of Jacob's Troubles........58-62
    God's Two Witnesses........60
    End of Troubles; "Second Coming"........62, 63
    End of 1,000 Year Reign........65, 65
    Final Judgment........65
    Eternity........66-68
    Festivals and Sabbaths foreshadow........82B7
  Of Messiah........3A3, 33-37, 57A1
  Withheld for a Time........20A1, 49B1, 97B4

Psalm 23 100
Rapture of the Church.... 56
Rest.... 77B2
Revenge.... 113A4
Rewards.... 86B2
Riches.... 88
Ruth.... 19
Salvation Through Christ.... 74
Samaria Lost.... 25
Samuel and King Saul.... 20
Sanctification.... 89
Satan.... 27B2, 53, 54, 58B, 85B3, 86A1
Second Coming of Christ.... 55
Sexual Immorality.... 71B1, 121A5
Shadrach, Meshach, and Abed-Nego.... 26
Signs in God's Plan.... 38B, 39, 40A1, 45
Signs of the Apostles.... 40A1, 40B2, 42A2, 44B3
Signs and Gifts.... 49, 59
Signs, False.... 51, 52, 59B1
Sin.... 71-73
Snares of the Devil.... 85, 86
Solomon.... 21, 22
Spirit vs. Flesh.... 47A5, 87
Spiritual Growth.... 94
Spiritual Maturity.... 90
Submission.... 113
Temple.... 8B4,22A3,30B3,60A2,68,,88A1-2
Ten Commandments.... 16
Two Commandments.... 116B3
"Tongues".... 41, 50
Trials and Temptations of Believers.... 93
Tribulation: .... See Prophecy of Last Days
Trivia:
    Forests in Egypt.... 122A1
    Left-Handed Slingers.... 122A3
    Slavery.... 122A2
Truth 13B2, 14, 16B3,51A4,85A4,88A,95B1,97A6
Warfare of Spirit vs. Flesh.... 87
Warnings of Defilement.... 91
Watch for Christ's Return.... 86
Wisdom.... 22B, 98
Word (Food) of God.... 95-98
Works.... 81
World and Its Riches.... 88
Youth.... 123

INDEX OF BIBLE PASSAGES

Syntax of index entries: **a**:b, c, d-e. . **[**f**]** **/**

a	chapter number
:	colon delimits chapter number from verse(s)
b	single verse number within chapter #a
,	comma separates verses or passages in list
c	another single verse in list for chapter
d	first verse in a passage
-	hyphen should be read as "through"
e	last verse in a passage
.	1 or 2 periods ends verses and precedes page number, or another chapter/verse entry on same page
[ ]	brackets enclose the page number of entry
f	page number of index entry
/	slash following page number ends index entry

Other examples of Syntax:
a:b. **a**:d-e..**[**f**]** **/** **a**:b,c,d..**[**f**]** **/** **a**:d-e. **[**f**]** **/**

All chapters and verses are indexed in numerical order.

At least I have attempted to do so.

You can probably imagine how difficult it has been to create and maintain the topical and passage index references. So, maybe you will want to participate in building the next edition of the BMB by going to the BusyMansBible.com website and submit any corrections you discover (I hope to pay some type of a bounty on those). Also, suggestions of additions or changes are definitely desired. My hope is that at least the indexes can be set up as wiki pages, and a community bulletin board for discussion can thrive in support on improving the BMB. ☺

Old Testament

Genesis

1:1-27..[1]/ **1**:26,27..[13]/ **2**:16-24..[110]/ **3**:1,4..[1]/
3:5,6,12..[2]/ **3**:16..[110]/ **3**:17-22.**6**:1-8..[2]/
7:1,8-12,23,24..[2]/ **8**:21..[71]/ **9**:6..[114]/ **9**:9-13..[2]/
18:18./ **17**:3-8,10.**22**:15-18..[3]/ **25**:32,23.**27**:6-37..[3]/
32:24-29..[4]/ **33**:17..[35]/ **35**:10-12..[3]/
37:28.**45**:26.**46**:3,4..[4]/ **49**:10..[34]/ **50**:17,20..[4]/

Exodus

3:6,14,15..[5]/ **4**:10..[4]/ **6**:2,3..[5]/ **6**:5,6..[4]/ **6**:7..[5]/
7:22.**8**:6,7,18,19..[52]/ **9**:14-16.**10**:1,2.**14**:18,21..[5]/
14:22,23..[122]/ **14**:31..[5]/ **15**:26..[105]/ **20**:1-18..[16]/
24:10,11,17..[8]/ **33**:1..[10]/ **33**:18-23..[8]/ **34**:5-7,14..[7]/

Numbers

12:3,6-8..[4]/ **16**:28-31..[72]/ **24**:1..[52]/ **24**:17b..[33]/
26:58,59..[121]/

Leviticus

5:17..[72]/ **17**:11..[73]/ **19**:31..[52]/ **20**:13..[121]/
23:41,42..[35]/ **25**:44,46..[122]/

Deuteronomy

2:34.**3**:4-6,8..[16]/
2:9b,10,11a,19b,20,21a,22a..[17]/
3:4-6..[18]/**4**:2,9,10,12..[16]/ **4**:15-18..[17]/
4:32-36..[8]/ **4**:37..[76]/ **6**:6-9..[96]/ **7**:16..[17]/
7:19..[111]/ **8**:3..[96]/ **8**:5..[92]/ **11**:26b..[11]/ **12**:2-5..[8]/
13:1-3..[51]/
17:17,18..[22]/ **18**:10-12..[20]/ **18**:18,19..[34]/
18:20-22..[51]/ **21**:17b..[24]/ **21**:18,21..[123]/ **22**:5..[121]/
23:3..[19]/ **28**:58..[5]/ **31**:24-26a,29..[17]/ **32**:3,4..[7]/
32:20b,39..[17]/ **34**:9-12..[17]/

Joshua

4:22-25..[17]/ **5**:6..[16]/ **5**:12..[17]/ **6**:20,21,25..[17]/
10:12-14,40./ **11**:19-21..[18]/ **23**:14./ **24**:2-7..[18]/
24:19..[7]/

Judges

2:7,10,11-22..[19]/ **20**:16..[122]/ **21**:10,11,14..[121]/
21:25..[19]/

Ruth **4**:10,13,16,17..[19]/

I Samuel

3:1.**8**:4-7.**9**:2.**10**:24..[20]/
15:22,23,35..[20]/ **16**:7,12,13..[21]/ **27**:8-11,15-19..[20]/

II Samuel

6:16,21,22.**7**:8,9..[21]/ **7**:12-16..[34]/ **7**:21..[95]/ **7**:23..[7]/
12:9,10..[21]/ **12**:13,14..[122]/ **12**:22,23..[102]/
12:24,25..[21]/ **23**:1,2..[96]/ **24**:1,10,15,16..[121]/

I Kings
2:11,12.**3**:2,3,5,10-13..[21]/ **3**:25-27..[22]/ **8**:2..[35]/
10:22-24..[22]/ **11**:2-9..[22]/ **11**:11-13..[23]/
17:21-24.**18**:37,38..[23]/ **19**:8-13..[10]/ **19**:14-18..[23]/
22:19-23..[117]/

II Kings
2:7b-14,22-24..[24]/ **4**:32-35.**5**:10,11,13..[24]/
6:15-17..[24]/ **17**:18,24-26,32,33..[25]/
18:1-5..**32**:30b,31..[25]/

I Chronicles
6:1-3..[121]/ **16**:23,24,29,34..[69]/ **22**:6-8..[22]/ **28**:9..[10]/

II Chronicles
6:18..[8]/ **7**:1,2,11,12,14,15..[22]/ **7**:14..[105]/ **7**:16..[8]/
9:30,31...[23]/ **10**:15,19,.**11**:5,12,13..[23]/ **12**:1,9,14..[23]/
16:9..[69]/

Ezra
1:1,3,7.**3**:1,8.**4**:23,24.**5**:5.**6**:15..[30]/ **8**:21..[102]/ **9**:12..[30]/
10:1..[102]/ **10**:2,3..[30]/

Nehemiah **9**:5b-35..[31]/

Job
1:6-12..[54]/ **1**:21..[88]/ **2**:1-7..[54]/ **5**:17..[92]/
19:25,26..[36]/
40:15-24; **41**:1-34..[119]

Psalms
1:1,2..[98]/ **4**:4..[9]/ **8**:1-9..[99]/ **9**:10a..[5]/ **9**:16..[69]/
12:1-4..[21]/ **16**:10..[36]/ **19**:1..[9]/ **19**:7..[98]/
22:16-18..[36]/ **22**:22..[101]/ **23**:1-6..[100]/ **30**:3..[33]/
30:4,5..[69]/ **32**:3-6..[101]/ **33**:1-3.**34**:1-3..[100]/
34:19,20..[36]/ **35**:13..[102]/ **37**:8..[91]/ **41**:4..[24]/
41:9..[36]/ **45**:6,7..[34]/ **51**:1-5,16,17..[100]/ **53**:1-3..[71]/
63:1..[99]/ **63**:6..[101]/ **68**:1,4..[6]/ **68**:17..[117]/
68:18..[36]/ **68**:33..[9]/ **69**:10..[102]/ **69**:21..[36]/
74:13,14a..[119]/ **74**:14b-17..[120]/ **77**:3-6..[101]/ **90**:4..[9]/
99:8..[7]/ **103**:1-4..[100]/ **104**:1-4..[120]/ **104**:5-9..[120]/
104:25,26..[119]/ **105**:1-5..[7]/ **105**:7-44..[6]/
106:8-11..[6]/ **110**:1,2..[34]/ **117**:..[69]/ **118**:1,8,9,14..[69]/
119:105..[96]/ **131**:1..[98]/ **135**:13..[5]/ **136**:1-9..[100]/
138.2d..[95]/ **147**:4,5..[9]/ **148**:4..[120]/ **150**:106..[99]/

Proverbs
3:11,12..[92]/ **8**:13..[115]/ **13**:24..[123]/ **16**:18,19..[115]/
18:14..[87]/ **18**:15..[96]/ **19**:18..[123]/ **20**:27..[13]/
22:6.**23**:13,14..[123]/ **28**:13..[91]/ **29**:15..[123]/
30:5,6..[95]/ **31**:10-31..[112]/

Ecclesiastes
3:11..[76]/ **3**:12,13..[99]/ **3**:14,15..[76]/ **5**:1,2..[107]/
7:16..[98]/ **7**:20..[71]/ **9**:11..[75]/ **11**:9,10.**12**:1..[123]/

Isaiah
7:14..[37]/ **8**:19..[52]/ **8**:20..[96]/ **9**:6,7.**11**:1-5..[34]/
13:9-13..[63]/ **14**:12-17..[53]/ **28**:9-11..[41]/ **28**:16..[35]/
28:18..[57]/ **29**:6..[100]/ **34**:4..[65]/ **35**:5,6a..[35]/
38:20..[99]/
39:5,6..[25]/ **40**:3..[38]/ **40**:10,11..[11]/
40:12-14,25-28..[10]/ **42**:1-8..[36]/ **45**:5-8..[93]/ **47**:10..[71]/
49:5-9..[35]/
49:25..[52]/ **52**:10..[11]/ **52**:13-15..[33]/ **53**:1-12..[33]/
58:8,9..[9]/ **55**:10,11..[95]/ **57**:15a..[9]/ **57**:15b-18..[10]/
58:1,2..[30]/ **58**:3-8..[102]/ **59**:21..[96]/ **60**:15,16..[36]/
62:2..[35]/ **62**:5..[66]/ **63**:8b,9..[33]/ **63**:12..[5]/
66:22-24..[66]/

Jeremiah
15:1..[25]/ **17**:9-10..[13]/ **23**:6-8..[7]/ **23**:24..[10]/
24:5-7..[25]/ **27**:5..[120]/ **30**:7..[62]/ **30**:9..[66]/
31:33-34..[67]/ **45**:23,24..[122]/ **48**:10..[51]/ **51**:15,16..[91]/

Lamentations **3**:23B-28..[93]/

Ezekiel
11:5..[14]/ **13**:3,6..[51]/ **14**:13,14..[25]/ **28**:12-19..[53]/
33:1..[82]/ **36**:22,23a..[7]/ **36**:25-27..[68]/
37:11-14,22-27..[66]/ **38**:3,8,15,16,19-23..[64]/ **39**:6,7..[65]/
39:25,29.**43**:7,10,11..[68]/ **44**:9.**47**:1,9,11,12,21-23..[68]/

Daniel
2:20-22..[7]/ **2**:45..[28]/ **2**:27-42..[29]/ **2**:44..[65]/
3:15-19,21-26..[26]/ **4**:37..[26]/ **6**:1-4,10-13,16-23..[27]/
6:25a,26a,28..[27]/ **7**:2-6..[28]/ **7**:7,8..[58]/ **7**:9,10..[8]/
7:11-14..[58]/ **9**:24-27..[57]/ **10**:1-7,11-13..[26]/
10:20,21..[27]/ **11**:1..[27]/ **11**:2-31..[28-29]/
12:1,6b,10-12..[60]/ **12**:2,3..[65]/ **12**:4-13..[57]/

Hosea **11**:9..[99]/ **13**:14a..[35]/

Joel **2**:28-29..[42]/

Amos 8:11,12..[97]/ **9**:6..[120]/ **9**:15..[66]/

Jonah **2**:6..[35]/

Micah **5**:2..[37]/

Habbakuk **2**:4..[115]/

Zechariah
1:12..[30]/ **7**:12..[96]/ **10**:12..[8]/ **12**:1b..[13]/
12:8-11..[67]/ **12**:10..[36]/ **13**:1,2..[67]/ **13**:3-5..[52]/
13:8b,9..[61]/ **14**:1,2..[61]/ **14**:3-7,12..[62]/ **14**:8..[35]/
14:16..[68]/

Malachi
3:1..[38]/ **4**:2..[35]/**4**:5..[60]/

New Testament

Matthew

1:2-17..[118]/ **5**:3-10..[115]/ **5**:16..[113]/ **5**:18..[95]/ **5**:32..[113]/ **5**:46..[90]/ **6**:3,4..[109]/ **6**:5-8,9-14..[101]/ **6**:16-18..[102]/ **6**:21-24..[88]/ **6**:27,28..[72]/ **6**:31-34..[103]/ **7**:1a..[83]/ **7**:6..[89]/ **7**:7..[103]/ **7**:13,14..[115]/ **7**:21-23..[51]/ **8**:16,17..[39]/ **10**:33-36..[93]/ **12**:36,37..[86]/ **12**:39..[123]/ **13**:10-12..[68]/ **13**:33..[88]/ **16**:18,19..[42]/ **17**:11-13..[38]/ **17**:16-21..[104]/ **18**:10-14..[116]/ **18**:10-14..[116]/**18**:15..[122]/ **19**:16,17,21-26..[71]/ **20**:22,23..[46]/ **21**:21,22..[104]/ **22**:30-32..[118]/ **22**:37-39..[116]/ **23**:3-12..[82]/ **24**:6-18..[55]/ **24**:23,24..[52]/ **24**:27,29-31..[63]/ **24**:38a,39a..[120]/ **24**:36-38,39b,43,44..[55]/ **25**:37-40..[116]/ **25**:41..[73]/ **26**:41..[85]/ **28**:19..[45]/

Mark

1:4,5..[38]/ **3**:29,30..[122]/ **3**:32-35..[107]/ **4**:10-12..[115]/ **4**:13-19..[114]/ **4**:33,34..[115]/ **5**:30-34.**6**:4-7..[104]/ **6**:56..[39]/ **7**:7,8..[82]/ **7**:9-13..[123]/ **7**:20-23..[72]/ **7**:25-28..[122]/ **8**:12..[123]/ **8**:19-21..[38]/ **8**:37,38..[115]/ **9**:1..[115]/ **9**:19..[123]/ **9**:23,24..[105]/ **9**:39,40..[121]/ **9**:44,45..[73]/ **10**:6..[120]/ **10**:7-9..[113]/ **10**:25-27..[80]/ **11**:22-25..[105]/ **12**:26,27..[56]/ **12**:35-37..[115]/ **13**:10..[55]/ **13**:14..[59]/ **13**:19,20..[57]/ **13**:21,22..[52]/ **13**:30..[123]/ **13**:31..[96]/ **13**:32-37..[55]/ **14**:10,34..[40]/ **14**:38..[87]/ **14**:61,62..[116]/ **15**:22-28..[40]/ **6**:15-20..[40]/

Luke

1:3,8-11,13-19,23,24,26-28,30-37..[37]/ **1**:41,42,46,48..[116]/ **2**:3-7..[37]/ **2**:11.**3**:16,17..[38]/ **2**:22,23..[115]/ **3**:23-38..[118]/ **4**:1-3.**5**:20,53,54..[38]/ **6**:45,46..[81]/ **9**:40,41..[123]/ **11**:17,18,21..[54]/ **11**:9-13..[103]/**11**:24-26..[121]/ **11**:27,28..[82]/ **11**:29..[38]/ **12**:46-48..[86]/ **15**:10.**16**:22-24..[117]/ **17**:20,21..[115]/ **18**:1-8..[103]/ **18**:25..[123]/ **18**:29,30..[114]/ **24**:39-43..[116]/

John

1:1-4,10-14..[11]/ **1**:17..[16]/ **1**:18..[13]/ **1**:29-32..[38]/ **3**:3-18..[74]/ **3**:19-21,36..[73]/ **5**:18..[12]/ **5**:28,29..[65]/ **6**:14,26,27..[38]/ **6**:33-35..[12]/ **6**:44..[75]/ **6**:63..[87]/ **7**:2,31,37-41..[39]/ **8**:7,8,10,11..[38]/ **8**:56-58..[12]/ **8**:31-32..[97]/ **9**:2,3,32,33..[39]/ **10**:25..[38]/ **10**:27-30..[78]/ **11**:4..[39]/ **11**:25..[74]/ **11**:35,36,39,40,42-44..[39]/ **12**:9-11..[39]/ **12**:16-18..[39]/ **12**:37,38,42..[40]/ **12**:44-48..[12]/ **14**:2,3..[118]/ **14**:6-11..[12]/ **14**:12-14..[104]/ **14**:16-18,25-28..[14]/ **14**:30..[53]/ **15**:4,5..[87]/ **15**:7,8..[104]/ **5**:12,13..[105]/ **15**:14,15..[14]/ **15**:19..[88]/ **15**:22-25..[72]/ **15**:26,27..[14]/ **16**:7-13..[14]/ **16**:22-29..[105]/ **16**:33..[106]/ **17**:9-14..[12]/ **17**:16-19..[88]/ **17**:20-22..[13]/ **18**:36..[40]/ **19**:28-31,33-37..[40]/ **20**:17..[13]/ **20**:21,22..[40]/

Acts
1:11..[56]/ **1**:14..[41]/ **2**:1-17..[41]/ **2**:22,40-45..[42]/
2:38.**3**:16..[45]/ **4**:10..[45]/ **4**:12..[74]/ **4**:29,30..[44]/
5:1-5,8b-10a, 11-13..[42]/ **6**:2-6,8..[42]/
7:2-6,8-25,29-36..[15]/ **8**:13-18..[43]/ **8**:27-29,35-39..[46]/
9:15-17..[43]/ **9**:34,35,40-42..[45]/ **10**:25-28..[43]/
10:43..[45]/ **10**:44-48..[43]/ **11**:16..[45]/
11:20-22,24-26.**12**:2,3..[43]/ **13**:48..[75]/ **14**:3..[44]/
14:22,23..[102]/ **15**:8-12..[44]/ **15**:18..[9]/
15:28,29..[80]/**16**:30b-32..[74]/ **17**:24-31..[11]/ **18**:4..[47]/
19:1-3,6,8..[44]/ **19**:11-13,15-17..[44]/ **20**:29-32..[85]/
21:18,19..[44]/ **22**:16..[45]/ **24**:25..[94]/ **26**:9,10..[45]/
26:26..[40]/

Romans
1:19,20..[10]/ **1**:24-32..[71]/ **2**:11,12..[72]/ **2**:13-15..[83]/
3:23..[71]/ **3**:27..[80]/ **4**:4,5..[81]/ **4**:13-25..[77]/
5:1-5..[79]/ **5**:6-8,12-14..[73]/ **5**:15..[80]/ **5**:19..[73]/
6:2-5..[46]/ **6**:12-16..[81]/ **6**:23..[73]/ **7**:14-25..[87]/
8:1-4..[78]/ **8**:5-8..[81]/ **8**:12-16..[87]/ **8**:18-31..[13]/
8:22-25..[79]/ **8**:26,27..[103]/ **8**:28-30..[75]/ **8**:31,32..[78]/
8:38,39..[78]/ **9**:1..[83]/ **9**:11-24..[68]/ **9**:32,33.**10**:1-4..[82]/
10:9-11..[74]/ **10**:14,15..[114]/ **10**:17..[104]/ **11**:6..[79]/
11:22..[86]/ **12**:3..[105]/ **12**:5-16..[107]/ **12**:17-19..[113]/
13:1-7..[114]/ **14**:1-9..[84]/ **14**:20-23.**15**:1,2..[84]/
15:4..[95]/ **16**:17,18..[82]/ **16**:25,26..[96]/

Corinthians
1:10..[82]/ **1**:21-23..[49]/ **1**:26..[98]/ **2**:3-5..[48]/
2:6-8..[94]/ **2**:10,11..[13]/ **2**:14-16..[94]/ **3**:1,2..[95]/
3:3,4..[82]/ **3**:13-15..[86]/ **3**:16,17..[88]/ **4**:6,6..[98]/
4:9-11..[48]/ **4**:20..[95]/ **5**:1,2..[71]/ **5**:4-6...[78]/
6:1-4..[108]/ **6**:12..[83]/ **6**:15,16..[91]/ **6**:17,19..[88]/
7:3-6..[111]/ **7**:8,9..[112]/ **7**:14,15,27,28..[113]/
7:32-35..[112]/ **8**:1b-3..[98]/ **8**:6-10..[84]/ **9**:4-10..[47]/
9:14..[109]/ **9**:20-22..[47]/ **9**:37..[94]/ **10**:1-4..[45]/
10:11..[95]/ **10**:13-15..[93]/ **10**:23-30..[84]/ **11**:1..[51]/
11:3,5-16..[109]/ **11**:24-26..[107]/ **11**:27-32..[92]/
12:3-11..[49]/ **12**:13..[45]/ **12**:21-27..[108]/ **12**:28-31..[49]/
13:1,2..[90]/ **13**:4-7..[90]/ **13**:8-12..[49]/ **13**:13..[90]/
14:1-15..[50]/ **14**:16..[102]/ **14**:19-28..[50]/ **14**:33-38..[110]/
15:1,2..[85]/ **15**:8,9..[48]/ **15**:20-23..[73]/ **15**:29-32..[45]/
15:39-44..[117]/ **15**:45-49..[120]/ **15**:50-53..[55]/
15:54-58..[78]/ **16**:1,2..109]/

II Corinthians
1:2-5..[116]/ **1**:22,22..[78]/ **3**:16-1**8**..[??]/ **4**:2..[98]/
4:3,4..[75]/ **5**:6-8..[87]/ **5**:10,11..[86]/ **5**:17..[87]/
6:14-18..[89]/ **8**:9..[80]/ **9**:6-8..[109]/ **10**:4,5..[97]/
11:3,4..[80]/ **11**:5-10..[47]/ **10**:10,..[48]/ **12**:7-**10**,11-12..[48]/
12:14..[112]/ **13**:5..[83]/ **14**:1-15,19-28..[50]/

Galatians
1:6-9..[98]/ **2**:20..[87]/ **2**:21..[80] / **3**:2,3..[80]/ **3**:16..[36] / **3**:17..[4]/ **3**:24,25..[17]/ **3**:26-29..[108]/ **4**:9-11..[80]/ **4**:13,14..[48]/ **5**:4..[80]/ **5**:5..[79] / **5**:9..[82]/ **5**:12..[80]/ **5**:16-18..[87]/ **5**:19-21..[91]/ **5**:22,23..[87]/ **5**:24-26..[88]/ **6**:1-2..[108]/ **6**:6..[109]/ **6**:9,10..[108]/

Ephesians
1:4-11..[75]/ **1**:13..[78]/ **2**:1,2..[86]/ **2**:8-10..[80]/ **2**:14..[116]/ **2**:20-22..[86] / **3**:3,5..[95]/ **3**:8-12..[75]/ **3**:17-19..[98]/ **3**:20..[104] / **4**:1-3..[89]/ **4**:4-6..[45]/ **4**:7,8..[50]/ **4**:9,10..[73]/ **4**:11-16..[107]/ **4**:23..[13]/ **4**:26,27,29,30-32..[91]/ **5**:1,2..[89]/ **5**:3-7..[91]/ **5**:8-11..[88]/ **5**:12-14..[91]/ **5**:15-21..[90]/ **5**:22-33..[109]/ **6**:1-4..[111]/ **6**:5-9..[113]/ **6**:10,11..[93]/ **6**:12-17..[85]/ **6**:18..[101]/

Philippians
1:19..[13]/ **1**:21-23..[87]/ **2**:3..[108]/ **2**:5-8..[116]/ **2**:13-16..[90]/ **2**:21..[51]/ **2**:25-27..[106]/ **3**:3..[82]/ **4**:4-8..[99]/ **4**:9..[47]/ **4**:11,12..[103]/ **4**:13..[93]

Colossians
1:15-17..[11]/ **1**:23..[79]/ **1**:24..[118]/ **1**:26-28..[98]/ **2**:2,3..[97]/ **2**:8..[89]/ **2**:9..[11]/ **2**:12..[46]/ **2**:10,15..[117]/ **2**:16-18..[82]/ **2**:20-23..[80]/ **3**:8,9..[91]/ **3**:12-15..[108]/ **3**:16..[97]/ **3**:17..[101]/ **3**:18-21..[111]/ **3**:22,23..[113]/ **4**:1..[113]/ **4**:5,6..[89]/

I Thessalonians
1:5-8..[48]/ **4**:13-18..[56]/ **5**:1-6..[56]/ **5**:8..[79]/ **5**:16-22..[92]/ **5**:23..[13]/

II Thessalonians
1:8b,9..[73]/ **2**:3,4..[60]/ **2**:5-12..[51]/ **2**:13..[75]/ **3**:13-15..[108]/

I Timothy
1:4-6..[83]/ **1**:8,9..[72]/ **1**:12-15..[74]/ **2**:1,2..[101]/ **2**:3,4..[10]/ **2**:5,6..[12]/ **2**:8-10..[103]/ **2**:11-15..[109]/ **3**:5..[114]/ **3**:6-7..[115]/ **4**:1-3..[52]/ **4**:4,5..[101]/ **4**:6,7..[97]/ **4**:8,9..[121]/ **5**:9-15..[111]/ **5**:16-18..[109]/ **5**:20..[108]/ **5**:22..[44]/ **6**:3-5..[97]/ **6**:6-9..[103]/ **6**:10,17..[88]/ **6**:16..[9]/ **6**:20,21..[49]/

II Timothy
1:8b..[116]/ **2**:2,7..[96]/ **2**:11b-13..[78]/ **2**:15,14..[95]/ **2**:16-18..[49]/ **2**:19-21..[94]/ **2**:22..[83]/ **2**:23-26..[89]/ **3**:1-7..[55]/ **3**:9..[83]/ **3**:12..[93]/ **3**:13..[52]/ **3**:14-17..[95]/ **4**:2-4..[97]/ **4**:5-7..[48]/ **5**:23..[84]/

Titus
1:9..[97]/ **1**:15,16..[83]/ **2**:3-5..[111]/ **2**:6-8..[90]/ **2**:11,12..[81]/ **3**:5,6..[74]/ **3**:7,8..[81]/

Hebrews
1:1-3..[11]/ **1**:13,14..[117]/ **2**:3,4..[41]/ **2**:14-15a..[53]/
2:16..[118]/ **3**:6,12-14..[85]/ **4**:1-11..[77]/ **4**:12..[96]/
4:13..[9]/ **4**:15..[116]/ **4**:16..[101]/ **5**:7-10..[106]/
5:11-14,**6**:1-5..[94]/ **6**:10,11.**7**:19..[79]/
9:14.**10**:15-17,22,23..[83]/
10:24-25..[107]/ **10**:26..[85]/ **10**:35-39..[81]/ **11**:1,2,6..[104]/
11:3..[1]/**12**:1..[89]/
12:5-11..[92]/ **12**:18,19,21..[85]/ **12**:16,17..[86]/
12:12-15..[85]/ **12**:22..[118]/ **12**:26-28..[65]/ **12**:29..[5]/
13:1,2..[117]/ **13**:3..[114]/ **13**:5..[103]/ **13**:8,9..[51]/
13:15,16..[99]/ **13**:18..[83]/

James
1:2-4..[93]/ **1**:5-8..[106]/ **1**:12-16..[93]/ **1**:17..[9]/
1:18..[13]/ **1**:19,20..[91]/ **1**:25..[80]/ **1**:26..[91]/ **1**:27..[90]/
2:9,10..[72]/ **2**:17-24,26..[81]/ **3**:13,17..[94]/ **4**:2,3..[103]/
4:4..[88]/ **4**:5-8..[86]/ **5**:13-16..[106]/

I Peter
1:4,5..[78]/ **1**:6,7..[93]/ **1**:10-12..[14]/ **1**:13..[79]/
1:20,21..[75]/ **1**:23..[77]/ **2**:2,3..[95]/ **2**:13-15..[114]/
2:18..[113]/ **2**:19-21..[93]/ **3**:1-7..[111]/ **3**:20,21..[46]/
4:8-10..[107]/ **4**:13..[93]/ **4**:14..[122]/ **4**:19..[106]/
5:5,6..[113]/ **5**:7..[92]/ **5**:8-10..[86]/

II Peter
1:3,4..[106]/ **1**:5-9..[90]/ **1**:10..[85]/ **1**:20,21..[95]/
2:4-11..[72]/ **2**:10,20-22..[85]/ **3**:5,6..[120]/ **3**:8,9..[9]/
3:10..[64]/

I John
1:4..[89]/ **1**:5,6..[91]/ **1**:7-10..[92]/ **2**:1,2..[98]/
2:3-6..[105]/ **2**:12-14..[94]/ **2**:15,16..[88]/ **2**:27..[96]/
2:28..[83]/ **3**:1,2..[12]/ **3**:1-3..[79]/ **3**:13-15..[90]/
3:16,17..[105]/ **3**:21..[83]/ **3**:22,23..[105]/ **4**:4,5..[88]/
4:6-11..[14]/ **4**:12,13..[12]/ **4**:16-18..[79]/ **5**:1-5..[90]/
5:6-8..[13]/ **5**:14-17..[106]/ **5**:18..[78]/ **5**:19..[79]/
5:20,21..[108]/

II John
9-11..[89]/

Jude
6..[117]/ **9**..[54]/ **14,15**..[56]/

Revelation
3:9,10..[56]/ **3**:14b..[12]/ **3**:19..[92]/ **3**:20,21..[106]/
6:7,8..[60]/ **6**:12-14,17..[64]/ **7**:4..[59]/ **7**:9,14,15..[65]/
8:7,9,11,12..[61]/ **9**:4-6,14-16,18,20,21..[61]/ **10**:4,7..[64]/
11:2,3,6,7,11,12..[60]/ **12**:1-9..[58]/ **12**:10,11..[54]/
12:12-14,17..[58]/ **13**:1-8.**14**:3,4..[59]/ **4**:6,7,10,11,13..[60]/
14:16..[64]/ **16**:11..[61]/ **16**:12-16..[62]/ **16**:17-21..[63]/
17:1-6..[61]/ **17**:10-13..[58]/ **17**:15-18..[62]/ **18**:20,21..[63]/
19:11-15,19-21..[62]/ **20**:1-8..[63]/ **20**:9,10..[64]/
20:11-15..[65]/ **21**:1-5..[65]/ **21**: 9-12,16-25..[67]/
22:12..[64/ **22**:18,19..[96]

REARFACE – CONT.

I suggest that you use the "Contents" in the front of the BMB, and the Index of Topics in the back, to help you as you try to follow your intuition, heart and the Spirit of God in seeking to know the truth about the subject.

6. Reread in reverse order, the material sandwiched between the BMB core and the BMB topical index.

Go back to the "BMB Challenges" sections, just before the Topical Index, and launch into a light research project on the subject that most caught your interest. I think that those "challenges" should be reread in reverse order. They flow from theory, to application; and therefore in reverse, more work on these or any similar application should help lead into better assimilation of the theoretical. Kind of like a physics class, where you are told about the theories and laws, and then you do some experiments. Often you then repeat the experiments, and maybe tweak them a bit, until the theories and laws are better proven to make sense to you.

REARFACE – CONT.

Note that I purposely placed the Index of Verses and Index of Topics all the way in the back, rather than just after the Bible passage "core" section, so they would be easier to find for rapid reference lookups. I had earlier planned to have them just after the BMB Core, and have all the BMB Challenges setup to be read in reverse, from the back, for fun, but that challenge was not practical, for index access.

3. Read it in the order you choose, using the Topical Index in the back.

Use the Topical Index in the back of the BMB (just before the verse index) as a way to study in the BMB, starting in the back, then jumping here and there as you choose different topics of interest. Listen to your heart as you read the Topical Index, and see if it stirs up an appetite in you, much like a menu of spiritual food. This approach can be most beneficial for a busy person to truly ingest and digest some spiritual food in short sessions, because you will be diving into scripture with some degree of actual hunger. I really think George W. Cable would approve, because his whole approach to Bible study stressed the need of a hunger for Truth, leading to the scripture being fully metabolized in us in order to grow our heart and affect our actions.

4. Reread and reorganize and add and embellish your own notes and scriptures you have added in the back.

The BMB has a blank page at the end of the core Bible section, and a little extra space on some pages where you can make notes and add other scripture references, etc. I encourage you to make this book a starting point for organizing scripture passages you find worthy of indexing and correlating to others, either in this BMB or your own Bible study work book. When I was in school, I did not actually study very much because I was able to make A's too easily. Whenever I had a test that covered a lot of stuff, requiring me to memorize many names, term and key facts like dates, I would figure out how I would arrange all the info I would need into a "crib sheet" that had to fit on one very small piece of paper. That exercise of analyzing to organize, then actually writing it on the page in what I figured to be the optimal structure for access during a test, was always sufficient to enable me to not need or use the crib sheet, and yet make A on the exam. I never made less than an A on any Final exam in high school or college. It works!

5. Go to the page after the chronological Section I – page 69 – and ponder the verses I proposed as being centrally important, with the idea of challenging my propositions.

I intentionally put that page in the middle of the BMB so as not to prejudice you, the busy reader by calling attention to it up front, despite the traditional thinking that "such important analysis" should be in the front to help guide your thinking.

REARFACE

The New Busy Man's Bible (BMB) actually introduces new dimensions of study and referencing of the basic doctrines of the Bible – almost a far eastern approach like what might have existed if Zen Buddhism had been founded on Jesus instead of Buddha. This book is meant to help you get to "know the Bible frontwards and backwards" figuratively speaking. So why not expect someone to read or study it in reverse? I have to admit that this idea owes some inspiration to the Japanese produced Animé graphic novels that were so popular with my step daughter Amanda in her early teens. They are translated into English, but they are read from back to front. "Like, how cool is that!"

So, in keeping with the figure of speech "frontwards and backwards" it is reasonable to assume that either the backwards reader of this book has already used this study aid from front to back, or is sufficiently quirky as to not need, much less follow any basic guidance. Upon reflecting on this, and considering how I have used it over the past 24 years, I concluded that there actually are a few meaningful study methods for starting from the rear of the BMB.

1. Read it in Reverse.

No kidding! Literally read the BMB scripture passages pages 1-123 in reverse page order, starting at the last passage on each page, and then reading each preceding passage. That should stimulate thoughtful reconsideration of each column and each page, and each section, considering that each section, page and column were planned to start with the most pre-eminent passage, and then build logically when read in their presented sequence. It seems reasonable to expect to gain fresh perspective and a refreshed, reinforced understanding from a reverse reading, at least in part because you are moving from the passages, in some way the least significant of the column, and also the most recently read (assuming you read the BMB front to back just prior to this), to the first, and most significant or foundational passage of each column, page, or section.

2. Read it along side the Bible, using the Index of Verses in the back.

Use the Index of verses in the back of the BMB to facilitate a study of the Bible, book by book, using the BMB to place the verses indexed there into a doctrinal or chronological context. As you read in your Bible, take the time to look in the index to know as you read when you can find a verse in the BMB, and note and read some of the context verses in the BMB. For example, if you are reading the book of Acts, when you get to chapter 2, verse 38, you will find it on page 45 column B in a section on the subject of baptism, along with several other important verses about baptism, including a few others in Acts.

Re-Dedication

*This book is for **You**,*
*If **You** are one of those few, who,*
if your teenage child tried to sneak your Ferrari out at night,
but crashed through the garage and
parked it in the pool,
would laugh because you discounted the apparent truth of his deserving punishment and your right to anger, and choose the real Truth of his needs
for forgiveness and
a grasp of the Truth of your Love for him,
and
you don't take your Self too seriously,
and can therefore take Truth more seriously,
and even be willing to enjoy learning about Truth
with me,
a man who likes to write long run-on sentences like William Faulkner, with lots of alliteration, yet realizes that others may not appreciate that so much and can probably best learn about Truth by simply reading passages from the Bible, without much or any commentary from any one, much less me ,
if only I can show them by example that they can indeed do so;
then
you might just be one of those I feel will enjoy and profit as much from this book as I,
*and I thus Dedicate it to **You** :*
*the **Busy Truth Seekers** -*
those fabulous few followers of conscience
who, while heroically busy working, whether
business of family, factory field or office,
actively resist their intimidating cultural frame
and their own flesh 's incessant drive
for recognition and fleeting fame ,
and whose heart is kept fresh, fertile and
fed with Truth by a mind focused
on finding spiritual fulfillment based solely on the fullness of Truth, no matter how unpopular they feel from feedback from fraudulent friends defaming them for being fanatical or fundamentalists or other unflattering affronts, and
*those unoffended by my offers of Faulkner-affected paragraphs full of **F**'s for fun and effect, when finally finished.*

The New Age Busy Man's Bible

Study And Enlightenment Toolset
For the Last "Generation"
In A New Age

(the Zen Method of Bible Study)

www.ingramcontent.com/pod-product-compliance
Lightning Source LLC
Chambersburg PA
CBHW071510170626
46811CB00007B/2792